Maxim

Play

The Last Ones: 'The writer was and remains a poet — his poetic soul is felt in the best parts of the play.' *Berliner Tagblatt*

Vassa Zheleznova: 'You begin to understand why Stalin found Gorky so dangerous. Vassa is a lonely workaholic who sacrifices everything to the cause of profit; her daughter-in-law is a dedicated puritan ready to sacrifice his child to the cause of revolution. Today, they both seen like victims of a merciless ideal.' *Guardian*

The Zykovs: '*The Zykovs* leaves the outside world quiet and implicit, if constantly threatening, and within the symbol of the divided family stresses more the struggle between work and idleness than between exploitation and suffering.' *TES*

Egor Bulychev: 'Their lack of faith coupled with the desire for it is so surprising in all these father figures from the past. This is probably one ingredient of the tragedy of your great "merchant characters" and their "attractiveness" as literary types.' K. A. Fedin (Letter to Gorky)

Maxim Gorky was born Alexei Maximovich Peshkov in Nizhny Novgorod, 225 miles east of Moscow, in 1868. By 1878 both his parents were dead and he spent his youth as a nomadic labourer. In 1898 his collection *Stories and Sketches* was published and proved an immediate success. His plays include *The Lower Depths* (1902), *Summerfolk* (1904), *Children of the Sun* (1905), *Barbarians* and *Enemies* (1906) and *Egor Bulychev* (1932). His other books include *Childhood* and *My Universities* and the novel *The Mother*. A socialist from his early days, he never joined the Communist Party. He offered qualified support to the Soviet state after 1918, living abroad from 1924 to 1932. In 1934 he became head of the Writers' Union but his work showed an increasing awareness that something had gone wrong with the revolution. He died in 1936.

MAXIM GORKY

Plays: 2

The Last Ones
Vassa Zheleznova
The Zykovs
Egor Bulychev

Translated and introduced by Cathy Porter

Methuen Drama

METHUEN DRAMA WORLD CLASSICS

Published by Methuen Drama 2003

1 3 5 7 9 10 8 6 4 2

First published in 2003 by
Methuen Publishing Limited

A CIP catalogue record for this book is available from the British Library.

ISBN 0 413 76940 2

Typeset by SX Composing DTP, Rayleigh, Essex
Printed and bound in Great Britain by
Cox and Wyman Ltd, Reading, Berkshire

These translations are fully protected by copyright. All enquiries concerning the
rights for professional or amateur stage production should be made before
rehearsals begin to: Rosica Colin Agency, 1 Clareville Grove Mews, London
SW7 5AH.

Contents

Maxim Gorky: A Chronology

1868*   16 March: Born, Alexei Maximovich Peshkov,
          in Nizhny Novgorod, 225 miles east of Moscow.
          Mother from a family of dyers; father a joiner,
          later a wharf-manager.

1871   Father, aged thirty-one, dies of cholera, caught
          from his son.

1873   Mother leaves Alexei to be brought up by his
          grandparents.

1879   Mother, aged thirty-seven, dies of consumption.
          Grandfather sends Alexei away to earn his own
          living.

1879–1884 Nomadic labourer: boot-boy, errand-boy, bird-
          catcher, dishwasher on Volga steamers, assistant
          in an icon shop. Self-education begins.

1884   Discovers Chekhov's short stories. Arrives in
          Kazan, hoping to enter University, but fails to
          get a place. Works as a stevedore, meets students,
          intellectuals, workers, revolutionaries. Works in
          a bakery. Studies the violin, tries to fall in love,
          but fails at both.

1887   Death of Grandmother and Grandfather.

1887   December: tries to commit suicide, succeeds only
          in damaging left lung.

1888   Works in a fishery on the Caspian Sea, then as a
          railway night-watchman. Arrested for the first
          time on suspicion of subversive activities.

1889   Toys with Tolstoyism and dreams of setting up a
          Tolstoyan commune. Goes to Moscow, hoping
          to meet Tolstoy, but fails to find him at home.
          Shows his verse to the elderly Populist writer
          Korolenko, whose gentle criticism causes him to
          tear up his manuscripts and vow never to write
          again.

with Chekhov in Yalta and is encouraged to write for the theatre. Soon begins work on the play, *The Lower Depths*, but has the idea for another play, *Philistines*, as well.

April–May: Imprisoned in Nizhny Novgorod for taking part in student demonstration in St Petersburg.

May: birth of daughter, Katya.

September: Completes *Philistines*.

1902   February: Elected Honorary Academician in *Belles Lettres*. Election cancelled on instructions of Tsar Nicholas II, leading to resignation in protest o Chekhov and Korolenko.

26 March: Premiere of *Philistines* given by Moscow Art Theatre on tour in St Petersburg.

May–August: Gorky exiled in Arzamas.

June: Completes *The Lower Depths*.

18 December: Première of *The Lower Depths* at the Moscow Art Theatre.

1903   January: *The Lower Depths* staged at Max Reinhardt's Kleines Theatre in Berlin and runs for over 500 performances. Soon afterwards: London premiere by Stage Society. Following meeting with Lenin's supporters in Moscow, Gorky gives considerable financial support to the Social Democratic Party.

1904   April: Reads first draft of his play, *Summerfolk*, to Moscow Art Theatre company. Following criticism of the text by Nemirovich-Danchenko, Gorky reworks it extensively then offers it to other theatres.

10 November: Premiere of *Summerfolk* at Passage Theatre, St. Petersburg.

1905   9 January; Gorky involved in the organisation of the workers' demonstrations which are brutally suppressed in the slaughter of 'Bloody Sunday'. Gorky drafts proclamation calling for 'a united struggle against the Autocracy' and is again arrested and imprisoned.

14 February: Released from the Peter and Paul Fortress following an international outcry. Completes his next play, *Children of the Sun*, during his imprisonment.

12 October: Premiere of *Children of the Sun*, at Vera Komissarzhevskaya's theatre in St Petersburg, twelve days before the first Moscow Art Theatre performance.

27 November: First meeting with Lenin in St Petersburg.

December: Organise supplies for the Moscow armed uprising.

1906   4 January: Takes refuge in Finland, but is forced to leave after five weeks. Moves on to Berlin. Gorky is accompanied by the actress, Maria Andreeva, who is now his common-law wife though Gorky has never formally divorced.

March: *Barbarians* published and given first performance in Riga.

10 April: Arrives in New York in order to campaign against a loan to the Tsarist government and to raise funds for the Bolsheviks. Meets figures from the artistic and political spheres, including Mark Twain and H.G. Wells, but is attacked in the Hearst press for his 'immoral' relationship with Andreeva and forced out of public life.

During the Summer: Lives privately with the Martin family, first on Staten Island and then in the Adirondacks. Completes his novel, *The Mother*, and the play, *Enemies*.

August: Daughter dies of meningitis in Nizhny Novgorod.

13 October; Gorky and Andreeva sail from New York for Italy.

2 November: Arrive on Capri, where Gorky spends the next seven years.

December: *Enemies* published in Stuttgart and St Petersburg. Serialisation of *The Mother* starts in

Appleton's Magazine, New York, followed by translations into numerous other languages.

22 February: Premiere of *Enemies* in Poltava, despite complete ban on the play following publication.

1907   April: The publishing house, Znanie (Knowledge), starts serialisation of *The Mother* in Russia.

May: Attends Fifth Congress of the Russian Social Democratic Party in London. Meets Shaw and Thomas Hardy, and re-encounters H.G. Wells.

1908   January: Completes the play, *The Last Ones*, which is banned in Russia for its portrayal of the police as 'inveterate scoundrels' but performed in Tashkent in June.

June: Lenin visits Gorky on Capri.

Publication of *A Confession* the novel in which Gorky attempts a fushion of Marxism and Christianity, to become a key text in the 'God-building' heresy of Russian Marxism.

1909   July–December: With Bogdanov and Luna-charsky sets up a school for revolutionary Russian workers on Capri. Lenin attacks 'God-builders' and refuses to have any part in the school.

1910   July: Lenin and Gorky reconciled – Lenin visits Gorky again on Capri.

During the Summer: Completion of two further plays, *Queer People* and *Vassa Zheleznova*.

September: Premiere of *Queer People* at the New Dramatic Theatre, St Petersburg.

1911   February: Premiere of *Vassa Zheleznova* at the Nezlobin Theatre, Moscow.

Stanislavsky visits Capri and discusses the development of his 'System' with Gorky.

1912–1913   Writes *Childhood*, the first part of his autobiographical trilogy.

1912   April: First edition of *Pravda* appears in Russia, with considerable financial assistance from Gorky. But due to the cooling of his relations with the

Bolsheviks he contributes no articles to the paper.

1913   February: On the three hundredth anniversary of the Romanov dynasty an amnesty for political exiles guilty of no violent crimes is announced. Lenin urges Gorky to return but he remains apprehensive.

July: Completes *The Zykovs* but refuses to give the play to the Moscow Art Theatre because he objects to their political staging of Dostoevsky.

31 December: Returns with Maria Andreeva to St Petersburg.

1914   During the Summer: Works on the second part of his autobiography, *My Apprenticeship*.

1915   December: Launches new monthly literary journal, *Letopis* ('Annals').

Opposes Russia's participation in the Great War.

1917   April: Founds and edits *New Life*, a daily newspaper which becomes the most widely read amongst the intelligentsia. In his column 'Untimely Thoughts' Gorky regularly criticises all factions, including the Bolsheviks. After the February Revolution in 1917 he opposes Lenin's plans for a further Bolshevik rising. He himself is attacked by the Right as a Bolshevik and pro-German, and by the Leninist Left as a proponent of 'false unification'.

1918   July: Premieres of *The Last Ones* and *The Zykovs* in the newly named Petrograd.

New Life forced to cease publication. Gorky is reconciled with Lenin but remains critical of the Bolshevik regime.

December: Elected to the Executive Committee of the Petrograd Workers' and Soldiers' Soviet and to its presidium.

1918–1921   Throughout the Civil War and after, Gorky regularly intercedes with Lenin to protect intellectuals and sets up organisations to improve their living conditions.

1921   16 October: Is persuaded finally by Lenin to

leave Russia for medical treatment abroad, at the same time distancing him from hostility within the Party. He recuperates at a sanatorium in the Black Forest.

1922--1924   Travels about Europe. Completes *My Universities*.

1924   21 January; Death of Lenin.
April: Gorky settles in Sorrento.
Continues autobiographical writings.

1926   January: Completes *The Artamanov Business*.

1927   22 October: Gorky's thirty-fifth anniversary as a writer is celebrated at the Communist Academy in Moscow and he is declared to be 'a proletarian writer'.

1928–1932   Spends the winters in Sorrento and the summers in Moscow, eventually returning to Russia for good.

1930–1932   Completes his final trilogy of plays, *Somov and Others, Egor Bulychev and Others, Dostigaev and Others*.

1932   September: Gorky's fortieth anniversary as a writer. He is awarded the Order of Lenin, the Gorky Literary Institute is founded in Moscow, and *Egor Bulychev* is given simultaneous premieres in Moscow and Leningrad, initiating the revival of his earlier plays. Nizhny Novgorod is renamed Gorky.

1933   September: Premiere of revised version of *Enemies* at the Pushkin Theatre, Leningrad, followed shortly by a second production in Moscow.

1934   10 May: Membership ticket No 1 of Union of Soviet Writers issued to Gorky.
11 May: Death of son, Maxim.
August–September: First All-Union Congress of Soviet Writers. Gorky elected chairman. Delivers opening and closing address.

1935   October: First performance of *Enemies* at Moscow Art Theatre.
December: Gorky completes revision of *Vassa Zheleznova*. Over next five years it is staged by almost every major Soviet theatre.

1935–1936   Gorky is twice refused a passport to travel abroad.
              18 June: Gorky dies of a lung infection associated with his tubercular condition. Rumours of suspicious cirucmstances have never been clarified.

* Dates for events in Russia before 1918 are given according to the 'old style' or Julian calendar which was thirteen days behind the Gregorian calendar adopted in the West.

Introduction

'The harder things were for me, the stronger and wiser I was,' wrote Gorky in *My Childhood*. 'I realised a person is created through resistance to his environment.' Huge and clumsy, with the appearance of a tramp and the soul of a poet, he was born in Russia soon after the abolition of serfdom and rose from poverty to become the most celebrated playwright of the revolution – an intensely romantic figure compared abroad to Tolstoy, Chekhov and Dostoevsky – who threw his considerable authority behind the Bolsheviks. Outside Russia, however, only a handful of his plays are performed, and most in the West will be unfamiliar with these dark melodramas about merchant life on the Volga where he grew up, and the strong against the weak.

Gorky was born Alexei Peshkov in 1868 in Nizhny Novgorod, the son of a poor shipyard carpenter and he spent his early years in the house of his grandfather, who had worked his way up from hauling barges to running a small dye-works. When he was three, they moved downriver to Astrakhan, where his brother Maxim was born and his father was employed as a shipping agent. He died shortly afterwards in a cholera epidemic and they returned to Nizhny Novgorod – Maxim died on the way and was buried in Saratov.

The business was unable to keep up with modern dyeing techniques and faced ruin. 'Hatred filled my grandfather's house like a fog,' he wrote. Also living there were his two uncles and their families, waiting for the old man to die, so the young Gorky was often whipped to an inch of his life. His mother remarried – a man who beat her then disappeared – and the family lived in penury in a basement. From his grandmother, though, he learned of a gentle God of love and heard stories of spirits and saints, and at night they would go to the woods to gather herbs and berries which they sold at the market. He picked rags and paper from the streets and gave the money to her. He was bullied at school for it, falling in with a gang of boys who stole from the timberyards.

When Gorky was eleven his mother died of tuberculosis and his grandfather sent him to earn his living in a shoeshop, sweeping the floor and heating the samovar. At twelve, he was apprenticed to a draftsman. The house was steeped in alcohol and piety, and on Sundays he would go to church and wander through the city, peering at the 'one-kopeck panoramas' behind people's windows. That spring he stole twenty kopecks and ran away to sleep rough by the river with the loaders. He worked as a pantry boy on a steamer, where the cook encouraged him to read; then he would return to the draftsman's house, catching songbirds to sell at the market and reading illustrated newspapers and penny-dreadfuls at night by the light of a tallow candle. He was beaten for it – so badly once that doctors wanted to inform the police, but he demanded instead the right to read and a neighbour gave him novels by Turgenev, Flaubert and Dickens.

He worked as a cabin boy, then for a icon painter. There were wild vodka sessions, where he met heretics and Old Believers (followers of the Old Russian Orthodoxy) who had been persecuted and sent to Siberia. He both admired and detested their humility and patience, 'that virtue of trees and rocks', and he read voraciously – Tolstoy, Gogol, Dostoevsky – struggling to apply Tolstoy's ideas of non-resistance to the life he saw around him and particularly men's cruelty to women. 'Buried in fiction, I regarded women as the best, most important element in life,' he wrote.

When he was fifteen he worked as a nightwatchman at a building site, armed with a club. But 'possessions displeased me', and he dreamed of a better life. Determined to make something of himself, he travelled down the Volga to Kazan, hoping to enrol at the university where Tolstoy had studied and gain in a year the certificate that would win him a scholarship.

He arrived penniless, he lived in the cellar of a ruined house with his equally penniless friend Evreinov, who taught him all he knew from his own reading, mainly philosophers of the French Enlightenment. But Gorky lacked knowledge and, abandoning his dreams of further education, he began work as a casual labourer on the docks, living with another student in a house full of jailbirds, prostitutes and revolutionaries – later immortalised as the Volga flop house in which he set his play *The Lower Depths*. The he moved out and worked in a bakery, sleeping at nights by the stove.

The bakery was one of his 'universities', and the story he wrote fifteen years later, *Twenty-Six Men and a Woman*, movingly evokes the airless, inhuman atmosphere in which twenty-six men toil sixteen hours a day and set out to deflower the beautiful girl who comes to buy bread.

He met socialists, joining a political study group and calling himself a Marxist, but he disliked their worshipful attitude to the workers, and preferred being with them to talking about them. He knew drudgery, the squalid tenements where people lived and the cruel inequalities of tsarism, but he was fascinated, too, by people like his grandfather who emerged from the lower depths to run their own businesses, and the Volga merchants and shipping magnates who were opening up pre-revolutionary Russia to capitalist development. These self-made, strong-willed millionaires and entrepreneurs – constantly veering between extremes of joy and cruelty – inspired some of the most powerful characters in his plays, such as Zykov, Bulychev, Vassa Zheleznova.

Life in the bakery cast him into a deep depression, and at the age of nineteen he bought an army pistol, went to the river and shot himself in the chest. The bullet punctured his lung but avoided his heart, and after a second attempt with hydrochloric acid he was summoned to an ecclesiastical tribunal at the Theodore Monastery and excommunicated for seven years for his 'atheistic act'; the shot permanently damaged his lung, and he suffered the first symptoms of TB.

In 1888, Gorky worked in a village on the Volga for his friend Romass, a former revolutionary and political exile who ran a shop and wanted to share his large library with the peasants. The peasants burned the library down and Romass moved on, while Gorky wandered from village to village working as a nightwatchman. In 1889 he set out on foot to meet Tolstoy in Moscow, then returned to Nizhny Novgorod, where he fell in love for the first time, with a married woman.

In the next two years he wandered in earnest, on foot and by freight train to the Don steppes, the Ukraine, the Crimea, the Caucasus, and down the Volga to the Caspian Sea, working on the docks and in a salt mine, harvesting grapes, composing poetry in his head and recording his conversations with the vagrants, revolutionaries and labourers he met. His first story was published in Georgia, where he was working at the Tiflis railway depot, and it was there he renamed himself Maxim Gorky – Maxim after his dead brother and Gorky meaning 'bitter', which was his father's nickname.

He had already come to the attention of the police when he returned to Saratov. He wrote a daily column for the local paper and married eighteen-year-old Ekaterina Volzhina, a proofreader and revolutionary, with whom he had two children. Between 1893 and 1899, he published *Stories and Sketches*, and his first novel, *Foma Godeev*, the story of a 'superfluous man'. When more stories came out in 1900, their spellbinding narrative and crude, powerful message of revolution made him instantly popular.

At the age of thirty, Gorky was Russia's most talked about writer. His rise from provincial obscurity was dramatic, and fame abroad soon followed. Interviews and photographs of him flooded the press. He made money, and gave much of it to political causes. He corresponded with Chekhov, and gratefully accepted his criticisms of his verbiage and lack of restraint, and his house became a focus and meeting place for socialists and writers.

In 1900, he protested against the drafting of students into the army, and wrote his first play, *The Petty Bourgeois*, and his novel *The Three of Them*, about three friends trying to live by their revolutionary ideals. It was seized by the police and he was banished to the Crimea. People carried him to the train on their shoulders and greeted him en route. Forbidden to stop in Moscow for fear of demonstrations or to visit Chekhov in Yalta, he ignored these orders and stayed with the sick Chekhov, before moving his wife and children into a house next to where Tolstoy was staying.

He was exiled to Arzamas, south of Nizhny Novgorod, where he wrote *The Lower Depths*, and in 1902 the Moscow Art

Theatre staged four performances of *The Petty Bourgeois*. The director, Nemirovich Danchenko, battled with the censors for every word. The police replaced the ushers and surrounded the theatre on horseback, and it was performed with numerous cuts on the assumption it would be a flop. But the truthful, naturalistic text, the acting and sets made it a triumph, and when *The Lower Depths* opened later that year Gorky was fêted as the successor to Chekhov and a national hero.

During the run of *The Lower Depths* he fell in love with the leading actress, Maria Andreeva, a Bolshevik already married to a railway official, who became his common-law wife, working with him finding new writers for the socialist publishing house Znanie (Knowledge). He was savaged in the press by the Union of the Russian People, and attacked by a member of a Black Hundreds gang who tried to stab him in the heart, but this only increased his popularity in Russia's factories, drawing rooms and universities.

In 1904 his third play, *Summerfolk*, was staged in Moscow, and Russia went to war with Japan. Sixteen months later the Russian fleet was at the bottom of the Japanese Sea and a humiliating peace treaty was signed. People's lives were desperately hard. There were strikes and food riots, and when Gorky joined a delegation of writers who petitioned the Interior Minister in St Petersburg asking him to allow a peaceful workers' demonstration they turned away. He was there when on 9 January 1905, soldiers outside the Tsar's Winter Palace killed three hundred people in the Bloody Sunday massacre that sparked the first Russian revolution. 'So it has begun,' Gorky wrote to his first wife in Nizhny Novgorod. 'History takes a new colour when soaked in blood.'

Arrested for trying to set up a 'provisional government', he spent a month in the Peter and Paul Fortress – where he wrote his fourth play, *Children of the Sun* – and the next eight months living under police surveillance in Riga.

He returned to the capital that autumn after the Tsar granted the new government, the Duma, and dropped charges against him. He met Lenin, also back from exile, and worked with him on the first legal Bolshevik newspaper, *New Life*, which was defended by eight Georgian Bolsheviks against Black

Hundreds attack, and in December he distributed weapons to workers in Moscow during the General Strike, turning his flat there into an operations centre for the street fighting. It ended in a bloodbath, and he left Russia with Maria Andreeva to escape arrest, mobbed at the station by the usual crowds of admirers.

For the next eight years they lived in exile – from Finland and Scandinavia to Berlin, where *The Lower Depths* had been in continuous production for over a year, then Paris, and finally New York, whose 'brazen wealth, based on the poverty of the people' provoked his article 'City of the Yellow Devil', and where he wrote his play *Enemies* and his novel *The Mother*, about the strike movement in Nizhny Novgorod.

Late in 1906, they finally sought refuge in Italy, and were welcomed by crowds of radicals in Naples, where he addressed packed meetings about the Russian revolution, before leaving for the island of Capri. In Capri, they unofficially adopted a twenty-eight-year-old wanderer and revolutionary called Zinovy, who renamed himself Peshkov, and later took French citizenship and became an eminent Diplomat. It was there the exiled Bolsheviks Bogdanov and Lunacharsky, with whom Gorky organised a training school for workers, recruiting them from the factories and bringing them to the island with false papers for lectures about literature, philosophy and underground struggle. Like Bogdanov and Lunacharsky, he thought politics should be reformed and 'spiritualised' in a sort of 'religion of the people', and his religious preoccupations at this time are apparent in the three plays he wrote there – *The Last Ones, Vassa* and *The Zykovs*.

*

Originally entitled *The Father, The Last Ones* was written in 1908, as terrorists roamed the streets of Russia shooting unpopular members of the police. It depicts the family of a brutal police chief, Kolomiitsev, tearing themselves apart after an attempt on his life. The characters' names ironically reflect the then fashion in Russia for symbolism and allegory – Kolomiitsev's daughters are Nadezhda, Vera and Lyubov (Hope, Faith and Love), their mother Sofia (Wisdom), his dying brother Yakov (the biblical Jacob). The action is set in Yakov's flat, nailed and shuttered against the terrorists outside, and the dialogue is dark and internal, heavy with family secrets and hints of incest and illegitimacy. Careers and lives are bought and sold with money and sexual favours. Vera prepares to sell herself in marriage to prop up the family finances. Alexander, Kolomiitsev's son, ransacks Yakov's money to advance his career. Nadazhda sells her body to her husband's superiors to promote his. Fedosia the nurse mutters riddles in her corner, and the crippled Lyubov watches from the other. Her role as the family Cassandra finally leads us to the truth of her birth, and when Yakov dies it seems the family's last link with life is gone.

The Last Ones was performed only once in Russia during Gorky's lifetime, in Tashkent when its publication in Znanie was savaged by censors and critics alike for portraying the police as 'inveterate scoundrels', undermining family values and the authority of the state. Its first performance in translation was in Berlin's Kammerspieler in 1910. It was revived in Berlin in 1991. It was staged two years later at Dublin's Abbey Theatre in this, its first English translation.

Vassa Zheleznova is also about social and family breakdown in the aftermath of 1905. He wrote it in Italy in 1910 and returned to it six months before his death in December 1935, to produce a second harsher and darker version in which he exposes the barbarity of small-town life before the revolution with its greedy merchants, anti-Semitism, corruption and child abuse. This is the version translated here. Like *The Last Ones*, it shows different aspects of a disintegrating family after the sudden death of their husband and father, arrested for raping a twelve-year-old girl. It is set in two rooms of the Zheleznovs' house in Kazan, presided over by the ruthless widow Vassa, owner of a large Volga shipping firm, who runs her two daughters and her alcoholic brother as she runs her business, negotiating with workers and shipping agents, buying and selling land. Around this family Gorky creates a large cast of servants, hangers-on, friends and a vivid panorama of provincial Russia that is both chilling and excruciatingly comic. It is his skill as a writer to see Vassa's humanity despite her murderous cruelty, and though he intends to give the last word to her daughter-in-law, the revolutionary Rachel, it is Vassa we remember and we warm to her as we hate her.

The earlier *Vassa* premiered at Moscow's Nezlobin Theatre in 1911 and was revived frequently after the revolution but, apart from its title it has little in common with this version, with its infinitely sharper plot, dialogue and politics. It was first performed in 1935 in Leningrad's Collective Farm Theatre and subsequently at every major Soviet theatre. It was staged in this translation at the Gate Theatre, London, in 1991.

The Zykovs is set in the same period, and was written in 1913, after Gorky was invited by the Moscow Art Theatre to write a play to be performed that spring. 'A man dances as if breaking his chains, then suddenly a ferocious beast bursts through and he hurls himself at all he sees, tearing, biting, destroying,' he wrote in *My Universities*. In Antipa Zykov and Egor Bulychev, he created two of his most memorable heroes of this type – successful businessmen, unstoppable and elemental, despising the human race and others' perception of them. Antipa is a wealthy timber merchant, all Russian soul and feeling, who commits the unthinkable in the first act by stealing his son's fiancée, Pavla, an unworldly convent-bred girl. Torn between her Tolstoyan ideals of non-resistance and her worldly love of Antipa but unable to realise them with him, she sinks into despair while Antipa drowns in alcohol, and his sister Sofia is left to run the estate.

'Everything's upside-down, no one knows their place,' says Tarakanov the book-keeper as the melodrama unfolds. Pavla's mother, the genteel Tselovaneva, moves in and laments the comforts of her little house; lecherous Muratov the forest-warden and Antipa's business partner Hevern have designs to marry Sofia for her money; Stepka the servant knows and sees everything and Sofia dreams Chekhovian dreams of meeting 'good people'.

Gorky's plays have the same laughter through tears as Chekhov's – the same provincial settings and philosophical discussions, but there's always a sense of the world of work, the forests, timber-mills and railways and the river, where people labour and fortunes are lost and made. There is little hidden dynamic; the characters are onstage together most of the time with their flaws and contradictions. Pavla speaks the truth, but is naive and weak. Antipa is brutal, abusive and uneducated, but there's an honesty that draws us to him as he rails against drabness, snobbery and stagnation.

Critics hated *The Zykovs* when it opened in 1918 at Petrograd's (formerly St Petersburg) People's Theatre and panned it as a 'blatant apology for bourgeois individualism, which denigrates the young Russia as greedy, bloodless and degenerate.' Despite this it was performed regularly in Soviet Russia, and became one of Gorky's most popular plays.

To his annoyance the Moscow Art Theatre staged a version of Dostoevsky's anti-revolutionary novel *The Devils*, and in 1913 he had handed in this pro-revolutionary play in protest to be read at Moscow's Free Theatre. In that year, to commemorate the three hundredth anniversary of the Romanov dynasty, the Tsar declared a political amnesty for some exiles · including Gorky, and some Moscow students wrote to him: 'We firmly hope we are about to welcome the flowering of a new spring, and like to believe we will welcome it with you.' He went back alone, trailed by the police. He found the anti-German atmosphere in Moscow unbearable, and suffered a worsening of his TB. 'Everything is rotten,' he wrote to Andreeva.

Two years later, over a million Russian soldiers had been killed in the war with Germany, the Tsar was under the influence of the sinister Rasputin and only the Bolsheviks were calling for peace. Regiments deserted *en masse*, peasants rioted, there were food riots and demonstrations and beggars, speculators and child prostitutes filled the streets.

He published *My Childhood* in 1913, the first volume of his autobiography, a touching account of his early years, followed by *With People* and *My Universities*, and used the royalties to fund an anti-war publishing house and the paper *New Life* in which he denounced Bolshevik extremism on culture and free speech. But as the Allies gathered forces to topple the revolution he joined the Bolshevik party again, so when people stormed the newly renamed Petrograd in February 1917, demanding bread and peace and invading the barracks, he helped arm the Bolshevik Red Guards who appeared on the streets to keep order.

Three weeks later the Tsar abdicated, and the Duma formed a new 'Provisional Government'. There were more strikes and demonstrations and by the summer the peasants' revolt was beyond the point of no return and the soldiers were calling for revolution. On September 25, soldiers and sailors stormed the Winter Palace and arrested the cabinet. The Bolsheviks were in power.

He set *Egor Bulychev* in this period between February and October 1917 and wrote it in 1931 as the first (unfinished) part of a trilogy that would span the period from the revolution to the thirties, and included *Somov and Others* and *Dostigaev and Others*.

Like Antipa, Bulychev runs a successful timbercompany and has pushed his family and his freedom to the limit in orgies of drink and violence, and is now dying of cancer. The play is set in Kostroma on the Volga and the character of Bulychev is based on a merchant Gorky knew named Bolshakov, who called the priest to his room and confessed to raping his niece, then ordered his wife and daughter to remove the icons and died.

It opens in the spring of 1917. Rasputin holds sway at court, wounded soldiers pour into the town from the front, deserters hide out in the forests, and the once-powerful Bulychev lies on the sofa waiting to die; a bear is shot, but his hunting days are over. Surrounding him are his daughter and her husband; his wife, his illegitimate daughter Shura and his lover Glafira – the family servant. All but Shura and Glafira hope to profit from his will and if necessary change it. The merchant Dostigaev (who later had his own play) plots with Bulychev's sister-in-law Melania, the Mother Superior of a convent, to drive him mad. The play ends in a glorious deathbed farce of lunatics, mystics and faith-healers, while crowds outside the window sing for those killed defending the revolution and the new world to come.

*

The Western powers ignored the Bolsheviks' peace proposals in the hope they would collapse, and over the next three years Soviet Russia was invaded from every direction by the armies of fourteen states. Whilst accepting the necessary rigours of

Communism during the war, Gorky tried to soften them, petitioning Lenin in the ensuing famine for extra rations for writers and artists. In many cases he saved them from the secret police – the Cheka – and headed committees to protect museums and monuments and for famine relief.

He believed the future belonged to the committed, not the sceptical, but his idolisation as a writer and figurehead of the revolution made his relationship with the new government a difficult one. In 1921 his All Russia Famine Relief Committee was suddenly closed down by the Cheka, and he left with Maria Andreeva for Germany where he was treated at government expense in a TB sanatorium in the Black Forest. For the next three years he lived in Berlin and Italy, surrounded by friends and working on his new novel, *Klim Samgin*. Emigré writers accused him of having sold out to the devil, but he loved his country and longed to go back.

In 1928, the year of the first Five-year Plan, he returned with his son Max and was welcomed home as a hero. There were meetings and demonstrations in Moscow, and he produced articles and lectures on the value of work 'which makes everything beautiful', and the redeeming power of literature. 'Art is the beauty people have been able to create even under the yoke of subjugation,' he wrote.

Intoxicated by the new Russia, he met delegations of young writers, walked the streets of Moscow in disguise talking to people, and made long journeys to Armenia, the Caucasus, Nizhny Novgorod and Kazan, visiting schools, factories and delinquent colonies, and writing enthusiastically about the Arctic hell of the Solovetsky Island prison-camp in the White Sea.

Egor Bulychev was premiered simultaneously in Moscow and Leningrad, *The Lower Depths* was in constant production, the new Gorky literary institute opened in Moscow, and the town of Nizhny Novgorod took his name during the Soviet period. The authorities housed him and his family in a three-storey mansion, with secretaries and a motorcar, but he was watched closely and felt uneasy living in such splendour. He was deluged with mail, much of it hate-mail, and the police extended its protection over him by vetting his staff.

In May 1934 his son Max died suddenly of pneumonia.

Confused, and drowning in adulation, he sank into a deep depression from which he never fully recovered. By then, according to the revolutionary Victor Serge, he was no longer a man but an institution. 'I caught a glimpse of him once, leaning back alone on the rear seat of a big Lincoln car,' he wrote. 'He seemed remote from the street, remote from the life of Moscow, reduced to an algebraic cypher of himself. He hadn't aged, rather thinned and dried, his head bony and angular under his Turkish skullcap, his nose and cheekbones jutting, his eye-sockets hollow as a skeleton's.'

Three months later he told six hundred delegates from fifty countries at the First Congress of Soviet Writers: 'Nowhere else in the world has there been a state where literature and science have benefitted from such fraternal aid as in the Soviet Union'. In the spectacular purges which followed Kirov's assassination that year, books were banned, writers were arrested and his friends disappeared – it made Gorky desperate but he said nothing. He made friends with officials at the Ministry of Culture, received Stalin at his house, and, astonishingly, amid the show-trials and conspiracies he celebrated his 'will of iron', and called on writers to be 'engineers of human souls'. Yet he still wrote, racked by tuberculosis, oxygen cylinder at hand, completing his revision of *Vassa* and perhaps putting his true feelings about the monster in the Kremlin into its bloodthirsty heroine.

In May 1936, at the age of sixty-eight, he caught influenza which spread to his lungs, and on the morning of 18 June he died. Stalin personally organised the funeral, and thousands paid their respects to his body at the Hall of Columns, where it lay in state attended by senior ministers. His ashes were buried at the Kremlin wall in a massive ceremony on Red Square, and as his canonisation continued in death, people began to wonder if it might have been suspicious. There were rumours that Stalin had killed him, and autopsies on his body and those of his two nurses revealed traces of poison. In 1938 in a final posthumous insult, several members of the secret police as well as prominent Bolsheviks and doctors were arrested on, among other things, the 'medical assassination' of Gorky and his son Max.

His naivety and optimism were exploited by the regime and it finally broke him, but his spirit and writing survive. Set in the landscapes of his wandering years and his childhood, with their sparkling dialogue and deep understanding of character, the plays are written with the passion and truthfulness that enabled him to survive his difficult and extraordinary origins. His Zykovs, Zheleznovs, Bulychevs and Kolomiitsevs live for us almost a century after his death.

The Last Ones

The Last Ones was first produced in this translation at the Abbey Theatre, Dublin on 3 March 1993. The cast was as follows:

Ivan Kolomiitsev	Tom Hickey
Sofia	Ingrid Craigie
Alexander	Declan Conlon
Pyotr	J.D. Kelleher
Nadezhda	Catherine White
Lyubov	Susan Lynch
Vera	Zara Turner
Yakov	Nick Dunning
Mrs Sokolova	Fedelma Cullen
Pavel Dmitrevich Leshch	Eamonn Hunt
Yakorev	Liam Cunningham
Fedosia	Doreen Keogh
Natalya	Sarah Jane Scafe

Director Katie Mitchell
Designer Vicki Mortimer
Lighting Designer Tina McHugh
Musical Director Helen Chadwick

Characters

Ivan Kolomiitsev, *retired police chief*
Sofia (*Sonya, Sofiushka, Soniushka*), *his wife*
Alexander (*Sasha*), *his son, twenty-six*
Pyotr (*Petya*), *his son, eighteen*
Nadezhda (*Nadya*), *his daughter, twenty-three*
Lyubov (*Lyuba*), *his daughter, twenty, a hunchback*
Vera, (*Verochka, Vera*), *his daughter, sixteen*
Yakov (*Yasha, Yashenka*), *his brother*
Mrs Sokolova, *mother of suspected terrorist*
Pavel Dmitrevich Leshch (*Pasha*), *Nadezhda's husband*
Yakorev, *police constable*
Fedosia, *the family nurse*
Maid

Act One

A large and comfortable drawing room with screens at the back, behind which is a narrow white bed with a red blanket. A large bookcase divides the room in two, the right side larger than the left. On the left is a fireplace. A carpet hangs over the back of the bookcase. Against it stands an upright piano. Opposite is a wide sofa and a small window. At the back of the room a door leads to the dining room, where a light is on. If a stool is drawn to the piano, access to the dining room is blocked.

In a deep armchair by the fireplace, **Yakov** *sits reading a book. He has grey curly hair, and a gentle, clean-shaven face. Behind his armchair is a writing desk, on which stands a tall lamp with a green paper shade. Seated in an armchair by the desk is* **Fedosia**, *old and very deaf. She has a long piece of grey knitting and a ball of wool on her knees, and mumbles to herself incessantly. In the dining room the* **Maid** *moves around silently, laying the table for dinner.*

Also in the dining room is **Sofia**. *She has a pale but still youthful face, and is staring anxiously into the distance. She hears* **Yakov** *raking the coals in the grate, then enters slowly. She hesitates a moment behind the bookcase.*

Sofia   Am I disturbing you?

Yakov (*with a welcoming smile*)   How can you ask!

Sofia   I thought you might be busy.

Yakov (*removing his pince-nez*)   Doing what?

Sofia   I wanted to ask you – Mrs Sokolova, the mother of the boy who shot at Ivan, wants me to receive her. D'you think I should?

Yakov (*uncertainly*)   I don't know . . . She has a right to see you, as his mother . . . But why you, not Ivan?

Fedosia (*mumbles without raising her head*)   Wait and see, wait and see . . .

Sofia   You think the boy did it?

Yakov   Me? I believe the terrorists – they say he's not one of them.

Sofia   I believe them too.

Yakov   Why don't you sit down?

Sofia (*hangs her head*)   I can't.

Yakov   You look so tired.

Sofia (*quietly*)   I'll be even tireder if I sit down. (*Still more quietly.*) Yakov, forgive me, I must ask you for money.

Yakov (*hurriedly, with embarrassment*)   Take it, don't ask – it's in my desk, top drawer on the left. It's not locked.

Sofia   I hate robbing you.

Yakov   You're not robbing me, Sonya!

Fedosia (*mumbles*)   Go ahead, he'll soon be dead!

Lyubov *enters from the dining room, wearing a shawl over her shoulders to hide her crippled back.*

Sofia (*pensively*)   We move into your house when you're sick, we drive you into a corner . . .

Yakov (*embarrassed*)   That's enough now, Sonya.

Sofia   There, I took a hundred.

Lyubov *moves the stool to the piano and starts playing softly.*

Yakov   Listen, I want to offer you . . .

Sofia   I must go, tell me after dinner, will you? (*Goes to the dining room.*)

Yakov (*picks up his book*)   Whenever you like.

Fedosia (*humming a lullaby*)   'Sleep, Yasha, sleep . . .' (*Mumbles inaudibly, as though rocking a cradle.*)

Sofia (*stops behind* **Lyubov**, *who ignores her*)   Let me pass, Lyuba.

Lyubov   I'm not stopping you.

Sofia   You're in the way.

Lyubov   I'm always in the way, Mother.

Sofia (*steps on the sofa and jumps round her daughter's stool*) Don't be cross . . .

Lyubov (*leaps up*)   You're only doing that so you can blame me!

Sofia (*quietly, exiting*)   I've never blamed you for anything.

Lyubov *rises and enters* **Yakov**'s *part of the room.*

Yakov (*quietly*)   How angry you are.

Lyubov (*calmly*)   Angry? Everyone says that. People hate me like a wet autumn or cold winter.

Fedosia (*hums*)   'Praise the Lord, our Lyuba's here . . . !'

Lyubov (*loudly*)   Stop it, Nurse!

Fedosia   What? (*Rakes her hair with a knitting needle and smiles at her.*)

Yakov   You complain too much, Lyuba.

Lyubov   People complain about wet autumns and cold winters, they're no good to anyone either. How much did she take?

Yakov   A hundred. Why?

Lyubov   Why not give it to her in one go, then she won't have to beg? You can see how it humiliates her!

Yakov (*embarrassed*)   I know, I was just about to.

Lyubov (*prompting him*)   After all, you're awfully rich.

Yakov (*smiling*)   I was. The aluminium ruined me.

Lyubov   Why aluminium?

Yakov (*sheepishly*)   Here's this extraordinary metal, I thought, wouldn't it be splendid if people could use it? Iron is dark and heavy, brass is dense . . .

Lyubov (*sighs*)   You're a funny man!

Fedosia (*sighing too*)   Lord, Lord, forgive us sinners . . .

Lyubov   Have you made many mistakes in your life?

Yakov (*grins*)   No, the mistakes were always made by others!

Lyubov (*stares into his face*)   I know one mistake you made.

Yakov (*anxiously*)   Really? What was that?

Lyubov   Not marrying my mother . . .

Yakov (*alarmed*)   Please, Lyuba, keep out of it, it's too complicated. If I were you I'd . . .

Lyubov   So who *am* I?

Yakov (*lowers his eyes*)   You ask such strange questions . . .

Lyubov (*persistently*)   Why can't I make you angry? I infuriate everyone else, why not you?

Yakov   I don't know!

Lyubov   Mother would have been happier with you than with that drunk.

Yakov   Lyuba, darling, please, what makes you say that?

Lyubov   He fathers diseased, unintelligent children, then leaves them penniless for Mother to bring up . . .

Fedosia (*seizes on the word 'penniless'*)   'A penniless monk is a joy to God . . .'

Yakov (*to* **Lyubov**)   That's no way to speak of your father! Nurse, please be quiet!

Fedosia   Yes, sir.

Lyubov   Why not? I don't want to be the daughter of a man who has people shot . . .

Yakov (*wistfully*)   What a hard heart you have, Lyuba.

Lyubov   . . . then runs like a coward when they shoot back at him.

Yakov   He's retired – he's old and sick.

Lyubov   Does that excuse him? He's only sick because he drinks.

Yakov (*shocked*)   Why do you say that?

Lyubov   Dr Leshch says so – d'you like Dr Leshch?

Yakov (*fidgets in his chair*)   Hush, he'll hear.

Lyubov   Leshch is a prison doctor. What an honour to have a man like that in our family. Shall we go to the dining room?

Yakov   I can't – I can't listen to this . . .

Lyubov (*shrugs*)   All right, sit down. Your heart is it? (*They hear voices outside.*) Who's that? Mother's little darlings are back!

Yakov   They are your brother and sister, Lyuba.

Lyubov (*thoughtfully*)   I don't think it's healthy to love people you pity . . .

Yakov   You're even hard on yourself!

Vera (*enters the dining room, followed by* **Pyotr**)   Uncle!

Fedosia (*loudly*)   My babies, my last-born!

Vera   Uncle, Uncle – we met such an interesting man!

Yakov   Have you been skating, Pyotr? You'll be ill again!

Pyotr (*distracted*)   Rubbish!

Vera   Three men came up to us on the street . . .

Pyotr Drunken idiots, Black Hundreds, they followed us making obscene remarks.

Vera I shouted, 'Our father's Ivan Kolomiitsev!'

Lyubov (*mutters*) Get down on your knees! Take off your hats!

Pyotr *throws a sidelong glance at her.*

Vera (*to* **Lyubov**) We were scared – we thought if we told them who we were . . .

Lyubov (*smiling*) But they cursed you even more?

Pyotr (*warily*) How did you know?

Vera I don't understand. You'd think people like that would respect authority! It's the revolutionaries who don't!

Yakov (*gently*) No one in Russia respects anything any more.

Lyubov Then what?

Vera Suddenly this young man appeared. A real gentleman. I was about to whack the one closest to me with my skates, but he –

Pyotr (*grins*) Vera was raring for a fight.

Vera – he shouted 'Leave them alone!' (**Fedosia** *laughs silently*.) Then they started shouting at *him*! It was terrifying! Then he whipped out a revolver (*laughs*) and they ran off down the street . . . !

Fedosia (*listens to her and laughs*) My darlings, happy, happy, happy . . . !

Pyotr . . . swerving to dodge the bullets!

Lyubov (*quietly*) Like Father.

Vera What?

Lyubov Father did that.

Pyotr (*sternly*)   How do you know?

Lyubov   Because . . .

Vera   What did she say?

Pyotr   Nothing. Go on!

Vera   He was very good-looking.

Pyotr (*thoughtfully*)   Then this other man came up, Maximov his name was. He had a gentle voice – he spoke so simply . . .

Vera   Dark, with a pointed beard and dreamy eyes. I expect he writes poetry.

Lyubov   Didn't you have your revolver, Pyotr?

Pyotr (*frowns*)   I can't always take it with me, I hate guns.

Vera   Coward!

Yakov   Listen, children, let's not tell your mother about this.

Vera (*disappointed*)   But I want to tell her!

Yakov   Not now, all right?

Vera   All right.

Pyotr (*thoughtfully*)   He walked us back. I wish we could have invited him in.

Vera   Oh, Petya, that would be excellent!

Lyubov   What makes you think he'd come?

Pyotr   Why shouldn't he?

Nadezhda (*enters the room*)   Why is everyone crowded here together, Uncle? Aren't they disturbing you?

Yakov   Not a bit! We always have a chat before dinner!

Nadezhda   You know the criminal who shot at Papa? Well, he's ill!

All look at her in silence.

My husband says he's not faking it either.

Pyotr (*anxiously*)   Why hasn't he been tried yet?

Nadezhda   He still hasn't confessed.

Pyotr   I've the strangest feeling, as if he's with us . . .

Vera   Where?

Pyotr   Just behind the door . . .

Nadezhda   Don't be absurd!

Pyotr   . . . standing there, waiting to be forgiven.

Nadezhda   He's not *that* stupid!

Sofia (*enters greatly perturbed*)   Who's waiting to be forgiven?

Nadezhda   The young man who shot at Papa.

Sofia (*looks around the room*)   What d'you mean?

Yakov (*soothingly*)   Pyotr feels as if the young man is with us, waiting for us to forgive him.

Sofia (*in a strange voice*)   The revolutionaries think they're right.

Lyubov   Like all tyrants.

Pyotr *slips quietly out of the room.* **Vera** *stands sulkily behind* **Fedosia**'s *chair, taking paper flowers from the lampshade and sticking them in her hair.* **Lyubov** *stares at everyone from the corner.* **Nadezhda** *preens herself, humming softly.*

Lyubov (*seriously, to* **Vera**)   The flowers don't suit her.

Vera   Yes they do.

Sofia   Where's Alexander? And Pavel Dmitrevich?

Nadezhda   My husband is dressing – he's just returned. By the way, Mother, he tells me the criminal is ill.

Sofia (*nervously*)   Ill? What's the matter with him?

Nadezhda   It seems he's gone mad. (*Sardonically.*) You're not sorry for him are you, Mother dear?

Sofia   I said nothing.

Lyubov (*grinning*)   Why not – scared?

Nadezhda   Our mother's becoming very odd!

Vera   Don't annoy her or she won't buy me my new skates!

Lyubov (*to* **Sofia**)   Tell me, *are* you sorry for him?

Sofia   I'm sickened by all this evil – so many trials, prisoners, executions . . .

Yakov (*sighs*)   It's growing worse every day.

Nadezhda   It's the price we must pay for living in peace.

Lyubov   Even the Hindus no longer believe peace necessarily brings happiness.

Sofia   The terrorists say the young man had nothing to do with it.

The others look at her in amazement. **Lyubov** *picks up a book and observes them closely over it.*

Nadezhda (*after a pause*)   They're revolutionaries, Mother! How unbelievably naive you are!

Sofia *smiles sheepishly and sits down on a chair, hanging her head and looking suddenly older and softer.*

Alexander (*calls from the dining room*)   Has the post come yet?

Nadezhda   There's a letter for you on the drawing-room table. Vera, go and brush your hair, you look a fright.

Vera   I don't want to!

Nadezhda   Don't pull faces, child, you're a mess, men hate it!

Vera   Men, men! When I was little, people scared me with the devil. Now it's men. (**Nadezhda** *marches her out.*)

Yakov (*quietly*)   What's troubling you, Sonya?

Sofia (*startled*)   Me? Nothing.

Alexander (*calls again*)   When's dinner ready?

Sofia   Soon.

Alexander (*enters whistling*)   Ah, a little meeting! About finances? Or domestic politics?

Lyubov   What a wit!

Alexander   Cripple!

Sofia (*reproachfully*)   Alexander!

Alexander (*ignoring his mother*)   How are the old legs today, *cher oncle*?

Lyubov (*exits through the door behind the screen*)   Get rid of him, Mother!

Alexander (*narrows his eyes*)   What's this? Our little revolutionary in a huff? Bloody Jew!

Sofia (*entreating*)   Go to the dining room, Alexander.

Alexander   Is that an order, *Maman*?

Sofia (*sadly*)   I don't want to see you . . .

Alexander   What do I hear? Our mama has finally lost interest in me?

Yakov   That will do, Alexander, you should be ashamed!

Alexander   *Bien* . . . I've a small matter to discuss with you, Uncle.

Sofia   He won't give you any more.

Alexander   What makes you so sure?

Sofia   I've asked him not to.

Alexander   Is it true, Uncle?

Yakov   Of course it is, if she says so.

Alexander (*furious*)   'If *she* says so.' How gallant! I shall remember that. What do *you* think?

Yakov (*embarrassed*)   Me? I've promised her . . .

Alexander   Commendable behaviour!

Yakov (*gently*)   Forgive me, Alexander, but this life you're leading — drinking and gambling all night . . .

Alexander   One can hardly gamble during the day.

Sofia   Look at yourself! You're losing your hair!

Alexander   I've the face of a healthy young man, baldness merely adds to my distinction. True, I'm a little pale, for I must waste my energy wondering where my next crust of bread is coming from. My parents brought me into the world but failed to provide me with the means to survive . . .

Sofia   Stop, I beg you.

Alexander   My respected papa grew rich from bribes, and lost it all at the card tables.

Yakov (*sadly*)   How cynical you are, Alexander . . .

Sofia (*quietly, crushed*)   Do you know what you're saying?

Alexander   Absolutely. Thanks to Father's losses at the club, I am now ruined.

Yakov   That's an appalling thing to say, Alexander! Why do you torment your mother?

Alexander   Give me twenty-five roubles, *cher oncle*, and I'll go!

Yakov   Help yourself, it's on the desk . . . Tell me – have you no pity for your mother?

Alexander (*frankly*)   I don't expect anyone to pity a
dissolute young man trying to get a job in the police force.
I'll smash a few faces, grab a few bribes and end up with a
revolutionary's bullet in my guts. Some career, eh? (*Exits
with a forced laugh.*)

Yakov (*after a pause*)   How like his father he is!

Sofia   Why did you give him the money? He'll only stay
out all night again!

Yakov   What could I do? I wanted to get rid of him.

Sofia   We're robbing you, Yakov – why d'you let us?

Yakov   That's enough, Sonya, I want to help you and I
will! When Ivan returns . . .

Sofia   Your money won't last for ever.

Yakov   It's only money, Sonya.

Sofia   Money . . .

Fedosia   Sonya, darling, is my little Andryusha Ryazanov
still alive?

Sofia (*loudly*)   No, Nurse, I told you, he's dead.

Fedosia (*shakes her head*)   That's right, they shot him . . .

Sofia (*matter-of-factly*)   No, it was Borodulin they shot.

Fedosia   I remember, I remember – I was his wet-nurse
too. So many babies . . .

Sofia (*looking at the old woman but addressing* **Yakov**)   Do you
remember Ryazanov? He shot the peasants in her village –
he killed the family of his own wet-nurse!

Fedosia   Yes, yes, so many . . . !

Yakov (*quietly entreating*)   Sonya, we have to talk – about
Lyuba.

Sofia (*defensively*)   Why?

Yakov   I think she knows – she's searching . . .

Sofia   Everyone's searching for something these days.

Yakov   People are so cruel to her.

Sofia   You mean me?

Yakov   No, of course not! You simply – pay her less attention.

Sofia   She's cruel to me though – she's the same with everyone.

Yakov (*quietly and significantly*)   Everyone except me, Sonya.

Sofia (*after a pause*)   No! She mustn't know, she can't! I love her so much, but it's the guilty love of a guilty woman. I'm afraid she'll find out, and I – I love her from a distance. I can't get close to her or talk to her . . .

Yakov   It's pointless, Sonya, you must talk to her, tell her the truth.

Sofia   I can't.

Yakov   Tell her later then, but you must tell her! You're in such a despairing mood, these terrible times are crushing the life out of you . . .

Sofia   I'm searching for something too. What must I do? My children are being destroyed, how can I save them?

Yakov   Be calm, Sonya! Who knows . . .

Sofia   God Almighty, I am calm! I worry endlessly, but I am calm!

Yakov   Stop, Sonya! You're shattered by the attempt on Ivan's life, and the press baying for blood and writing lies . . .

Sofia   Lies? Is that what you think?

Yakov   They exaggerate. Of course Ivan – he's too . . .

Sofia   Come, let's be honest. We know very well they're not lying.

Yakov   It's hard for a man to be honest when he has five children . . .

Sofia   How can you – you don't believe it yourself!

Yakov   Everything's against us! It's impossible to be true to oneself!

Sofia (*paces the room, removes the flowers from* **Fedosia**'s *hair and throws them in the fire*)   We know this man with five children – we know him better than the newspapers do. We know he's a gambler and a drunk, that he made his gambling den next to his children's nursery and had a string of mistresses. For ten years he humiliated his wife constantly. The women he had! He corrupted Alexander and I did nothing to stop it. He got drunk, he dropped Lyuba and crippled her – and I let it happen! And now it's too late. Yes, yes, it's too late . . .

Yakov (*shaking his head*)   You could have . . .

Sofia   I know . . . You're – gentle. Yes, I could have lived happily with you. You're an honest man. But I was thirty-five years old when I realised that, and Lyuba was already ten. I put you out of my mind for ten years. I didn't even think about you until Ivan joined the police. As a landowner he was promoted immediately – you'd never do that, you'd rather die! Then another ten years of torture and humiliation for us both – soon he was a complete wreck, rotten through and through. When they shot him I actually felt sorry for him – I was ready to forgive him everything. But no, he behaved like a coward, a wretched, despicable coward!

Dr Leshch *appears from the dining room, a middle-aged man with a large yellow face. He listens, advances cautiously and gives a little cough.*

Leshch   Apologies for the intrusion! Has Nadya told you the suspect is ill?

Sofia   What's that to me?

Leshch   What a strange thing to say – you aren't indifferent to the boy's fate, are you? Surely it's in your interest that he receives the proper punishment? (*Feels* **Yakov***'s pulse, looking at the ceiling.*) What sort of night did you have?

Yakov   Bad.

Leshch   And the heart?

Yakov   Slow.

Sofia   Has he confessed?

Leshch   No. Appetite?

Yakov   Poor. The baths make me weak.

Leshch   Of course. As I predicted.

Sofia   Maybe he didn't do it?

Leshch   I don't know. That doesn't concern me. You must continue with the baths.

Fedosia (*smiling*)   Will you cure me, Doctor? Cure me, eh? (*Chuckles quietly.*)

Leshch (*gravely*)   It seems they're taking Alexander on as assistant superintendent. However, it will cost him five hundred roubles.

Sofia   We have to bribe *them* now, do we?

Leshch   Naturally.

Sofia   But we've no money.

Leshch   Of course. But presumably Uncle Yakov here understands his family's predicament . . .

Sofia   He has no money either . . .

Leshch (*stares coldly at her*)   I beg your pardon? You speak as if *I* were demanding it from you!

Yakov (*hurriedly*)   It's all right, Sonya, I can give him five hundred . . .

Sofia (*to her son-in-law*)   You think my son will prosper in the police force?

Leshch   I am a truthful man, as you know, and I tell you in all honesty, it's all he's fit for. I've a low opinion of him -- I can't conceal it from you. His instincts are good, but fundamentally he's subaltern material – an anarchist, a creature of infirm will, with neither education nor inner discipline . . .

Yakov   Not only do you pass judgement on everyone, you do so at inordinate length.

Leshch (*affably*)   The cause lies in the superabundance of their failings!

Sofia (*to* **Yakov**)   I don't want him to join the police force.

Yakov (*murmurs*)   What can we do?

Leshch   Frankly I don't see what else to do with him. He has a certain military bearing, and his position ensures him a decent rank. I don't suppose he'll make a bad policeman – here in the provinces!

Yakov (*cautiously*)   The main thing, Sonya, is that he'll leave home and the children will be free of his influence. Let me give him that five hundred.

Sofia (*shrugs*)   I don't know -- what should I do?

Yakov (*to* **Leshch**)   Who will this money go to?

Leshch   I'm duty-bound not to divulge the recipient's identity.

Yakov (*embarrassed*)   No, no, I see, of course.

Leshch   See it from my side, as broker in the matter. When's dinner ready?

Sofia   Let's go. (*Helps* **Yakov** *up*.)   So now I've sold my son . . .

Leshch (*in a pontificating tone*)   Those who sell shall gain much.

Sofia   It feels – wrong . . .

Yakov (*shuffles to the door*)   What can we do! The machinery of our life is oiled by bribes.

Leshch (*follows him out*)   Personal independence is impossible without them.

Nadezhda *comes out of the dining room to meet them.*

Leshch   What is it?

Nadezhda   Just a minute, Pavel. (*Leads him back into* **Yakov**'s *room*.) Did you get it?

Leshch (*grudgingly*)   What a question – as though I intended to keep it from you!

Nadezhda (*kisses him*)   Don't be cross, darling! Five hundred, yes? And you get two?

Leshch   For God's sake, keep your voice down!

Nadezhda   So you'll buy the garnet cross you promised me? My heart's set on it!

Leshch   Of course I will – I'm a man of my word! Come, they're sitting down to dinner! (*Shouting is heard outside the room*.) What's happening?

Both listen.

Nadezhda (*startled*)   It's Father!

Leshch   Well, what a surprise!

Ivan (*from the dining room*)   Why didn't anyone meet me at the station?

Sofia   We didn't know you were coming . . .

Ivan   I sent a telegram!

Sofia   Don't shout . . .

Leshch   Let's wait till he cools down.

Nadezhda (*sighs*)   What a comedian!

Ivan (*at the door of the dining room*)   You haven't the courage to walk down the street with a man sentenced to death by criminals – even though that man is your father?

Sofia   Sit down and eat your dinner, Ivan.

Ivan (*goes into* **Yakov**'s *room*)   I don't want dinner! Nadya, why did no one meet me?

Nadezhda   We weren't expecting you!

Ivan   Lies! Lies! I know what you're thinking! The day I retired I became worthless in your eyes!

Leshch   You might at least say good evening, sir.

Ivan   Oh, you here? Good evening!

Leshch   The criminal who . . .

Ivan   Who raised his bloody hand against me – yes?

Leshch   Well, he can't stand trial now.

Ivan   Why not?

He collapses on the sofa. **Pyotr**, **Vera** *and* **Sofia** *appear in the doorway of the dining room, followed by* **Alexander**. *From the door behind the screen,* **Lyubov** *enters* **Yakov**'s *room. She stops by* **Fedosia**'s *chair and pensively strokes her hair. The old woman mumbles and laughs quietly, nodding her head.* **Leshch** *and* **Nadezhda** *stand by* **Ivan**.

Sofia (*from the dining room*)   Dinner's ready!

Ivan   I'd choke on your food!

Alexander   Drink some vodka then.

Ivan (*to* **Alexander**)   Why didn't you meet me at the station?

Alexander   Stop it, Father!

Ivan (*with feeling*)   I'm hurt – don't I deserve better from my children?

Yakov   That's enough now, Ivan!

Lyubov (*approaches her father, coldly*)   Will you stop this ridiculous performance?

Ivan (*bridles*)   Ridiculous? (*Addressing all present.*) Is that how she addresses her father, the figurehead of public order and decency?

Lyubov (*evenly*)   Let me pass please, I'm hungry.

Ivan (*threatening*)   And whose bread do you intend to eat, hunchback?

Yakov (*shouts*)   Ivan, for God's sake!

Lyubov (*calmly and loudly*)   I eat the bread of your brother.

Sofia   Please, Ivan, not in front of the servant. You should be ashamed.

Ivan (*looks around*)   Me? Why?

Lyubov   Don't you dare speak to me like that!

Ivan (*looks around distractedly*)   That's enough!

Yakov (*leans on* **Pyotr**, *speaking with quiet agitation*)   What's got into you, Ivan? Have you taken leave of your senses? Go – leave us in peace . . . !

Ivan (*goes into the dining room*)   I won't eat at the table with that Jew.

Yakov, **Pyotr** and **Lyubov** *remain while the others follow him out.*

Yakov (*quietly*)   What is it, Lyuba?

Lyubov (*quietly*)   What do you think?

Ivan (*mournfully, from the dining room*)   Whence this spirit of contradiction and family enmity?

Alexander   Your very good health, Papa!

Yakov and **Pyotr** *go silently into the dining room, leaving* **Lyubov** *behind. She looks around and hugs her shawl to her.*

Fedosia (*leans forward in her chair, looks at* **Lyubov** *with a smile, beckons to her and whispers*)   Come here, Lyubushka, come here . . . ! What's our warrior shouting about?

Leshch (*from the dining room*)   Your health, sir, welcome home! Let's drink to family happiness! Long may we remain strong and united!

Act Two

A gloomy corner of the dining room with an old-fashioned clock on the wall, a bulky sideboard and a large table, half hidden behind the stage. A wide arch draped with a dark curtain separates the dining room from the drawing room. This room is bigger than the dining room and crammed with old furniture. The right corner is lit by a small electric light; beneath it **Vera** *sits on the sofa with a book in her hands.* **Pyotr** *paces between the chairs as if looking for something. At the back of the room by the window* **Lyubov** *kneels on a chair, holding on to the back and staring out of the window.*

Pyotr (*quietly*) I just want the truth.

Lyubov (*turns to face him*) You'd better not tell Mama you two quarrelled.

Pyotr (*suspiciously*) Why not?

Vera (*angrily*) Stop disturbing us, Petya!

Lyubov Why worry her?

Pyotr What if Maximov is right though?

Vera (*hotly*) You should be ashamed! How can you think that of Papa!

Pyotr (*pensively*) Be quiet, Vera, you're just stupid.

Vera And you're conceited.

Pyotr (*insistently*) Why don't you say something, Lyuba?

Vera He met an interesting man and it turned his head.

Lyubov (*climbs off her chair*) What do you want me to say?

Pyotr You're older than me -- you should know. Maximov shouted that Papa was a coward and took bribes, and . . .

Vera (*jumps up*) Don't you dare repeat things like that while I'm in the room, or I'll tell Mama!

Pyotr (*gazes at her*)   Go on, tell her! See if I care!

Vera (*runs off*)   I will! I will! See if I don't!

Lyubov (*worried*)   Vera, don't! This is terrible, Pyotr!

Pyotr   I know it is, Lyuba. It's terrible to hear people say things about Father. Is it true he ordered some prisoners to be flogged, and two of them died? Is it true?

Lyubov (*after a pause*)   Listen, Petya, it's not always so good to tell the truth.

Pyotr   What, just me?

Lyubov   No, I mean everyone.

Pyotr   Why?

Lyubov   There's no point.

Pyotr (*warily*)   I suppose not.

Lyubov   If you sow on barren ground, how will it ripen?

Pyotr (*hurt*)   Is that what you think of me! You're just angry with the world because of your back.

Lyubov (*smiles*)   A fine gentleman tells you the truth in fine words and you believe him, but you don't believe me because I'm a cripple. Cassandra was a cripple – they didn't believe her either.

Pyotr (*thoughtfully*)   Don't confuse me, I'll find out for myself. (*Pauses.*) I'm sorry I said that, I'm just unhappy – and angry . . .

Lyubov (*quietly*)   I pity you.

Pyotr (*gloomily*)   But I . . . I won't lie – I don't pity anyone! (*Makes for the door.*)

Lyubov (*seriously*)   You think silence is as bad as lying?

Pyotr   What do you mean? Of course it is!

Lyubov *stands there frowning.* **Nadezhda** *crosses the room in her housecoat, her hair loose over her shoulders.*

Nadezhda (*calls out*)   Vera! The horrid girl's gone off with my hairpins. Why are you staring at me like an owl, Lyuba?

Lyubov   What do you want?

Nadezhda   What will become of the girl! It's beyond belief - she's so rude! What on earth is Mother thinking of? You're just abnormal, you always were. It's frightful - you don't do a stroke! You should help Mama keep an eye on her . . .

Lyubov   Is Father in bed?

Nadezhda   Of course. And I'm getting dressed for an evening at the Attorney's!

Lyubov (*looks at her and smiles*)   Aren't you depressed by your life, Nadya?

Nadezhda   Me? With a beautiful body like mine? Only the abnormal are depressed.

Lyubov   Is that what your Leshch says?

Nadezhda   I can speak for myself.

Lyubov   And think for yourself too?

Nadezhda   Save your breath, you won't hurt me . . . Ah, there's Vera. I'll teach her to run off with other people's things.

She runs out of the room. **Fedosia** *enters through the door on the right.*

Fedosia   Lyubushka darling, naughty Alexander's hidden my knitting, can you find it?

Lyubov (*picks up the knitting from the sofa and gives it to her*) Here you are.

Fedosia   What a scamp. I nurse him and feed him and bring him up to be a fine young man – and I give the world a parasite. That's what our life is like – they're either fools or villains.

Lyubov (*smiles*)   You're right, Nurse, your babies didn't turn out very well, did they?

Fedosia   What's that, dear? (*Sits down at the table and disentangles her knitting, mumbling as usual.*)

Pyotr and **Sofia** *enter the dining room talking.* **Sofia** *sits on the sofa while* **Pyotr** *sprawls on the floor at her feet.* **Vera** *runs in and sits next to her mother, tidying her hair.*

Pyotr (*thoughtfully*)   He said the time would come when people would fly through the air as easily as riding a bicycle . . .

Sofia   Did he discuss politics?

Pyotr   Yes, politics too. It was amazing! He talked about everything!

Sofia (*insistently*)   What did he say about politics?

Lyubov   Listen to you, Mama, still the police chief's wife!

Pyotr (*trying to recollect*)   I can't remember. He was so interesting, he had such intelligent eyes. But I think he's ruthless – he said hundreds of the strong must perish, and thousands of the weak . . .

Sofia (*anxiously*)   Why perish?

Pyotr (*smiling*)   I don't remember – I didn't really take it in . . .

Sofia   You think he was a – revolutionary?

Pyotr   Mama, how can you?

Sofia (*sighing*)   Those people are clever, Petya.

Vera (*to her mother*)   Are you angry with Petya?

Sofia (*quickly*)   Well, yes, a bit. Now tell me . . .

Pyotr Then a young lady arrived – Natalya Mikhailovna – and she started talking about books.

Vera (*wheedling*) Please let me go and see him, Mama, he knows respectable ladies!

Sofia It's a bit awkward, we don't know him.

Lyubov Don't you think Vera's relationship with Kovalyov is awkward for her?

Sofia At least her father knows him.

Lyubov Does that make him respectable?

Sofia Hush, Lyuba. (*To* **Pyotr**.) Did he know you were Kolomiitsev's son?

Pyotr (*not answering at once*) Of course he did! (*Stands up and walks away, muttering angrily*.) Kolomiitsev's son – as if it were a disease!

Vera Do you hear that, Mother? Petya's awful! Please can we invite him home, Mama, please?

Sofia I'll think about it.

Vera Please, Mama, the house is so dull – the only people we ever see are policemen and soldiers!

Ivan *enters the dining room, his hands behind his back. He looks at the clock and wags his finger menacingly at it, then opens the sideboard and pours himself a glass of wine. He gulps it down and peers into the living room, waving his arms and twirling his whiskers.*

Fedosia Sofiushka, it's time you found a wife for Alexander! And Verochka. So many babies there'll be! (*Laughs soundlessly.*)

Pyotr *stands before her and scowls.*

Ivan Who's in here?

Sofia The children.

Ivan And you!

Sofia   What do you mean?

Ivan   You should say, 'The children and I are in here.' Why is it so dark? You know I hate darkness – I need light!

Fedosia (*mumbles*)   'They came to town, hunted him down . . .'

Pyotr *lights the lamps.* **Sofia** *looks sad and* **Lyubov** *mocking.* **Vera** *hangs her head.*

Ivan (*to* **Pyotr**)   Why aren't you doing your lessons, boy?

Pyotr (*staring back at him*)   I've done them already, Father.

Ivan   Don't lie to me, numbskull! You'll go without dinner at school tomorrow and your father will take the blame. I'm ashamed of this family – nobody lifts a finger!

Lyubov   Show us how, then.

Ivan   You, work? What could you do?

Lyubov (*calmly*)   I'm not bad at drawing – I could forge money.

Ivan (*steps towards her*)   I'll . . . (*He meets her gaze and lowers his voice.*) Kindly leave the room! Pyotr and Vera, you too, I want a word with your mother.

Vera *and* **Pyotr** *hurry from the room.* **Lyubov** *goes more slowly. The end of her shawl gets caught on a chair and she stops to disentangle it.* **Fedosia** *lifts her head and looks at* **Ivan**, *who only then notices her.*

Ivan   Why's the old crone still here? Pack her off to the poorhouse!

Sofia   Don't, Ivan . . . !

Ivan (*loudly*)   Get out, Nurse, d'you hear? Clear off!

Fedosia (*rises from her chair*)   I can hear all right. I'm not made of wood. (*Goes to the dining room.*)

Ivan   Now then, Sofia, I've decided to make some changes in this house . . .

Sofia   Which isn't yours.

Ivan (*snaps*)   I know that, it will be when he dies though -- don't interrupt me, woman. Clearly I must involve myself personally with the house and the children. When I was working I was too busy to notice how badly you'd brought them up, and I intend to correct that, as from now. (*Thinks for a moment.*) First, I'll block up the front window in my room and make a new door into the corridor. Then Lyubov must find a job. She'll never marry of course -- no one in his right mind would want anyone so deformed or vicious . . . !

Lyubov *disentangles her shawl and turns towards the drawing room, but the quiet voice of her mother stops her.*

Sofia   Don't forget who is to blame for Lyuba.

Ivan (*quietly*)   God, I don't! You never stop reminding me! (*Lowers his voice.*) Perhaps you told her -- is that why she hates me? Well, is it?

Sofia (*flustered*)   No, of course not . . . I don't know if you dropped her by accident or threw her on purpose, out of jealousy. Nurse saw it -- Fedosia knows everything . . .

Ivan (*menacingly*)   I forbid you to mention it again. I don't know who dropped her, and that's that!

Sofia   You did. You'd been drinking.

Ivan (*quietly, bending over her*)   Maybe it was you? How can you prove it wasn't, or that she's mine? How do I know she isn't my niece?

Sofia (*to his face*)   Is that why you reject her?

Ivan   Be quiet!

Sofia   How dare you accuse me of being unfaithful to you! You had dozens of women . . .

Ivan   Of course I did! It's a man's right! I can have as many as I like!

Sofia   So why can't I?

Ivan   Don't be absurd, you couldn't if you wanted to! As I was saying, Lyubov must find work, as a village teacher perhaps – there's nothing for her here, and she's a bad influence on Pyotr and Vera. By the way, Kovalyov says he'll take Vera for five thousand.

Sofia (*alarmed*)   Kovalyov? That invalid? He's sick!

Ivan   So where do I find a son-in-law who's decent and healthy? Did you find Nadezhda her husband? Of course not, she did. Vera hasn't the wit or the manners to get one herself, she's too bloody impertinent. Kovalyov's got his priorities right, he's set his sights on that assistant inspector's job. Now you get Yakov to give Kovalyov the five thousand – plus a bit for us, to cover the wedding. (*With a grin.*) He can't refuse you. (*Anxiously.*) What's up? Why are you looking at me like that?

Sofia (*quietly*)   Everything's gone dark.

Ivan (*relieved*)   Get your eyes examined then!

Sofia (*anxiously*)   I can't see.

Ivan (*irritably*)   Have them examined, I said. We've a doctor in the house!

Sofia (*quietly, recovering*)   God . . . I'm afraid . . .

Ivan (*looks around, scowling*)   When I walk down the street everything goes dark too. They shoot you and put bombs under you even when you've retired, it's all the same to those animals! (*With sudden sincerity.*) Tell me Sonya, am I really that bad?

Sofia   I . . . don't know.

Ivan (*grins*)   What, after living with me for twenty-seven years?

Sofia   Everything's different now, it's frightening and confusing. People say appalling things about you - they say you're worse than bad.

Ivan (*contemptuously*)   You mean the papers! To hell with the papers!

Sofia   And people. People read the papers. (*Wearily.*) Why did you order those prisoners to be flogged?

Ivan   It's not true! It wasn't me! They resisted arrest! They were flogged before I arrested them!

Sofia   They were flogged on the way to prison too!

Ivan   They were singing songs! They defied me! We had a mutiny on our hands! You know me, I'm a hot-tempered man, I won't be defied. They were troublemakers, enemies of the state -- hard labour's too good for them, they should be hanged. I did nothing illegal, they had to be silenced . . . !

Sofia   Two of them died, two boys . . .

Ivan   Those two? Lazy, good-for-nothing layabouts, a tap on the head would have finished them off! (*Pauses, then throws up his arms and speaks more sincerely.*) All right, I'm partly to blame, but they provoked me . . . I'm not as bad as some, and they don't get shot at . . .

Sofia   All right, we've more important things to discuss - the children, our children. The two boys you killed were children too, just children . . .

Ivan (*shrugging*)   Why should I care?

Sofia   Because your children will judge you for it.

Ivan (*angrily*)   What? My own flesh and blood pass judgement on me? I served in the police for them, I sacrificed everything for them – and nearly my life too! Mind what you're saying!

Leshch (*from the dining room*)   May I?

Ivan   Of course.

Leshch (*looking at them*)   Kovalyov is here.

Ivan (*to his wife*)   Go and see him! I'll be along in a minute. Be – you know, pleasant to him and so forth – all right?

Sofia *silently leaves the room.* **Leshch** *smiles.*

Ivan (*sarcastically*)   What's the joke?

Leshch   I know what you're up to.

Ivan (*severely*)   Is that so? Listen, my respected friend, you're in danger of compromising me – badly!

Leshch (*raises his eyebrows*)   Indeed? You amaze me.

Ivan   How much did you pay the police for Alexander?

Leshch   Alexander? Three hundred.

Ivan   But my brother gave you five.

Leshch   Quite.

Ivan   So where's the other two?

Leshch *silently taps his breast pocket.*

Ivan   That makes things extremely difficult!

Leshch   What, for me?

Ivan   For everyone – what if Yakov finds out?

Leshch   Who'd tell him?

Ivan   What if I . . . ?

Leshch (*seriously*)   You'd better not! I advise you to forget it!

Ivan (*threatening*)   Don't you talk to me like that . . . !

Leshch   Forget it, I said – just as you forgot to pay me the three thousand outstanding on your daughter.

Ivan (*wearily*)   What do you need all this money for? Haven't you enough?

Leshch   Nadya doesn't think so.

Ivan   I see, yes. By the way, I don't suppose you could advance me twenty?

Leshch (*frowns*)   It wouldn't be convenient, it's too much.

Ivan (*surprised*)   Too much?

Leshch   Twenty roubles at twenty per cent, then . . .

Ivan (*barely controlling his temper*)   What are you saying, sir?

Leshch   All right, ten! You don't want it? As you wish . . . Now I've news for you. The daughter of Fedyakov the baker is bringing a paternity suit against you.

Ivan (*indignant*)   Who? Oh, her! She'll never prove it.

Leshch   Of course it can't be proved – but the scandal will be enormous.

Ivan   The slut!

Leshch   And Trusov the delivery boy has lodged a complaint against you . . .

Ivan   What?

Leshch   You burst his eardrum when you punched him the other day.

Ivan (*after some thought*)   Remember the fable about the donkeys kicking the wounded lion? I am that lion!

Leshch   Quite possibly!

Ivan (*sincerely*)   Yes I am! They want to disgrace me because they're afraid I'll join the police again. They're jealous! Everyone's against me, plotting against me . . . !

Leshch (*solemnly hands him a roll of banknotes*)   Death to the vanquished!

Ivan (*takes the money*)   We shall see, my dear fellow! Now you must help me. You've a hand in everything, there's nothing you can't do with that brain of yours!

Nadezhda *slips into the dining room in an elegant low-cut dress, her bare neck adorned with a cross of red stones. She stands in the corner listening.*

Ivan   One good turn deserves another. Tomorrow in the club I'll introduce you to Muratov – you know, the merchant fellow.

Leshch   Why?

Ivan   His nephew's in prison. They found some pamphlets on him, he kept the wrong company – that sort of thing. The boy needs a medical certificate to get him out. I know him, he's a splendid boy! The pamphlets were an unfortunate accident . . .

Leshch (*solemnly*)   If he's a splendid boy, of course we must help him.

Ivan   His uncle dotes on him – he'll do anything. He won't grudge us three hundred . . .

Leshch   Three hundred? This is politics!

Nadezhda (*enters*)   Come, Pavel, time to go!

Ivan   What a woman, eh? A real devil!

Leshch (*leaves the room*)   I'll just examine Uncle Yakov . . .

Ivan (*calls after him*)   Examine my wife, will you, sir? She's complaining of her eyes . . . Look at you, woman – lovelier by the day!

Nadezhda   Because I've no children.

Ivan (*sighs*)   Too true, Nadya, they make us old and tired. Children – how much that means . . . Yet of all my five children only you bring me joy.

Nadezhda (*wheedling*)   Poor Papa, life's been so hard for you! You used to love giving your little girl nice presents, but now you've no money you've lost that joy.

Ivan (*crestfallen*)   It's true, I have.

Nadezhda   I know, ask Uncle for some!

Ivan   It's already been tried!

Nadezhda   . . . then you could buy me a dozen pairs of silk stockings. Remember you used to buy me stockings?

Ivan   I remember, my poor girl, I remember.

Leshch (*enters*)   I'm ready. (*Quietly, to* **Ivan**.) Uncle Yakov's in a bad way.

Ivan (*quietly*)   Meaning?

Leshch   It's his heart – he's very weak!

Ivan   I see . . .

Nadezhda   You must talk to him, Papa.

Ivan   Why? What about? He has no children – I'm his only heir.

Leshch (*significantly*)   Are you sure? Come, Nadya, let's go.

Nadezhda (*offers her cheek to her father*)   Good night, Papa darling!

Ivan (*kisses her*)   Enjoy yourself, sweetheart, God be with you! (*Alone in the room, he walks deep in thought to the sideboard, pours himself a glass of wine and drinks, muttering.*) Talk to him? Maybe I should . . .

Pyotr *enters the drawing room from the right and slumps into an armchair, his eyes closed, his head lolling forward.* **Ivan** *peers at the clock, opens the door and moves the hand. It strikes eight.* **Pyotr** *opens his eyes and looks round.* **Ivan** *stands scowling and preoccupied in the middle of the room, whistling 'God Save the Tsar'.* **Pyotr** *firmly goes up to him.*

Pyotr   Father!

Ivan   Well?

Pyotr   I want to ask you . . .

Ivan   What?

Pyotr   It's not easy, I'm scared . . .

Ivan (*peers at him*)   Speak up, boy, spit it out!

Pyotr   Maybe you'll hate me – please don't be hard on me, I want to tell you the truth . . .

Ivan   You should always tell your father the truth.

Pyotr   I want to speak to you man to man . . .

Ivan (*astonished*)   You wha-at? (*Seizes him by the shoulder and shakes him, speaking in an angry whisper.*) Are you ill? Did you – catch something? You little . . . !

Pyotr (*indignantly*)   It's not – let go, you don't understand! I'm not ill!

Ivan (*relaxes his grip*)   Is it true?

Pyotr (*quietly*)   Please, Father, take your hands off me!

Ivan (*irritably pushes him aside*)   What are you trying to say then?

Pyotr   Wait – I can't . . .

Ivan   Don't play games with me, Pyotr!

Pyotr (*runs off to the dining room*)   It's no good! I can't!

Ivan (*sternly*)   Wait, come back I said! (*Looks at the clock and grows calmer.*) No time, unfortunately . . .

Yakov *enters, clutching the walls and chairs.*

Ivan (*looks at him and clicks his tongue sympathetically*)   What's the matter, brother? Legs not so good this evening? Poor old warriors, weary of the fray . . .

Yakov (*stammers in his distress*)   I heard you shouting, Ivan, and I . . .

Ivan (*apologetically*)   Yes, I was a bit. I know, a father shouldn't shout! Sit down, old man, remember the song about the two grenadiers? (*Sings tunelessly but with emotion.*)

Two grenadiers in a Russian jail
Broke out one day and for France set sail . . .
(*Forgets the rest of the words.*) Tum-tiddly-tum-ti-tum . . .

Forgive me, Yakov, I must be off.

Fedosia (*comes in*)   What are you doing, Yasha, walking on your own? You'll fall.

Yakov (*to* **Ivan**)   Stay, please – I'm begging you! We must talk.

Ivan (*looks at the clock*)   Sorry, brother, out of the question!

Yakov   It's serious, we need to discuss Lyuba.

Ivan (*frowns*)   God, you look ill. I know, we've things to discuss – about the children and so on . . . (*Decisively.*) But it must wait. Till tomorrow, my friend! (*Goes out before his brother has time to reply.*)

Yakov (*calls after him*)   Come back, Ivan! Tomorrow may be . . . (*Waves his arm and goes to his room.*)

Fedosia   Round and round like a rolling stone, no seed, no growth . . . What d'you expect? Can't find treasure unless you dig for it . . . I'll keep an eye on you – guard you, watch you . . . ! (*Goes off trailing her knitting behind her.*)

Vera *runs into the living room dragging* **Yakorev**, *a good-looking young man in the uniform of a police inspector.* **Pyotr** *follows, looking gloomy and distracted.*

Vera   Sit down! Go on!

Yakorev   Am I frightening you?

Vera   Heroism's always frightening – it's supposed to be!

Yakorev   Very true. So he took a shot at me, whereupon I grabbed my revolver, threw myself to the ground to get a better angle, and aimed at his – pardon, Miss – his stomach . . . to ensure a serious injury. After I'd fired three shots one of the attackers, who turned out subsequently to be Nikolai

Ukhov, a student at the art school, was wounded slightly in
the leg . . .

Vera (*waves her arms*)   No, no, not like that!

Yakorev (*surprised*)   How d'you want me to do it? You can
check my notes if you like, I'll bring you a copy!

Vera (*firmly*)   No, not from the notes! It must be different,
understand?

Yakorev (*grinning*)   But if I diverge from my notes it won't
be the truth!

Vera (*stamps her foot*)   Oh, how can you! Pyotr, tell him how
you have to describe frightening things.

Pyotr (*reluctantly*)   Cut the rigmarole, Yakorev.

Yakorev   Why? It's exciting.

Pyotr   That's nothing to be proud of . . .

Vera   Yes it is, Petya!

Yakorev (*offended*)   How can you say that? I nearly
sacrificed my life – you gentry should understand . . .

Pyotr   Well, I don't. And I won't. And if I did, I certainly
wouldn't shake your hand.

Vera   What do you mean by that, Petya?

Yakorev (*rising to his feet*)   Don't get above yourself, sonny.
If you think you're superior to me because I didn't go to the
Gymnasium, I shall take it as a personal insult . . .

Vera (*gleefully*)   Wonderful, Yakorev! See, you *can* be noble
and passionate – like a real hero!

Yakorev (*raises his voice, to* **Pyotr**)   I think your behaviour
is despicable.

Vera   Now then, don't swear.

Pyotr (*coolly*)   I don't give a damn what you think of me –
you were scared and took a potshot at some schoolboys . . .

Vera It's not true, Petya!

Yakorev (*angrily*) Scared? Me?

Pyotr (*airily*) Yes, you! You panicked and fired, without the slightest provocation . . .

Yakorev (*menacingly*) That's a very serious allegation, young man.

Poytr (*mockingly, to his sister*) He should be arrested, you silly girl, and you make out he's some sort of hero!

Vera (*flustered*) He is – he's just no good at describing it!

Yakorev I'm not staying here to be insulted! I'll talk to you later, Pyotr Ivanovich!

Pyotr (*sneering*) Is that a challenge?

Vera (*clasps her hands delightedly*) Oh no, Petya dear, must it come to a duel?

Yakorev (*ponderously*) We'll see – I'll think about it. (*Goes to the door.*)

Vera (*follows him*) You were wonderful, Yakorev, you noble soul! It's true, Petya's so conceited these days. He met this man, you see – I think he was a revolutionary – and ever since . . .

Vera and **Yakorev** *leave the room.* **Pyotr** *goes to the sideboard, pours himself a glass of vodka and gulps it down.* **Yakov** *emerges from his room, walking as quickly as he can.*

Yakov Pour me some of that water, Petya.

Pyotr It's not water.

Yakov Vodka? Why are you drinking vodka?

Pyotr I – I've a toothache.

Yakov Oh, Petya, Petya! Never mind, give me some water . . .

Pyotr (*hands him a glass*) Is someone crying?

Yakov   Yes.

Pyotr   Is it Mama?

Yakov (*leaves the room*)   No, it's Lyuba.

Pyotr   I'll go to her.

Yakov   No. Don't disturb her . . .

Pyotr (*roughly*)   I wasn't going to . . .

Sofia *enters with* **Mrs Sokolova**, *a grey-haired woman with an anguished face. She holds herself very erect and speaks quietly, with an inner strength that automatically commands respect.*

Mrs Sokolova   You know why I've come.

Sofia (*unsure how to conduct herself*)   I received your letter . . . Petya dear, leave us.

Mrs Sokolova *looks at* **Pyotr**. *He walks towards her, staring into her face. He bows and tries to give her his hand, but* **Sofia** *comes between them.*

Sofia (*agitatedly*)   Please, Petya! (*To* **Mrs Sokolova**.) Why don't you sit down?

Exit **Pyotr**.

Mrs Sokolova (*remains standing; she speaks firmly, and although barely able to restrain her emotion, her voice remains powerful*)   I've come to tell you that my son is innocent. He didn't shoot your husband! Please understand, Misha is not a terrorist! He could never take another person's life! Of course he's a revolutionary, like all decent people in Russia today, but –

Sofia   *Decent* people?

Mrs Sokolova   Of course. Surely you don't disagree?

Sofia (*after a pause*)   I don't know.

Mrs Sokolova   Your husband made a terrible mistake – it wasn't Misha! An understandable mistake perhaps, but it must be put right. My son's been in prison for five months and he's ill, that's why I've come. He can't stand much more – I'm so afraid! I'm sure you understand! You're a mother, you know what it's like to fear for your children! For pity's sake, tell me you understand! (*She clutches* **Sofia**'s *hand and gazes into her eyes.* **Sofia** *bows her head, and both women are silent for a moment.*)

Sofia (*tersely*)   We've seen the terrorists' statement – they deny all knowledge of your son . . .

Mrs Sokolova   Quite. Surely that's enough for any honest person to admit their mistake . . .

Sofia (*quietly*)   Please don't be so hard on me!

Mrs Sokolova (*after a pause*)   I'm sorry, forgive me.

Sofia (*sighs*)   Maybe, it doesn't have to be like this . . .

Mrs Sokolova (*leans towards her*)   You're right. I feel you want to help me – you do, don't you? You know your husband is wrong and you want to help me?

Sofia (*anxiously*)   Yes, yes, I do! I'm sure your son didn't do it – I wasn't before, but I am now!

Mrs Sokolova (*squeezes her hand*)   We're both mothers – mothers are never wrong about their children . . .

Sofia (*uncertainly*)   What, never?

Mrs Sokolova   Mothers are always right, like . . .

Sofia (*with a hysterical laugh*)   It's not true! It sounds beautiful, but my God – me?

Mrs Sokolova (*insistently*)   No, a mother is always right, like life, like nature . . . She is the enemy of death. All children are dear to her heart, if her heart is healthy . . .

Sofia (*sadly*)   A healthy heart?

Mrs Sokolova   That's why you want to help me save my son.

Sofia (*sadly*)   I have sons – two of them – and they're good! This is the first time I've met you, but I feel I've known you all my life – like a sister . . .

Mrs Sokolova (*simply*)   We're all sisters when our children are in danger.

Sofia   How strangely you speak, you're so strong.

Mrs Sokolova   I am a mother.

Sofia   I want to save your son . . . Maybe it will help me save my own children . . . But have I the courage?

Mrs Sokolova   I'll come the day after tomorrow, in the morning – is that all right? Please persuade your husband to listen to me calmly.

Sofia   Persuade my husband? (*Quietly.*) Tell me, what do you think of him? Is he very evil?

Mrs Sokolova (*calmly*)   By all accounts, yes, very.

Sofia (*with a sheepish smile*)   Look at me – I'm forty-five years old, I've grown-up children, and I'm asking you about the man I've spent my whole life with! You must find me pathetic and ridiculous.

Mrs Sokolova (*gently*)   How long have you been a mother?

Sofia   Oh, I was just sixteen when I . . .

Mrs Sokolova   No, I mean spiritually?

Sofia *looks fearfully into* **Mrs Sokolova**'s *face and shakes her head, not understanding.*

Mrs Sokolova (*after a pause*)   Forgive me.

Sofia (*quietly*)   No, it's me . . .

Mrs Sokolova (*walks to the door*)   One more question. Why didn't you let your son shake my hand?

Sofia   I don't know, I was afraid. People are so quick to hurt each other . . .

Mrs Sokolova   He had such sad eyes . . .

Both leave the room. **Pyotr** *appears in the dining room in an agitated state, followed by* **Alexander** *in his police cap and uniform.*

Alexander (*angrily*)   Is Father here?

Pyotr   No, he's at the club.

Alexander   Where's Mother?

Pyotr   Why do you want to know?

Alexander (*shouts*)   Damn your cheek!

Pyotr (*restraining his temper*)   Don't shout at me! What an odd person you are . . .

Alexander   What did you say?

Pyotr   Why do you want to seem worse than you are?

Alexander   I'll pull your ears off, puppy!

Pyotr (*dodges out of the way*)   Listen, Alexander . . .

Sofia (*hurries into the room*)   Leave your brother alone!

Alexander   He was being insolent!

Sofia   You've no right to hit him!

Pyotr   He's getting his hand in for the police!

Alexander   Did you hear that, Mother? I'm the oldest. If you can't teach the boy manners and Father's too busy, I'll have to. Now get out!

Pyotr (*leaves the room grinning*)   I'm going, I'm going -- beloved brother . . .

Alexander   Say that again and I'll . . . Listen, Mama, you've put me in a ridiculous position. I have to celebrate with my colleagues when I join the ranks, and I'm strapped for cash. Not a bloody bean! Where do I get it, tell me that!

Fedosia (*enters the room*)   Sonyushka, come quick . . .

Sofia (*gently*)   We've no money, Sasha! Everything's been pawned . . .

Alexander   But I can't take bribes on my first day, you must see that. Help me – don't force me to . . .

Sofia (*with quiet melancholy*)   What can I do, Sasha dear?

Fedosia   Sonyushka, Lyuba is crying.

Alexander   Words, words – I'm sick of words!

Fedosia   You heathen, take your cap off! You should stand before your mother as before an icon! And you, look – gawping!

Alexander (*tears off his cap*)   Go to hell, you old . . . !

Sofia   Alexander, how dare you talk like that! I am your mother!

Alexander   And I might remind you that I'm your son – I've a right to your protection. It's your duty to fix me up. I need at least two hundred, my career in the police depends on it – my honour as a gentleman and an aristocrat.

Sofia (*sardonically*)   You're a shrewd boy, Sasha! You almost fooled me.

Alexander (*with mounting indignation*)   Poppycock! For heaven's sake, drop this *façon de parler*, *Maman* – two hundred roubles I need right now!

Sofia   Be reasonable, Alexander! Where would I find that?

Alexander   From Uncle Yakov, of course!

Sofia   We've robbed him enough. I'm ashamed to ask for more.

Alexander (*with malicious glee*)   How loyally you defend his interests! *Parole d'honneur*, one might find it a little suspicious . . .

Sofia   What? What are you saying?

Alexander   Why the dramatic whisper? I'm no longer a child!

Sofia (*with quiet horror*)   What are you hinting at?

Alexander   No need for hints! We all know Uncle can't refuse you anything.

Sofia   Why do you say such things, Sasha?

Alexander (*realising he has gone too far*)   Well, you know . . .

Sofia (*suddenly firm*)   Has your father said something?

Alexander (*tries to placate her*)   Well, yes. You know what a big mouth he has. But what's so terrible about following your heart? It's only female nature . . .

Sofia (*enraged*)   Be quiet!

Alexander *rises to his feet, shocked to see his mother so angry.*

Sofia   Your father – do you know . . . ?

Alexander   It's none of my business.

Sofia   Do you know what sort of man he is?

Alexander (*backs out of the room*)   Leave me out of it, I've enough to worry about . . .

Sofia (*stands as if rooted to the spot, looking with horror into the icon corner*)   Why hast Thou done this, Lord? With Thine almighty hand? Why, oh Lord, why?

Fedosia   What's up with him, Sonyushka?

Sofia (*murmurs like a child*)   Nurse darling, Nurse . . .

Fedosia   That's why I came, Sonyushka . . . Here's my last little one . . .

Pyotr *enters. He looks bright and excited and seems to have pulled himself together.*

Pyotr (*cautiously approaches his mother*)   Forgive me, Mama, I heard what she said – not everything, but I heard . . . Don't be angry . . .

Sofia (*dully*)   Wait, I . . .

Pyotr (*paces the room excitedly, not noticing his mother's condition*) Wasn't she magnificent? She was, wasn't she, Mother? Say yes!

Sofia   What? Who?

Pyotr   That woman – she came from another world!

Sofia (*quietly*)   Is that meant as a criticism of me?

Pyotr (*quickly*)   No, Mother, for heaven's sake! I just meant . . . !

Sofia   Do you love me?

Pyotr (*automatically, his mind elsewhere*)   Of course I do, Mother!

Sofia (*loudly*)   Why?

Pyotr (*also raises his voice*)   I just love you, that's all. But she was amazing, wasn't she, Mother? She was so proud! You must introduce me to her, I want to make friends with people like that – good people . . .

Sofia (*sadly*)   So only other people are good, are they?

Fedosia   I don't like him, that Alexander!

Pyotr (*confused*)   You don't understand, Mother – I didn't mean . . .

Sofia   No, darling – I deserve it . . . Don't go – where are you going?

Lyubov *leads in* **Yakov**. *She looks severe and drawn.* **Yakov** *is agitated, and looks pleadingly into her face.* **Sofia** *rises to her feet.*

Yakov (*quietly*)   Hush, Lyuba, treasure it . . . You didn't think I knew . . . Look, Sonya, she's helping me. Petya, will you leave us?

Fedosia (*to* **Yakov**)   He's slipped out again, naughty boy! Sonyushka, Lyuba was crying – that's why I came . . .

Pyotr (*sullenly, leaving the room*)   Come on, Nurse, let's go.

Yakov   We have to talk, we must settle this. I'm sorry, Sonya, but she knows. Lyuba . . . I told her . . . she knows . . .

Sofia (*sits down. Dully*)   So there we are, Lyuba, what do you want? What shall we do?

Lyubov (*quietly*)   Mother, is he really my father?

Yakov (*also quietly*)   Tell her, Sonya.

Lyubov   Well, is he?

Sofia (*lowers her head*)   I wish I could tell you . . .

All three fall silent. **Lyubov** *drops to the floor and buries her head in her mother's lap.* **Yakov** *stands clutching the back of the chair. They all begin to speak softly, as if someone in the house had died.*

Sofia   All I know is that the only healthy, honest days of my life were the days of your love, Yakov.

Yakov   Our love, Sonya.

Sofia   I was a real person, free of lies and filth -- when you loved me . . .

Yakov   And you loved me, Sonya!

Sofia   How could I, if I didn't go with you when you asked me? I sacrificed love to convention and habit – and was punished for it . . .

Lyubov (*firmly*)   He *is* my father, I know he is . . . !

Yakov   She's right, Sonya, she knows!

Sofia (*cautiously caresses her daughter*)   So be it . . . What now?

Silence.

Fedosia (*smiling at them*)   Having a nice chat?

Lyubov (*with quiet despair*)   Mother, Mother, why am I deformed?

Yakov (*gently*)   How can you say that at this sacred moment, blessed with the ashes of a dying love?

Lyubov (*turns on him coldly*)   Because I'm a cripple, and there's never a moment when I don't know it – Father!

Sofia (*slowly*)   Now I too must share your shame!

Lyubov   Is this the blessing of love, Father? No, now we've been discovered we . . .

Yakov (*pleading*)   Don't, Lyuba!

Sofia   Hasn't her suffering earned her the right to be cruel?

Lyubov (*sadly*)   Mother, Mother . . . How I pity you!

They sit in despairing silence.

Fedosia   Yasha, tell us something funny! Remember when you and Andryusha Ryazanov put on a comedy for us? And Sonyushka too. Lyuba wasn't born then. Nadya had the measles. Colonel Borodulin, her godfather, was . . .

Act Three

The large uncomfortable dining room. The breakfast things are still on the table, with chairs scattered around. **Ivan** *paces the room in a double-breasted jacket.* **Sofia** *is washing cups and saucers.* **Fedosia** *put them in the sideboard.*

Ivan   Is the Sokolova woman respectable?

Sofia   She commands respect, yes.

Ivan (*sceptically*)   Respect, hah! (*After a pause.*) I'd better put on my best uniform.

Sofia   It's at the pawn shop.

Ivan   Bugger it, you'll drag me there next!

Sofia (*calmly*)   I wouldn't get a brass kopeck for you.

Ivan   What! Who ruined me? You – your outfits, your tantrums . . .

Sofia (*keeping her temper*)   Your gambling, your women, your drinking . . .

Ivan (*looks at her and shrugs, then addresses her in a calmer tone*)   I won't argue, I must compose myself to receive her. I suppose all Kazan will hear about it – you'll regret it if they do, my darling. (*Wags his finger menacingly at her.*)

Fedosia (*mumbles*)   Yelling and fighting again . . .

Ivan   You're becoming insufferable, as coarse as a washerwoman and bad-tempered as the devil. I'm tired of your moods, I need peace of mind! I must conserve my energy for my children . . .

Sofia (*coldly*)   You've destroyed the children!

Ivan (*roughly*)   How dare you say that!

Sofia (*sighs*)   Yes, between us we've destroyed them. Can't you see how unhappy they are?

Ivan (*at his wits' end*)   I won't tolerate it – I'm a gentleman, Sofia, an aristocrat!

Sofia   You accused that young man of shooting you – how did you know it was him? Did you see him properly? Well, did you?

Ivan   Ah, I've got it – the mother's been indoctrinating you!

Sofia   Tell me honestly – swear before this icon and look me in the eyes   was it him?

Ivan (*furious*)   I've had enough! I know her game! I'll show her!

Fedosia (*hums*)   'O-ho-ho! The squire saw red and lost his head . . .'

Sofia (*goes up close to her husband*)   Ivan, you must tell the police it wasn't him! Tell them you were wrong!

Ivan (*alarmed by her tone*)   And if I don't?

Sofia   You will! I'm asking you – in the name of God, tell them . . .

Ivan   What if I'm convinced he's guilty?

Sofia   But you're not! I won't appeal to your heart – there's no point calling to the void. All I'm asking is that you admit your mistake – otherwise I shall tell Vera and Petya everything. Please, Ivan, for the sake of our children!

Ivan (*wavers*)   You're mad! This is appalling!

Sofia (*relaxes slightly*)   If you do as I say you'll be a better, more honest person.

Ivan (*brushes her aside*)   Stop it, Sofia! Of course I . . . Oh, to hell with the boy – it's true, I'm not sure, but someone did it! All right, I'll tell her it wasn't him! Satisfied? God, what a farce – it's insane!

Sofia (*quietly, weary with tension*)   My life is insane – and yours too.

Fedosia (*mumbles*)   Nurse 'em and care for 'em and they eat up your strength . . .

Pyotr *enters.*

Ivan (*to* **Sofia**, *shrugging*)   So what? Yes, boy, what is it?

Pyotr   Nothing.

Ivan   Why aren't you at school?

Pyotr   I didn't go. Are you quarrelling?

Ivan (*furious*)   How dare you?

Sofia (*weakly*)   Don't, Petya . . .

Pyotr (*calmly*)   Why not?

Ivan   See, Sofia? What did I tell you!

Pyotr (*smiles sadly*)   Aren't I supposed to care how my parents live?

Ivan (*unsure how to react*)   You're too damn young . . .

Pyotr   I know, I know – tell me, is it true you're marrying Vera off to Kovalyov?

Ivan (*startled*)   What's it to you?

Sofia   No, Petya, it's not decided yet.

Pyotr   Because poor Vera's in floods of tears.

Ivan (*shrugs his shoulders*)   Don't look at me.

Pyotr   But Papa, you called Kovalyov a vile brute . . .

Ivan   I did? When?

Sofia   Frequently.

Ivan (*looks from one to the other*)   What's this, an inquisition? Never in my . . . I'm your father, for Christ's sake! (*Storms out.*)

Pyotr (*after a moment*)   I forgot children shouldn't answer back.

Sofia (*thoughtfully*)   Perhaps it's no bad thing.

Pyotr   I wanted to ask Father if he told the truth about . . .

Sofia (*anxiously*)   No, Petya, please don't!

Pyotr   Why not, Mama? Because it hurts you? Is hurting people such a bad thing?

Sofia (*quickly*)   Yes, yes it is! (*More quietly.*) I don't know – perhaps it isn't . . .

Pyotr (*gently*)   See, Mama? With you, yes and no are inseparable friends! Doesn't it frighten you?

Sofia (*quietly*)   It terrifies me, Petya!

Pyotr   I think it would terrify me too. The thing is, Mama, I've made up my mind – I'm leaving school . . .

Sofia   But Petya, you can't, you must study!

Pyotr   Study what, Mama? The only useful things I learned there were about Father – I already know enough to –

Sofia   Stop, Petya, for God's sake!

Pyotr   All right, I'll stop! But God – whose God, Mama? Do you know?

Sofia (*despairingly*)   I know nothing any more, nothing, my darling!

Pyotr (*after a pause*)   It's strange, you don't love Father or respect him, yet you won't let me say a bad thing about him. Why is that, Mama? It was you who told me about him!

Sofia   I shouldn't have!

Pyotr   Why? Because it hurt me? We're too quick to pity each other. I think there's nothing worse than pity, Mama.

Sofia (*quietly*)   Yes, my friend, you may be right . . .

Pyotr   Your friend? That's the first time you've called me that . . . (*Pauses, then addresses* **Fedosia**.) Nurse, are you afraid of dying?

Fedosia   What's it to you?

Pyotr   Well, are you?

Fedosia   Leave me alone, it's none of your business!

Pyotr   I want to know!

Sofia   Leave her alone, Petya.

Fedosia   I've nothing to fear – I never offended death, I never offended anyone. Just don't play with it – you're too young to play with death.

Sofia   My God . . .

Pyotr (*quietly*)   Mother, you must tell Father I'm not going back to school. I tried talking to him but it's no good, we don't understand each other. Tell him . . . You see, I punched Maximov in the face for calling him an animal. I know it was wrong. Maximov was wrong though, he's not an animal, he's . . .

Sofia   Just a weak, unhappy man . . .

Pyotr   Who's always had power over others, that's what Uncle Yakov says. I want to talk to him about life, and why weak, unhappy men have power and people let it happen – and . . . and . . . What d'you call people like that? I must ask Kirill Alexandrovich.

Sofia (*her mind elsewhere*)   Who?

Pyotr   You know, Maximov, the man I told you about. He talked about flying, remember? I want to fly too – above the castles in the air. Look, here comes poor Verka, doesn't she look funny, Mama?

Vera (*weeping and distraught*)   Why won't you listen to me, Mama? I shan't marry that cretin! I'll leave!

Sofia   Nothing's been decided yet, child, I haven't had time to speak to your father . . .

Pyotr *goes to the sideboard, pours himself a glass of wine and drinks. No one notices. He taps the glass and clears his throat.*

Vera   No time! You never have time! He won't listen to you anyway.

Sofia   Don't be silly, there's no point in getting angry – is there, Petya?

Vera   Silly? You tell me to marry a bald, pot-bellied pervert with green whiskers, and I'm supposed to say, *Merci, Maman*, can I kiss your hand?

Ivan *(appears at the door in uniform and medals)*   Complaining again? It won't get you anywhere, my girl, I've made up my mind.

Vera *(through tears)*   They *are* green, Papa! Haven't you noticed?

Ivan   Stop blubbing, grow up! Look at Nadya's husband – he's hideous, but she's happy. Marriage is a serious business, child!

Vera   I *am* serious, they *are* green! You should lend him your hair dye!

Ivan   My . . . what?

Vera   Yours are mauve – at least they're original . . .

Ivan *(with quiet menace)*   Are you laughing at me, Miss?

Pyotr *(leaves the room)*   Mama, can you have a tragic farce?

Ivan *(shouts)*   For God's sake, punish her, Sonya! She's making a laughing stock of me!

Fedosia *(growls)*   Restless people, shouting and yelling! *(Stamps out of the room.)*

Vera (*weeps*)   You've made a laughing stock of *me*! What d'you need Kovalyov for? You've already got Leshch to make everything in this house repulsive!

Sofia   And you said the children loved you . . .

Vera   We do love you, Papa, but we're not your policemen . . .

Ivan (*looks distractedly from one to the other*)   You're all in it together. It's a bloody conspiracy – against your father!

Lyubov (*enters*)   Mama, my father is calling you – what's wrong, Vera?

Vera   You know what's wrong.

Ivan (*shocked*)   Father? Whose father?

Lyubov   Don't cry, Vera, there's no point.

Ivan   Don't tell her what to do! Vera, leave the room – quick, at the double! Lyubov, stay here. You heard me!

Lyubov   What d'you want?

The two stare at each other, **Ivan** *evidently not understanding why he has kept her,* **Lyubov** *calmly waiting for him to speak.*

Ivan   Father, you said – who were you referring to?

Lyubov   My father.

Ivan   Ah, I see! So you and I are – not related?

Lyubov   No. We're strangers.

Ivan   Well, you always treated me as your enemy!

Lyubov   Because I'm more intelligent than the others.

Ivan   You are a deeply evil person!

Lyubov   Like all cripples.

Ivan (*with emotion*)   You've infected my children with the spirit of contradiction and driven your mother half mad . . .

yes, now I understand – it's you who are to blame for everything, you're bent on revenge . . . !

Lyubov   Must you turn everything into cheap melodrama?

Ivan (*as if trying to convince himself*)   I always wondered where the evil in this house came from . . .

Lyubov   You had only to look at yourself.

Ivan   Now you listen to me –

Lyubov (*calmly*)   We've nothing more to say to each other.

Pause.

Ivan   So what happens now?

Lyubov   I shall leave here.

Ivan   I see. Where will you go?

Lyubov   That's my business. I don't think I've anything to thank you for. (*Leaves the room.*)

Ivan (*watches her, shakes his head sadly and mutters*)   My God, this is fertile ground for terrorism and anarchy . . . I'm so lonely! So lonely . . . !

Nadezhda (*enters*)   All alone, my lord and master? What are you mumbling, darling? Saying your prayers?

Ivan   Nadya, Nadya, you mustn't joke about God.

Nadezhda (*cheerfully*)   I'm not, Papa! Pray on! Thank Him for his infinite mercies!

Ivan (*sadly*)   I think He's forgotten me.

Nadezhda   Not any longer He hasn't!

Ivan   Do you know something I don't?

Nadezhda   It appears you're to be chief superintendent . . . !

Ivan (*thumps his chest*)   Me? Former police chief Kolomiitsev, a mere superintendent? Never!

Nadezhda   Oh, Papa, you're such a child!

Ivan   I won't accept it, Nadya, not at any price!

Nadezhda   Darling, pride is a beautiful thing, but one must eat! And how good bread tastes when one has earned it with dignity . . .

Ivan   I've always earned my own bread!

Nadezhda   And fed your little Nadya too. Listen, you're like the knights of old – one step back . . .

Ivan (*lost in thought*)   Chief superintendent, eh?

Nadezhda   And two steps forward!

Ivan   Two forward?

Nadezhda   That's right.

Ivan   Dammit, there's nothing a man can't do these days if he puts his mind to it!

Nadezhda   There, it's not so bad, is it, Papa?

Ivan (*sighs*)   You're a beautiful woman, Nadya, too good for that husband of yours!

Nadezhda   Papa, how can you? Think of all he's done for us!

Ivan (*merrily*)   Come, you know I don't mean it! But tell me, you don't love him, do you?

Nadezhda   That's my secret!

Ivan (*winks*)   Between the two of us though, he's an ugly bastard, isn't he?

Nadezhda (*pretends to be shocked*)   Papa, darling!

Ivan   He looks like a carp. Aren't you tempted to put a pair of horns on him, eh?

Nadezhda   How can you say such wicked things to your daughter? (*Puts her hands over her ears.*) I'm not listening!

Ivan (*pulls her hands away*)   Maybe he's a cuckold already, eh?

Nadezhda   Let go, Father, you immoral man!

Ivan (*laughs*)   Not till you tell me – has that carp got horns on him yet?

Nadezhda *tears herself away, laughing.*

Alexander (*enters the worse for drink*)   Having a laugh? Wonderful! *Bonjour, Papa!* Give me your hand, sister!

Ivan (*admiring his son*)   Now that's what I call a man!

Nadezhda (*stands beside her brother*)   Not a bad couple, eh, Papa?

Ivan (*touched*)   My children! You're the only two who bring me joy – healthy, happy, honest . . .

Nadezhda (*to her brother*)   Guess what? It looks as if Father will be chief superintendent!

Ivan (*winks, as though the matter were already decided*)   For now anyway . . . The first step on the ladder, from which I shall rise ever higher!

Alexander   Is it true, Nadya?

Nadezhda   The Attorney told my husband.

Alexander   My God, that Leshch is a genius!

Ivan   The carp, you mean? Of course he's a genius – for a fish!

Alexander   Papa, why don't you make me your assistant?

Ivan   Why not? Excellent idea!

Alexander   Between us we'll create heaven on earth in this dump. Girls, merchants' wives – and above them all God and the tsar, *père et fils*! An idyllic prospect!

Nadezhda (*shakes her head*)   I can imagine what you two will get up to.

Alexander   Bah! We're no worse than the others!

Leshch (*enters*)   May I join the discussion?

Alexander   Here he is - the genius of the house!

Ivan (*shakes* **Leshch**'s *hand*)   My dear fellow, Nadezhda told me . . .

Leshch (*disgruntled*)   I should have known! She's always on the scene half an hour before the murder is committed!

Nadezhda (*playfully*)   Oh, Pashka!

Leshch (*to* **Ivan**)   You must go to our friend Karpov the Attorney, and pay him for taking care of the business with the delivery boy.

Ivan (*joyfully*)   Already? Thank you, my friend, thank you! (*Looks at* **Nadezhda** *and tries not to laugh.*) Karpov, eh? Interesting name. (*Bursts into giggles.*) Very interesting . . .

Leshch (*stiffly*)   I don't see why you're laughing.

Nadezhda   So as not to weep with happiness!

Ivan (*barely able to control his emotion*)   I am happy, my friend, happy! Everything is going wonderfully, and I'm happy!

Leshch   You must be prepared to lay out a certain amount, of course. A position like this costs roughly seven hundred roubles – say a thousand.

Ivan (*becomes serious*)   Ah, I see. Things are a bit tight at present . . .

Alexander   And two hundred for me.

Vera (*peers round the door*)   Nadezhda, come here.

Nadezhda   What do you want?

Vera   You.

Nadezhda   Wait, I'm busy!

Ivan   Nadya, go and knock some sense into the girl about Kovalyov!

Nadezhda   Absolutely! I intend to get drunk at their wedding!

Leshch (*insistently*)   So what about the cash?

Ivan (*sighs*)   Where am I to get it?

Alexander   We could mortgage the house.

Ivan   But it's my brother's!

Leshch   Does Uncle Yakov's family mean nothing to him? He doesn't strike one as a selfish man, and his days are numbered, as it were.

Alexander   That's true.

Ivan   He'll get it back of course! Look, is the job in the bag?

Leshch   Definitely. People know you, you've an excellent reputation. All your – misunderstandings have been ironed out. But you must exert your authority! The days of anarchy are over, the government has the power to restore order and requires of its servants a firm hand . . .

Alexander (*stoutly*)   Thank God Petersburg's come to its senses!

Ivan   So what do you advise me to do?

Leshch   I'd advise you to find the money.

Ivan   Yes, yes, I know . . . Unfortunately, the Sokolova woman's coming to see me shortly – the mother of that . . .

Leshch (*sternly*)   Why?

Ivan   She wants me to say I was wrong – that I wasn't sure who fired . . .

Alexander (*sneers*)   That wouldn't be very clever, would it?

Leshch   What do you propose to do?

Ivan   I . . . ah – I haven't decided yet. I wonder if I should see her in view of my new position. What do you think? The new chief superintendent announcing he's made a mistake! It would make a pretty bad impression, wouldn't it?

Leshch   It certainly would!

Alexander   Think of your officers, Papa!

Leshch   For heaven's sake, this is no time for sentimentality! Be realistic – consider the position it would put your men in!

Ivan (*wavers*)   Yes, I suppose so. The colonel's a splendid man . . .

Alexander   And your card partner.

Ivan   God alone knows if it was the boy . . .

Leshch   Well, someone did it! These gunmen are all friends. In my view it's quite unnecessary to meet the woman. Now get hold of the money unless you want this opportunity to slip away. I warn you, Kovalyov has his eye on the job too.

Ivan (*through clenched teeth*)   Kovalyov? The little . . . !

Alexander   Be firm, Papa, be firm!

Ivan   Sofia will never forgive me if I . . . Damn the boy, he'd have done better to wound me!

Leshch (*inclines his head*)   It might indeed have been advantageous. A slight wound can frequently push a man up the ladder.

Ivan (*with a sour smile*)   If it doesn't knock him off first!

Alexander (*glances at his watch*)   Why don't you go and see Uncle now, Papa?

Ivan (*to* **Leshch**)   So, Pavel Dmitrevich, you can't oblige me?

Leshch   I consider you obliged to find me the money.

Alexander   I know you can do it!

Alexander *goes to the door whistling, then thinks better of it and approaches the sideboard. Enter* **Nadezhda** *and* **Vera**, *arm in arm. At first they don't see him.*

Nadezhda (*pleading*)   Come, Vera, you're being silly.

Vera (*angrily*)   And you're lying!

Nadezhda   Don't be rude, beastly girl! I only want to help you!

Vera   It's disgusting, you can't mean it!

Nadezhda (*pushes her away*)   Disgusting, eh?

Vera   I don't want lovers!

Nadezhda (*contemptuously*)   Ignorant brat!

Vera   Are you really unfaithful to your husband?

Alexander   Yes, are you, Nadya?

Vera (*to* **Alexander**)   Nadya says the only reason to be married is to have lovers!

Nadezhda   Don't listen to her, she doesn't know what she's talking about.

Alexander   It sounds like something out of a French novel. You mind what your sister says, Vera!

Vera   I won't! (*Runs from the room.*)

Nadezhda   Horrid obstinate child!

Alexander   A real devil!

Nadezhda   She's stubborn – and stupid . . .

Alexander   Never mind, Kovalyov will give her a box of chocolates and she'll be fine. Tell me, d'you think Leshch would give me the money if we mortgaged the house?

Ivan   Your hunchback is! *My* children respect me!

Sonia   Pyotr hates us. Nadezhda is a sensual animal without heart or brains . . .

Ivan   Like you – you were the same!

Sofia   You corrupted Alexander. Poor Vera is a silly girl . . .

Ivan   It's your fault! You raised them!

Sofia   I know, I've failed them.

Ivan   What d'you want of me? Tell me!

Sofia (*throws down the dishcloth*)   Listen, for ten years you've made war on children . . .

Fedosia   They're off . . .

Ivan (*grins*)   Which ones?

Sofia (*forcefully*)   The ones you searched, the ones you jailed and killed . . .

Ivan   This is rabid liberalism! Are you mad?

Fedosia   Cursing and swearing – time to be tired of it . . .

Sofia (*sadly*)   One boy was only seventeen – and what about the girl you shot in a search? You're soaked in blood – the blood of children! Remember how you used to shout 'They're just children'?

Ivan (*taken aback*)   What's got into you, Sofia? This is terrible!

Sofia   Yes, it's terrible!

Ivan   You believe these lies? It's not only young people who attack the state . . . You could get into serious trouble – what if Pyotr or Vera heard?

Sofia   I've no idea if it's wickedness or plain cowardice, but what you've done is vile.

Nadezhda   Don't ask *me*, I want it for myself. It's too small for the whole family of course, but for two it's perfect. My husband will soon be chief police surgeon – we'll need to entertain guests.

Alexander   It'll belong to all of us when Uncle dies.

Nadezhda   I know, but there are so many of us. If we mortgage it, Pavel and I would have first claim . . .

Alexander   You always get what you want, don't you!

Nadezhda   It's not for me, it's for Pavel.

Alexander (*embraces her*)   Don't be modest, I like it!

Nadezhda   You like it so much you can't keep your hands off it!

Alexander (*leers*)   I'll grab your last kopeck!

Nadezhda   Is that all you ever think about? Come, I've something to show you in my room . . .

Alexander (*follows her out*)   So won't you give me any?

Nadezhda   It's naughty to ask a lady for gifts!

Alexander (*laughs*)   Bah! Prejudice!

They exit. **Vera** *peers agitatedly round the door and waves* **Yakorev** *in.*

Vera (*in a whisper*)   In here! Quick!

Yakorev (*disgruntled*)   What's the fuss?

Vera (*quietly*)   Did anyone see you?

Yakorev (*lowers his voice*)   Just the maid. Why?

Vera (*looks round*)   There's nowhere to hide . . . What a stupid house, if it was summer you could jump out of the window!

Yakorev   Why the window?

Vera   It's what people do . . . Listen, they're trying to marry me off to Kovalyov.

Yakorev (*disappointed*)   Really? Never mind, congratulations.

Vera   And you must save me!

Yakorev   Save you? From what?

Vera (*urgently*)   You must – you're a hero! I've planned it . . . You'll hide me somewhere, then go to them and deliver a passionate speech. Say they've no right to coerce a girl's heart, you won't let them. Say you don't love me but you're willing to sacrifice your life for me – whatever you like, you know what to say. Then they'll cry and give me to you and you'll be my friend for life!

Yakorev (*smiles*)   They'll give me a kick up the –

Vera   Yakorev, don't be coarse!

Yakorev (*ponders*)   I suppose Kovalyov wants a fair bit for you . . .

Vera   They're giving him five.

Yakorev   Five? Are you sure? Well I never!

Vera   It's not important.

Yakorev   Five thousand – not important?

Vera   What's it to you?

Yakorev   Me? Well . . . Kovalyov won't give you up.

Vera   To you?

Yakorev   To anyone. Not for five thousand.

Vera   I don't understand, will you do it or won't you?

Yakorev (*thinking aloud*)   Hell, why not? I'm still young, time's on my side if I mess it up . . .

Vera   Well?

Yakorev (*decisively*)   All right, Vera Ivanovna, I'll do it!

Vera   See? I knew you would!

Yakorev   What have I to lose? It's risky – but God, it's tempting! Give us a kiss, Vera Ivanovna – for courage!

Vera   Here's my hand.

Yakorev   I don't want your hand! I want this! (*Grabs her roughly and kisses her on the lips.*)

Vera (*tears herself away*)   Ooh . . . Ugh . . . ! You smell of hair oil!

Yakorev (*laughs*)   That's not my hair – it's my moustache!

Vera (*pushes him to the door*)   Go on, I'll take you out the back way so no one sees you. It's a shame you can't jump through the window . . .

Yakorev (*from behind the door*)   Why should I?

Mrs Sokolova *enters. She paces the room, stops and looks around her.* **Pyotr** *runs in, bows to her embarrassedly and pulls out a chair for her.*

Pyotr   Have you come to see Papa? Please sit down, I'll call him!

He runs off. **Mrs Sokolova** *ignores the chair and continues to pace the room.* **Ivan** *and* **Alexander** *enter from* **Yakov**'s *room, followed by* **Pyotr**.

Ivan (*strikes an imposing attitude and does not offer* **Mrs Sokolova** *his hand*)   My respects, madam! My children . . . Alexander . . . Pyotr . . . You – ah – don't object to their presence?

Mrs Sokolova   It's up to you.

Ivan (*after a pause*)   Run along now, Pyotr . . . A nervous youngster, madam, a most susceptible nature . . . What are you staring at, boy?

Pyotr *quickly goes out.* **Mrs Sokolova** *gazes silently at* **Ivan**.

Pyotr (*shouts from behind the door*)   Mama, where are you? Mama, come quick . . . !

Ivan (*muttering, unable to contain his irritation*)   Sasha, tell Pyotr to stop that row at once . . . ! (*Clears his throat.*) Madam, I know the purpose of your visit. My wife has informed me of your request.

Mrs Sokolova (*calmly and coldly*)   I make no requests – I am merely offering you the opportunity to correct your mistake.

Ivan (*disconcerted by her manner*)   What do you mean, mistake? How do you intend to prove I was wrong?

Mrs Sokolova   I don't.

Ivan   You mean you can't!

Mrs Sokolova (*severely*)   Are you sure it was my son who fired the gun?

Ivan (*grows agitated*)   His appearance is striking . . .

Mrs Sokolova   You saw him only once – at the police station, the day after the shooting. Do you deny it?

Ivan (*with much pathos*)   Madam! Do not insult an old man! Surely you cannot suspect . . .

Mrs Sokolova   I am simply asking if you're convinced the young man at the police station was the one who shot you.

Ivan (*robustly*)   Convinced? But if I recognised him –

Mrs Sokolova   Don't you have the courage to confess your mistake?

Ivan (*his temper roused*)   You've no right to address me in that tone, madam. Your son is a revolutionary, they found him with –

Mrs Sokolova   You didn't answer my question – was it my son or not?

Ivan (*continues to shout*)   Leave me alone! I don't give a damn for your son, I've children of my own! I repeat – your son is a revolutionary!

Mrs Sokolova (*makes to leave*)   That doesn't excuse you.

Ivan (*follows her to the door*)   What did you say?

Mrs Sokolova (*from behind the door*)   I said – it doesn't excuse you.

Ivan (*quietly*)   In whose eyes?

He stands twirling his whiskers, glaring at the door. **Sofia** *enters, followed by* **Yakov,** *leaning on* **Pyotr.** **Vera** *runs in, then* **Alexander** *and* **Nadezhda,** *intrigued by the noise.*

Sofia   Has she gone?

Ivan (*wearily*)   The woman's a devil! She was harassing me.

Sofia   So you refused.

Ivan (*gently*)   Listen, Sofia . . .

Sofia (*fiercely*)   You promised you'd admit you were wrong – you promised me, Ivan!

Ivan (*more calmly*)   Hang it, I can't, not now. Don't you see? My position's changed – we must wait . . .

Sofia (*in horror*)   This is terrible! It will destroy us!

Pyotr (*shocked*)   How could you, Father?

Ivan   Silence, boy. (*Turns to his brother.*) Yakov, you're a sensible man . . .

Vera   Don't be upset, Petka . . .

Ivan (*to his brother*)   Help me, Yakov. Talk to the woman, calm her down . . .

Yakov (*weakly*)   You must get her back, Ivan!

Sofia   Run, Petya! Quick – call her back!

Ivan (*in despair*)   What are you doing? You're killing me!

Yakov   No, we . . . Think, Ivan, please, just think . . .

Sofia   Confess, Ivan! In the name of your children and your old age – for the love of God, confess, or we're ruined!

Ivan (*fretfully*)   I'm ruined already, a broken man! Nadya, what should I do? Tell me, Sasha! Tell them . . .

Nadezhda (*takes her father by the arm*)   Calm yourself, Papa!

Vera *looks at all of them in turn with frightened eyes.*

Alexander   Listen, Mama, you don't understand . . .

Ivan   Let's discuss it, Sofia . . .

Yakov   There's nothing to discuss, Ivan.

Nadezhda (*to* **Alexander**)   If the woman comes back, she'll . . .

Sofia (*wearily*)   Please, Nadya . . .

Alexander   Father's going to be chief superintendent – if he tells her he was wrong he'll lose it. It would look terrible.

Yakov (*with disgust*)   Enough! That's disgusting!

Alexander (*hurt*)   What do you mean, Uncle?

Nadezhda   Alexander is merely defending his family's interests!

Vera (*distraught*)   Who are you talking about, Mama? Who's coming back?

Sofia   Hush, child . . .

Ivan (*to* **Alexander**)   If I don't do as the woman says, Yakov won't give us the money.

Alexander   God, that's a point!

Nadezhda (*hotly*)   I'll get the money! My husband will give it to you! You can't risk it, you mustn't – think of your position . . .

Alexander   Well said, Nadya!

Pyotr (*runs in*)   Too late! She's already left . . .

Ivan (*relaxes*)   Thank God!

Yakov *sits in his chair, his head slumped on his chest. Behind him stands* **Sofia**, *dazed with horror. Beside her the breathless* **Pyotr**. **Lyubov** *sits in the corner, a calm spectator.* **Alexander** *and* **Nadezhda** *sit at the table.* **Ivan** *sits down with them.* **Vera** *stands behind him tenderly stroking his shoulder, gazing at everyone.*

Nadezhda (*quietly*)   I wish I'd kept my mouth shut . . .

Ivan (*wearily*)   Vera, pour me a drink. Thanks, Nadya, my legs are shaking . . . Thank God it's over . . .

Sofia (*murmurs*)   It's not over, far from it!

Ivan (*angrily*)   Keep out of it, woman! You did this to me, I see it all now!

Nadezhda (*reproachfully*)   Really, Mama, you're hopeless – so impractical!

Fedosia *enters. She stands by the sideboard and mumbles something, shaking her head.*

Sofia   What will happen, Yakov?

Ivan   I can't take any more – I'm trembling all over!

Lyubov (*to* **Yakov**)   We must leave this house!

Yakov (*mustering his strength*)   I'm ashamed to call you my brother, Ivan. I'm afraid for your future, your children – I'm afraid of what they'll say about you . . .

Nadezhda (*loudly*)   You've no right to speak for us!

Ivan (*rises to his feet*)   How can you say that, brother? Have I acted so badly? You don't mean it! You're wrong!

Lyubov (*to* **Yakov**)   We must leave! These people are dead – words won't wake his conscience . . .

Alexander (*smirks and hums*)

'Alexander woke up under the trees
And gave his Cassandra a hefty squeeze . . .'

Pyotr *reaches out to his father, trying to speak to him, then slumps unconscious to the floor.*

Ivan (*anxiously*)   What's up with him?

Lyubov (*calmly*)   You're killing this child too.

Sofia (*horrified*)   She's right, Ivan! Even him!

Nadezhda   For God's sake, he's only fainted, he knows he's not meant to run. Calm yourself, Papa, you must rest!

Alexander (*takes his father by the arm*)   Come -- rest!

Fedosia   Look – they've crushed the child . . .

Ivan   Wait -- what's wrong with him?

Yakov   Go, please!

Ivan   It's up to you of course -- you've the right to throw me out. But my children, I have the right to –

Nadezhda (*jumps up*)   Please, Papa – come!

Alexander   My, we're touchy today!

Fedosia   Silly people – always squabbling . . .

Ivan (*leaves the room*)   Poor boy – they persecute him . . .

Sofia (*lifts* **Pyotr**)   For pity's sake, be quiet!

Ivan, Nadezhda *and* **Alexander** *exit.*

Yakov   See, Sonya, the sick child and the murderer . . .

Sofia   Help me, Lyuba. Vera, help me.

Fedosia   Guarded them with my life -- now look . . .

Lyubov   The sick child goes to hospital, the murderer to jail . . .

Vera (*shouts*)   Stop talking about Papa like that! He's not a murderer! You're just a spiteful cat!

Yakov   Vera, darling . . .

Vera (*turns on* **Yakov**)   And you're no better! You've never done anything but make money. Papa has power over people -- that's why they shot at him! I know what you say about him - you say he's immoral and he drinks – but it's because you don't love him and it's not true! Bad people can't have power. Papa has power because he's good and clever! If he was bad, people wouldn't take orders from him . . .

Fedosia (*laughs*)   Listen to the girl – cuckoo, cuckoo!

Pyotr (*struggles to his feet*)   You're wrong about our father, Vera -- he is a bad man . . .

Vera (*with great effort*)   You don't understand! He's a hero! He risked his life to do his duty! Look at the rest of you! What do you do? What do you live for? You're not responsible for anyone! You just envy Father because you've nothing, nothing, nothing . . . !

Fedosia   My children, my babes, my last ones . . .

Act Four

Yakov's room. A fire smoulders in the grate. Yakov *reclines in an armchair, his legs covered in a rug.* Fedosia *sits knitting at the back of the room against the screen.* Ivan *paces around greatly perturbed, talking quietly to* Yakov. *In the adjoining room* Lyubov *stands beside the piano.*

Ivan   Is that your last word?

Yakov   Yes.

Ivan (*with emotion*)   You're an extraordinarily cruel man, Yakov! It was you who corrupted my wife – she was sweet and docile before . . .

Yakov   Save your breath! You're in a most humiliating position.

Fedosia   It's nice to hear human voices when they're quiet and friendly . . .

Ivan   Don't tell me what to do – I'm older than you.

Yakov   I said I no longer regard you as an honest man, but you still ask me for money.

Ivan (*almost sincerely*)   Yes, you insult me, and I ask you for money. Yes, you were my wife's lover, and I grovel at your feet! Do you imagine I enjoy it? Do you think I don't long for revenge? You're ill – that's your excuse. I am a normal healthy man – a father! You can't understand a father's soul – like a Jew can't possibly understand the soul of a Russian. Fatherhood is a sacred role, Yakov. A father is the origin of life. God Himself bears the sacred name of Father! A father must sacrifice everything for his children – his self-esteem, his honour, his life . . . I've sacrificed everything to fulfil this duty – I've trampled on my self-esteem and joined the police force as a humble superintendent. Me, a former police chief! In fulfilling this duty have I not endured my own brother's insults, and bared my breast to the assassins' bullets . . . ?

Fedosia   Agh, can't bear it, shouting again!

She gets up and goes out.

Yakov   Be quiet. Ivan . . . You have destroyed your children. You unhappy man. Do you know where Vera is?

Ivan   She'll turn up, little madam, they'll find her.

Yakov   And Petya? You've crushed the life out of him.

Ivan   He's a sick boy, you corrupted him, he must get away from here.

Yakov (*exhausted*)   I don't know what to say, no words can touch your heart.

Ivan (*lapses into bombast*)   My soul is robed in the crimson of truth – the arrows of your malice cannot touch me. I stand firm in my rights as a father; the wellspring of life. Ivan Kolomiitsev is resolute in his right to be true to himself.

Lyubov (*enters, to* **Yakov**)   Sorry to interrupt, Father, but it's not good for you to overexcite yourself. Ivan Danilovich, my father has told you he won't give you the money – he couldn't if he wanted to, it's gone to Mrs Sokolova as security for her son.

Ivan (*clasps his hands in horror*)   Yakov, how could you do this to me?

Lyubov (*smiling*)   You'd have got it if you admitted your mistake.

Ivan   And let Kovalyov get my job? Keep out of this, Lyubov Yakovlevna – you're too young to understand . . .

Lyubov   I was thinking of my father.

Ivan   I won't listen to any more of this. I accept I'm powerless to persuade you, brother, but what can I do? If you won't give me the money I'm ruined – not just me, Sofia and the children . . .

Lyubov (*coldly*)   Your children are ruined already . . .

Ivan (*ignoring her*)   Yakov, my life and that of my family now depends on a mere twelve hundred roubles – say a thousand. You're a good man, Yakov, and you're clever. They're discussing my appointment now, Leshch is there pushing for me. When it's confirmed I'll need the money. Now I'll leave you, brother – to face your conscience.

He stalks out, head held high.

Yakov *looks after him apprehensively.* **Lyubov** *grins.*

Yakov (*also grinning slightly*)   Look at the man, he's besotted with himself! When he was young he had a taste for amateur dramatics and it shows! (*Pauses.*) I've no choice but to give him the money.

Lyubov (*dully*)   What a repulsive, obnoxious creature . . .

Yakov (*anxiously*)   Lyuba, you're so hard, what's wrong with you?

Lyubov (*quietly and coldly*)   Tell me how I should be, then.

Yakov (*pauses*)   I can't . . . I'm shattered . . . It's happened too fast . . . All these years I've lived like a mole, alone with my love for your mother. Some people are destined to love one woman all their life, just as some writers write only one book . . .

Lyubov   And do it badly . . .

Yakov (*vehemently*)   Yes! They hide their mediocrity by flaunting the dubious merit of single-mindedness.

Lyubov (*thoughtfully*)   You're honest – but it'll do you no good.

Yakov (*quietly*)   Do you feel no pity for me?

Lyubov (*quietly, moving about the room*)   I feel angry that I can't do anything. I'd like to get Vera and Petya away from here, but I can't, it's beyond me . . .

Yakov   You're so cold.

Lyubov   It's anger at my own powerlessness . . . (*After a pause.*) Why did you let me stay in this den of filth?

Yakov   You know Sonya didn't want it known you were mine.

Lyubov (*smiling*)   Why are parents such children?

Yakov   That's cruel.

Lyubov (*coldly*)   You're right, and pointless.

Sofia (*enters in a daze*)   I couldn't find her. I don't know what's happened to her . . .

Yakov   Sonya, you're so pale . . .

Sofia (*distracted*)   Yakorev is here. He's being disgustingly rude.

Lyubov   I'm sure he knows something about her.

Sofia   What will happen to her? God is punishing me for you, Lyubov . . .

Lyubov   Don't be ridiculous, Mother, what has God to do with it? We're like the rubbish from some old building – a prison perhaps. We sprawl in the dust and people kick us and stumble and break their bones on us, and we barely feel the pain . . .

Yakov (*quietly*)   Please don't talk like that.

Sofia (*moans*)   Where is she?

Yakov   Is Nadezhda looking for her?

Sofia   And Alexander, and my son-in-law . . . Oh, the scandal!

Lyubov   We're facing worse than a scandal, Mother!

Sofia   I know, I know, it's as I said – we're haunted by disaster . . .

Ivan *enters noisily dragging in* **Yakorev**, *who is surly but composed.*

Ivan (*irately*)   Congratulate me on my new son-in-law! Filthy animal.

Yakorev   Don't talk to me like that.

Ivan   I'll smash your face in.

Sofia   Is Vera with you?

Yakorev   I know where she is.

Ivan (*threateningly*)   Hand her over at once.

Sofia (*pleading*)   Please let us have her back. You've no money, she'll be miserable with you. She'll make a dreadful wife – she's not right for you . . .

Yakorev (*looks at the floor*)   But she's already . . . We're already married . . .

Sofia *collapses in a chair.*

Ivan (*grabs* **Yakorev** *by the throat*)   Liar! You couldn't . . . She – how could she . . . ?

Yakorev   Take your hands off me. Let me explain . . .

Yakov   Let go of him, Ivan.

Lyubov   It's too late to be angry. (*To* **Yakorev**.) So she's your wife now, is she?

Yakorev *silently bows his head.*

Ivan (*shouts*)   Liar! I'll blow your brains out . . .

Yakorev   Let me explain . . .

Yakov   Yes, let him . . .

Ivan   Speak up, dog!

Yakorev   If you love your daughter don't talk to me in that tone.

Ivan   Are you threatening me?

Yakorev   It was Miss Vera herself who asked me to take her . . .

Ivan   Liar!

Yakorev   . . . and sent me to say that now it's happened, you must accept her wishes. You promised Kovalyov five thousand for her -- we'll take four. And when you're chief-superintendent you can take me as your assistant . . .

Ivan (*thickly*)   You little thief – how dare you . . .

Sofia   My God!

Yakov (*stammers in his haste*)   You mustn't stop them, Ivan. It's more sensible this way, don't you see? I'll give them the money, everything will be fine! They love each other – don't destroy that love. Love is a rare flower that blossoms only once in a lifetime – we must protect it . . .

Lyubov (*coldly*)   That's enough, it's bad for you. Come now – time for your bath.

Yakov   No, wait . . .

Lyubov (*helping him up*)   Don't get involved – everything's useless, especially your flights of poetry.

She leads him through the door in the corner of the room.

Ivan (*to* **Yakorev**, *shaking his head*)   What made you do it though? Why did you risk it?

Yakov (*shrugs*)   You see a good thing and you grab it.

Ivan   A good thing! Hear that, Sofia? Our constable regards our daughter as a good thing.

Sofia *sits looking straight ahead and plucking nervously at her dress.*

Yakorev (*philosophically*)   I'm a constable now, who knows where I'll end up?

Ivan   In jail if I've anything to do with it!

Yakorev   Don't shout at me, Ivan Danilovich! I'm your son-in-law now . . .

Vera *silently enters and runs to her father.*

Yakorev   Vera! What are you doing here . . . ?

Ivan (*howls at her*)   The shame. Get out of my sight!

Vera   Papa!

Ivan   I'll strangle you!

Sofia (*remains seated*)   Vera . . .

She stretches out her arms to **Vera**.

Vera (*firmly*)   I know, Papa, I've been a stupid girl and I've been cruelly punished, but you mustn't blame me . . .

Ivan   Ah, hear that, Sofia? She knows where the blame lies. Go on, girl.

Sofia (*quietly*)   Whatever possessed you, Vera?

Vera   Yakorev, go to the dining room!

Yakorev (*obediently leaves the room*)   I don't know what she's playing at . . .

Ivan   You heard her! (*To* **Vera**.) You've disgraced me. Vera, do you understand?

Vera   Listen, Papa, I'll marry Kovalyov now.

Ivan   Now? What decent man will have you?

Vera (*pleading*)   Kovalyov's not decent, he's a brute – you said so yourself.

Ivan   And you're a whore!

Sofia (*rises to her feet, menacingly*)   Be quiet.

Ivan   What . . . ? To hell with you, do as you want.

Vera   Yes, Papa, and you'll do as I want.

Ivan (*braces himself*)   I will?

Vera   Invite Kovalyov here – I'll do the rest.

Ivan (*warily*)   What about his five thousand? Where will you get it from?

Vera   The money doesn't matter.

Ivan   Doesn't matter, eh?

Vera   It's me he wants. He's got piles of money and he can always steal more.

Ivan (*genuinely shocked*)   Listen to her!

Sofia   Leave us for a minute, Ivan.

Ivan   With pleasure. Anything to get away from you – lunatics!

He exits.

Vera (*looks tearfully at her mother*)   See what I've come to, Mama . . .

Sofia (*silently embracing her*)   My child. Do you really love him?

Vera (*smiling*)   He's a wretched coward.

Sofia   So why did you do it?

Vera (*shrugs*)   I don't know . . . It's a bad dream, Mama, I never thought it would end like this. Are there no honest men, Mama? (*She shudders and weeps silently, staring at her reflection in the looking glass.*) Poor little Vera, you look like a whipped dog – your nose is red, your face is a mess . . . Mama, fetch my hero, will you? He is a hero, Mama, he is! Please don't say anything – you're to blame too, you know, and no one can tell me anything worse than I've told myself these last three days. I've turned into an old woman, Mama.

My heart is dead, it will never recover – never, as long as I live. The heart dies instantly, from the first blow. (*She looks at her mother, speaking harshly but without malice.*) I'll grow cold and bitter, like Lyubov, and delight in tormenting everyone who crosses my path. People are worthless, Mama, filth. Go on, fetch him.

Exit **Sofia**. **Vera** *remains alone, clutching her head and gazing into the distance with trembling lips. Hearing* **Yakorev**'s *footsteps, she quickly tidies her hair and forces her face into a calm, businesslike expression.*

Yakorev   What's happening? First you seem serious, then you rush home. Why didn't you wait quietly like we said, while I talked them round? I was almost there, and now . . . I don't understand . . .

Vera (*calmly*)   I changed my mind, that's all – I've decided to marry Kovalyov instead.

Yakorev (*slowly and angrily*)   Really?

Vera   Yes, really.

Yakorev   You won't get away with it!

Vera (*controlling her anger*)   What makes you say that?

Yakorev   I'll make damn sure you don't.

Vera (*flaring up*)   What! Are you serious?

Yakorev   Never more so. Try me.

Vera   What do you propose to do?

Yakorev   I'll make sure the whole town hears about it, that's what. Forget Kovalyov – even the waiters at the tavern won't touch you! I won't be trifled with, understand? I'm not a woman . . .

Vera (*giggles*)   Really? Don't – I'll die of fright!

Yakorev (*with mounting indignation*)   It's not funny – it's disgusting! You cooked up the whole thing, then . . .

Vera (*calmly*)   Then when I saw you for what you were – a thief, a coward, a mercenary little . . .

Yakorev (*furious*)   You'll regret that . . .

Vera (*scornfully*)   Be quiet!

Yakorev (*draws himself up to his full height with a shudder and peers around, as if afraid his boss might be hiding in the room, then threateningly*)   Right then!

Vera (*advancing on him*)   Listen, Constable. That girl who spent two nights with you – one against her will – no longer exists.

Yakorev (*sensing danger, mutters*)   Of course, I understand . . .

Vera   You don't, but you will. That silly girl has died, and a woman has been born who fears nothing and pities no one. You'll drag me through the mud? It doesn't bother me – you've already done that. What do I care if people say I lived with you? (*Laughs a dry laugh.*) I know I did! What will I do now? Live with Kovalyov of course – legally, not because I want him, just as I never wanted you. It's all the same to me. You don't like it? You rob me of my shame then try to scare me by threatening to tell everyone? Go ahead, I don't care. You don't frighten me, worm. Some villains are evil, some are just pathetic. Get out of my sight!

Yakorev (*listens to her initially with an angry smirk, but as her words gather strength he grows increasingly nervous, and finally stops her with an angry shrug*)   You – you seem to have forgotten it was you who initiated it . . .

Vera (*coldly*)   Get out, I said!

Yakorev (*mortified*)   If I'd known you were like this, I . . .

Vera   Yes, what?

Yakorev (*after some thought*)   I'd never have taken you in the first place . . . You deceived me. You can do me a lot of damage, I see that. Your father and brother are both in the

police – and now your husband. They'll tear me to shreds
. . . Look, I give you my word . . .

Vera (*shouts*) Get out!

He hurries out as **Sofia** *enters.* **Vera** *throws herself at her mother.*

Sofia (*alarmed*) Who was shouting? Was he being rough
with you?

Vera (*breathless with agitation*) He was a perfect gentleman,
Mama! I said to him – my darling, I love you . . .

Sofia But you told me . . .

Vera No, Mama. I said there were insurmountable
barriers to our happiness. I shall destroy them or die, the
hero replied . . . He is a hero, Mama. We opened our hearts
– it was beautiful. We both wept tears of ecstasy, two pure,
passionate souls . . . (*Recites.*)

'Two little stars in the heavens so bright
Spoke to the flowers of their pitiful plight . . .'

Then they betrayed the poor girl. As regards love, he kept
making excuses and I couldn't bear it, so I kicked him out.

Sofia My poor child, my poor darling . . .

Vera No, Mother, I shouted because I was suffering – I'm
in pain. Darling Mama, why did it happen? I only wanted
some pleasure. Tell me, can't people be happy and good at
the same time?

Sofia I don't know.

Vera (*seriously*) I'm like you, I don't know either. (*After a
pause.*) I'll never have children, it's too horrible, I wouldn't
know what to say to them . . .

The voices of **Nadezhda** *and* **Alexander** *are heard in the dining
room.*

Vera Are they looking for me? Help, hide me – don't let
them see me.

Sofia *leads her through the door in the corner.*

Vera (*on her way out*)   Mama, did you believe life was good when you were young?

Sofia   Yes, I did.

Vera   And now you think all heroes are liars?

Voices ring out from the dining room.

Alexander   Stupid creature, I'll box her ears.

Nadezhda   Little idiot - honestly.

Ivan   And what of her poor father?

Nadezhda (*peers into* **Yakov**'*s room*)   She's not here.

Ivan   Blow upon blow rain down on my head.

Alexander   We must marry her off to Kovalyov without delay.

Nadezhda   I couldn't agree more.

Ivan   What makes you think he'd want her?

Nadezhda   Don't worry, he'll want her.

The voices recede as they pass into the drawing room. **Pyotr** *enters looking very pale with a drunken smile on his face, and slumps in* **Yakov**'*s armchair with his eyes closed.* **Sofia** *emerges through the small door and pours a glass of water from the carafe by* **Yakov**'*s bed.*

Pyotr   Is someone crying again?

Sofia   You're back. Where have you been?

Pyotr   Who's crying?

Sofia   Vera . . .

Pyotr   So she's home . . .

Sofia (*moves towards him*)   Yes.

Pyotr   Impossible to escape . . . Not worth the effort . . .

Sofia (*quietly*)   Petya, have you been drinking again?

Pyotr   Only a little, Mama, just one glass.

Sofia   What makes you do it? Do you want to kill yourself?

Pyotr   Kill myself? I think it's pathetic when boys my age kill themselves.

Sofia   Oh my God, Pyotr. Where were you?

Pyotr (*smiling*)   I was with Kirill Alexandrovich. But I'm not going there again. They're ever so strict, Mama, they demand such a lot from you - understanding of life, respect for other people . . . And I . . . I'm like an empty suitcase that you take on holiday by mistake, and forget to pack . . .

Sofia   So they got you drunk?

Pyotr   Heaven forbid. It's all tea and philosophy and wise words with them – you don't even get jam with your tea. No, I called in at the tavern. It's fun there.

Sofia   Go to your room and sleep . . .

Pyotr   Sleep . . . You're always asleep, Mother – so cold and melancholy. Do you know a cure for melancholy?

Sofia   I know nothing. I'm afraid to speak. It's better to lie.

Pyotr   Silence is a lie, speaking is a lie. Off you go, wipe your eyes . . . Who's the water for? Vera?

Sofia *leaves the room and passes* **Lyubov** *and* **Yakov** *in the doorway.*

Lyubov (*to* **Yakov**)   Are you feeling better?

Yakov (*in a hoarse voice*)   Yes . . . a little . . .

Lyubov   The baths are obviously bad for you.

Yakov   I know, but Leshch . . .

Lyubov   We'll get another doctor.

Yakov   That would be awkward, Leshch would object.

Pyotr (*gets to his feet*)   Apologies, I've usurped your throne.

Yakov   Sit down, Pyotr, stay where you are. I'm going back to bed, I can't even sit these days.

Pyotr (*to* **Lyubov**)   Have you seen Vera?

Lyubov (*making* **Yakov** *comfortable in bed*)   So she's back?

Yakov   How is she?

Lyubov (*to* **Pyotr**)   Stay here, I'll go to her. (*She goes.*)

Yakov   Poor child, how sad . . .

Pyotr   Why pour vinegar on a wound, does it ease the pain?

Yakov (*startled*)   Why, you sound like Lyuba . . .

Pyotr   Lyuba sees more than we do, that's why she's so cruel. (*Hearing* **Nadezhda** *and* **Alexander**.) Aha, here, come sweet reason.

Yakov (*grimacing*)   I hope they don't shout . . .

Nadezhda (*enters*)   Where have you hidden Vera?

Alexander   Bloody comedy.

Pyotr   She's with Mama.

Nadezhda (*peers at him*)   Tidy yourself up, you're a mess! (*Crosses the room to the small door.*)

Alexander   How are you feeling, *mon oncle*? How's the old ticker? *Tant pis.* Let's have a smoke . . .

Yakov   Might I ask . . . ?

Alexander   Ah, *pardon*! I forgot tobacco's bad for the heart – as well as wine and women and everything else.

Pyotr   He likes a joke, doesn't he, Uncle?

Yakov (*sadly*)   Yes, he does.

Alexander   What are you doing here, brat?

Pyotr   Uncle, there's this boy at the gymnasium who's a real wit, and he said, 'If you want to live a carefree youth, don't ask questions or seek the truth . . .'

Alexander   Stuff and nonsense.

Nadezhda (*interrupts*)   Lyubov's too ghastly for words – she's finally gone off her head!

Alexander (*lights a cigarette*)   So what's new?

Nadezhda   Uncle, you've some influence over her – you must control her, she's corrupting Vera.

Yakov   Lyuba? Corrupting Vera?

Nadezhda   You should hear the things she says!

Yakov   Alexander. I asked you not to smoke.

Alexander Oh, *pardon*!

Yakov (*weakly*)   I won't argue with you, Nadya, I'm not well, but please don't talk about Lyuba like that . . .

Nadezhda   But she's putting vile ideas in Vera's head.

Ivan (*entering*)   Leshch still not back?

The small door bursts open noisily and **Vera** *runs in, followed by* **Sofia** *and* **Lyubov**.

Vera (*angrily*)   You and Mama are wrong. Papa is a good, wise man.

Ivan (*solemnly*)   Unhappy child. Did you ever doubt it?

Pyotr (*smiles sadly*)   Vera, how could you?

Vera   Papa, don't talk like that . . . waving your arms around. I may be bad, I may be unclean, but I'm your daughter, your own flesh.

Ivan   Yes, regrettably.

Pyotr   What a waste of a marvellous comedian.

Vera   Answer me, Papa – talk to me!

Yakov   Please go . . . it's too crowded . . .

No one hears.

Ivan (*pushing* **Vera** *away*)   You've no right to ask my forgiveness.

Vera   No right?

Ivan (*goes to* **Pyotr**)   What did you say, boy?

Alexander (*restrains him*)   Leave him to me, Father, I'll thrash him for you.

Sofia (*calmly*)   No you won't!

Pyotr (*steps out from behind his mother*)   All right, policeman, you want a fight?

Ivan   See that, Nadya?

Vera (*sobs*)   Please, Papa. I'm begging you . . .

Pyotr (*pale and trembling*)   Father, she has the right to know who you are. We both do – well I don't, but she needs to know if her father's an honest man.

Ivan (*stunned*)   What? What did you say?

Nadezhda   For heaven's sake, Petya!

Sofia (*in a slow, commanding tone*)   Let them speak!

Pyotr (*to* **Ivan**)   Do you think a bad, sick, dishonest man has the right to father children?

Alexander (*sneers*)   The right? Any man can have children, you donkey.

Pyotr (*drunk with emotion*)   Listen to me, Father! Do children exist to bear their fathers' sins? To justify and defend everything their parents do? We want to know – tell us how we're to live with your mistakes.

Ivan   Weakling! Failure! What the hell's he getting at?

Pyotr   How can you say that, Father? You gave me life, you raised me – I'm your son!

Vera (*plaintively*)   Don't, Petya!

Yakov (*in a low voice*)   Lyuba, tell them I can't . . .

Lyubov *doesn't hear.*

Pyotr   Tell us, Father, are you an honest man?

Vera (*insistently*)   Mama, make him answer, make him!

Ivan (*beside himself*)   You little . . .

Pyotr   There, Vera, listen to him!

Ivan (*reverts to his usual tone of pathos*)   Yes, depraved child, you listen . . .

Sofia   Stop, Ivan, before you destroy yourself. (*Drops to her knees.*) My children, forgive me!

Nadezhda   Mama, for heaven's sake! God, what a farce!

Ivan   To hell with the lot of you.

Sofia   I can only beg your forgiveness . . .

Lyubov (*throws herself at her mother*)   Get up, Mother, it won't do any good.

Sofia (*to her husband*)   Ask them to forgive you – it's all you can do.

Ivan (*storms out of the room, shouting*)   You want to drive me insane?

Nadezhda (*to her mother*)   Don't, Mother, you're destroying our respect for you!

Pyotr (*sadly*)   A tragic farce, Mama, that's what it is!

Vera (*passionately*)   But she means it.

Pyotr   What difference does that make?

Yakov (*quietly*)   Lyuba . . . Sonya . . . Listen . . . (*He struggles to get out of bed, gasps and topples over, opening his mouth as if trying to cry out.*)

Sofia   I have wronged each one of you. What will become of us?

Pyotr (*sees his uncle's face, shudders and goes to him, then announces solemnly*)   Uncle Yakov is dead . . .

All are momentarily stunned, then they cautiously approach the dead man.

Lyubov   The only way out of this house . . . The only way . . .

Pyotr   The other way – the death of the soul . . .

Sofia (*dazed*)   We've killed him.

Vera (*looks at everyone*)   Why am I not afraid?

Nadezhda (*runs out*)   Oh God, and my husband's not back!

Ivan (*in the dining room*)   I'll make some changes round here, you'll see!

Lyubov   Stop shouting.

Nobody stirs.

Ivan (*passes* **Nadezhda** *in the doorway*)   Well, madam! Have I got the job or not? (*Goes into* **Yakov**'s *room.*) He's dead . . . ! (*Stands on tiptoe and looks over the heads of* **Sofia** *and the children into his brother's face.*) Well, bugger me! Call a doctor! Get Leshch, he's just back . . .

Leshch (*enters*)   Where is the joy proper to such an occasion?

Nadezhda (*quietly*)   Uncle is dead, keep your voice down!

Leshch   Oh dear. (*Goes to* **Yakov** *and takes his hand.*) Yes indeed. Of course it was to be expected, but nevertheless, death is never welcome. Hmm . . .

All fall silent, as though waiting for something. **Alexander** *enters,*
realises what has happened, and looks relieved. **Ivan** *peers around*
anxiously, shifting from foot to foot, then clears his throat, closes his
eyes and starts to speak, at first quietly, then lapsing into his usual
bombast.

Ivan   Children, friends! As we gather here beside the body
of the dear deceased, in the face of the infinite mystery that
is for ever hidden from us . . . Yes, for ever – and, ah,
bearing in mind its reconciling power . . . I speak of death,
of course . . . Let us forswear our quarrels and arguments
and embrace, dear friends. Let bygones be bygones. We are
all the victims of these troubled times, whose poisonous
spirit pervades everything . . . Our only sure support is the
family, our one true fortress, yes, our fortress, and ah . . .

Pyotr *silently pulls the screen round his uncle's bed and looks sadly*
at his father.

Fedosia (*enters, mumbling*)   He's dead, that good, quiet
man . . .

Ivan   Our fortress, our defence against all enemies . . .

Sofia (*quietly*)   Stop it, Ivan . . .

Ivan *sulks, as if about to raise his voice, then looks at everyone and*
stamps out of the room. He is followed by **Leshch**, **Nadezhda**
and **Alexander**. *The others surround* **Yakov**'s *body.* **Vera** *curls*
up in a chair, weeping silently. **Pyotr** *stares dry-eyed at his mother.*
Lyubov *stands stern and motionless.* **Sofia** *looks at her children*
wildly, silently pleading with them.

Fedosia (*behind the screen*)   Queen of Heaven, take the body
of Thy wretched slave . . .

Pyotr (*dully*)   If I believed in God I'd enter a monastery.

Sofia   Lord God almighty! What a terrible life – and at the
end of it, death. Why, Lord?

Lyubov (*in a trance*)   Life and death are true friends,
Mother – two sisters.

Pyotr   Am I to blame? Or Vera? Or any of us?

Lyubov   Death humbly serves the cause of life. The weak and superfluous will perish . . .

Fedosia *mumbles inaudibly.*

Curtain.

Vassa Zheleznova

Characters

Borisovna Zheleznova (*Vassa, Vassilisia*), *early forties but looks younger*

Sergei Petrovich Zheleznov, *her husband, aged sixty, former captain on Black Sea ships and river boats*

Prokhor Borisovich Khrapov, *her brother, fifty-nine*

Natalya (*Nata*), *Vassa's elder daughter, eighteen*

Lyudmilla (*Lyuda*), *Vassa's younger daughter, sixteen*

Rachel Moiseevna, *Vassa's daughter-in-law, late twenties*

Anna Onoshenkova (*Anyuta*), *Vassa's secretary and confidante, mid-thirties*

Melnikov, *Vassa's tenant, clerk at the district court*

Evgeny, *his son*

Gury Krotkikh, *manager of Vassa's shipping company*

Liza
Polya } *housemaids*

Alexei Pyatyorkin (*Alyosha*), *former soldier and sailor, late twenties, with a helmet of coarse thick hair and sleek moustache*

Act One

The large office in the house where **Vassa** *has lived for the past ten years. There is a vast desk, in front of which is a safe and a light armchair with a hard seat. On the wall is a large brightly coloured map of the upper and lower Volga, from Rybinsk to Kazan. Beneath the map is an ottoman covered with a rug and piled with cushions. In the middle of the room is a small oval table, some high-backed chairs and a large leather armchair. French windows open on to a verandah leading to the garden. Two windows also overlook the garden. There are geraniums on the window sills. Between the windows stands a bay tree in a tub. A small shelf holds a silver-plated pitcher and matching ladles. Next to the ottoman is a door leading to a bedroom. Another door behind the table leads to various other rooms, including* **Anna***'s. It is morning. A late-March sun pours through the door and windows, and the room is bright and spacious.*

Vassa *and* **Krotkikh** *enter.*

Vassa   Three fifty for fifteen tons – that's seventy-five kopecks a ton and we pay the dockers twelve. They'll never accept it – they have to lug the stuff thirty yards or more. Most of them are on a rouble a day but they eat a lot – they die if they don't get meat. Sort it out, will you? Get an article in the paper, find someone to have a word with the men. You must know *someone.*

Krotkikh (*cheerfully*)   I certainly do!

Vassa   Good! It's the big shipping lines we must squeeze. We're small fry, we don't carry much. Our crews can drop it over the sides of the boats on to the wharf, we don't often use dockers anyway.

Krotkikh   Yes, but twelve kopecks isn't enough!

Vassa   Well, that's all they're getting! If big ships like the *Caucasus Mercury* raise their wages to fifty, we'll get more business and we can pay them more. Sorry, but that's it, I can't go any higher.

Krotkikh (*frowning*)   But Vassa Borisovna . . .

Vassa   Talk to the small craftsmen – the potters, the millers – offer them a discount so they'll ship with us . . .

Krotkikh (*proudly*)   We did all right last year, we're in the black!

Vassa   Doing all right won't keep us going, we must do better! Now move, I'm up to my ears in work!

Krotkikh *bows silently and leaves the room.*

Vassa (*listening for something*)   Anyuta! (**Anna** *enters from her room.*)   Quick, make copies of these! Was Gury cross?

Anna   A little.

Vassa   What did he say?

Anna   I couldn't make out, something about the conservatives.

Vassa   He would, he's a socialist. No, he believes in socialism like Prokhor believes in God – he prays because everyone else does, but he doesn't believe a word of it. You'd better not let him sweet-talk you. What were you two chatting about last night?

Anna   About the deal the socialists in Germany have hatched with the Kaiser.

Vassa   Huh, mind he doesn't hatch his socialism in you!

Anna   No, I've learned my lesson. It's Natalya he's after.

Vassa   I know. Well, our Nata's no fool.

Anna   And Lyuda too . . .

Vassa   He's just – versatile. (*The telephone rings.*) Yes, speaking . . . Good . . . I'll expect you. (*To* **Anna**.) It's my tenant, Melnikov.

Gestures to **Anna** *to leave the room. Stands at her desk, frowning and looking straight ahead, while her hands sort through papers and shuffle things around.*

Melnikov (*enters from* **Anna***'s room*)   Good morning to you, madam.

Vassa   Thank you. Leave the door ajar. Sit down. Well, what's the news?

Melnikov   Bad news, madam. The investigation's over and the findings have gone to the public prosecutor. The investigator assures me he has suppressed as much as possible.

Vassa   He'd have suppressed the whole thing for another three thousand.

Melnikov   Out of the question, I'm afraid. I've read the woman's statement – the procuress. She's poured her heart out as if to a priest.

Vassa   So there'll be a trial?

Melnikov   It's unavoidable.

Vassa   What will he get?

Melnikov   Possibly hard labour. (*Takes out some photographs.*)

Vassa   What are those?

Melnikov   The victims' pictures you wanted.

Vassa (*takes the pictures and looks at them*)   What do you lawyers call this – sort of thing?

Melnikov   What sort of thing?

Vassa   You know, messing about with children.

Melnikov   We call it depravity, madam.

Vassa   What a . . . foul word! (*She looks through the pictures.*) God, the shame of it. Who's this?

Melnikov   The daughter of your laundress, madam. Just twelve years old.

Vassa   God . . . Who took them?

Melnikov   The police. In the hotel room.

Vassa (*opens the drawer to put the pictures inside*)   Aren't they ashamed to photograph such things? I'll buy them.

Melnikov   Impossible.

Vassa   I'll give you a thousand – two thousand.

Melnikov   The police have the negatives. Please – I took them from the court files. (*Puts out his hand.*)

Vassa (*hands them back*)   So what now?

Melnikov   The prosecutor will file the indictment, charge the accused and arrest him.

Vassa   And the other two? What about the procuress?

Melnikov   All three will be charged of course.

Vassa   What about the prosecutor? Could he hush it up?

Melnikov   He could, but I doubt he will, this one has an eye on his career. Though there's a rumour the – ah – other parties may appeal.

Vassa   Hah! So we can appeal too! Try, please, I beg you. Offer the prosecutor whatever it takes, I need to bury it, wipe it out! I have my daughters to consider . . .

Melnikov   Vassa Borisovna, with infinite respect and gratitude for your generosity, I –

Vassa   Never mind that, we'll talk about gratitude when it's been decently buried. Now do something!

Melnikov   There's nothing I can do, my hands are tied . . .

Vassa   If you succeed, I'll tear up all your debts. I can put in another fifteen hundred, five thousand in all. That's enough, isn't it?

Melnikov   Yes, but - I am unable . . .

Vassa   What?

Melnikov   Wouldn't it be better if *you* -

Vassa   No, no, the prosecutor doesn't want me fussing around. I don't mind paying but I won't grovel. Besides, you know me, I don't mince my words. I couldn't do it. You must do it - today, please. Then ring and tell me how much. I wish you luck.

Melnikov   Allow me to take my leave. I shall go to the court at once.

Vassa   Off you go, quick! Remember, money's no object - for this!

Melnikov *exits.* **Vassa** *sits at her desk with her eyes closed, then pulls out the drawer, looks for something and finds a small box. She opens it and examines the contents, stirring them with a pen nib. There is a noise at the door. She slips the box in her pocket.* **Lyudmilla** *enters.*

Lyudmilla   Mama, darling, I had the most lovely dream! It was so lovely . . .

Vassa (*kisses her*)   Everything's lovely with you, Lyuda, even when you're awake!

Lyudmilla   But listen -

Vassa   Not now, tell me at dinner.

Lyudmilla   But Nata will laugh at me, or someone will interrupt and I'll forget it. It's very easy to forget your dreams. Please listen now!

Vassa   Run along, Lyuda - send Liza to me.

Lyudmilla   You're so horrid today, Mother!

Vassa (*alone, muttering to herself, imitating* **Lyudmilla**)   'So horrid today . . . !' Little fool! (**Liza** *enters*.) Liza, my brother says he told you to oil his padlocks, why did you disobey him?

Liza   I didn't have time, madam! I have to wait on everyone and clean the house – it's too much for me on my own! Can't you get a girl to help me . . .

Vassa   Forget it, I don't need any more people hanging around. The young ladies will give you a hand. You must just work harder – and sleep less.

Liza   I didn't sleep at all last night, madam!

Vassa   Is he in?

Liza   No.

Vassa   Tell the Captain I want to see him.

Liza *exits.* **Vassa** *stands, deep in thought, then snaps her fingers and taps her pocket.* **Zheleznov** *enters in his dressing gown. He has a heavy grey moustache, his curly hair is unbrushed, and his cheeks and chin are covered in several days' growth of beard.*

Vassa   Just up, or going to bed?

Zheleznov   What d'you want?

Vassa (*firmly shuts the door to* **Anna**'s *room*)   Don't shout, you don't frighten anyone.

Zheleznov *turns towards the other door.* **Vassa** *slips past him and shuts this too.*

Vassa   The prosecutor is bringing charges.

Zheleznov (*grips the back of the chair*)   I don't believe it, you're lying!

Vassa (*calmly*)   The trial is going ahead.

Zheleznov   Bloody swine! I lost nine thousand to him at cards and hinted I'd put another eleven his way . . .

Vassa   In a few days you'll be charged, arrested and thrown into jail.

Zheleznov   Skinflint, you've been sitting on your cash, the investigator wasn't paid – you didn't give Melnikov enough! Tell me, how much did he get?

Vassa   For depravity with little girls you get hard labour.

Zheleznov (*sits down shaking his head; in a husky voice*)   And you're glad . . .

Vassa   Think of your daughters, they're not married yet – while they're looking for husbands you'll be in jail. What decent man will take them? You've a grandson who's almost five . . . Murder would have been better than this filth!

Zheleznov   I should have murdered *you*! Murdered you and torn out your cruel heart and thrown it to the dogs! *You* got me into this, I don't know what I'm doing any more, you . . .

Vassa   Lies won't help you, Sergei. Who are you lying to? Yourself? Don't lie, I can't bear to listen to you. (*Goes to him and presses the palm of her hand against his forehead, pushing his head back and staring into his face.*) I'm asking you not to let this go to court. Don't disgrace your family. In all my vile, disgusting life with a drunken lecher I've not asked for much, but I implore you for the children's sake . . .

Zheleznov (*horrified*)   What? What are you saying?

Vassa   You know what I'm saying.

Zheleznov   Never!

Vassa   Must I beg? Must I go down on my knees?

Zheleznov   Go – leave me alone! (*Tries to stand up.*)

Vassa (*grips his shoulders and pushes him back in his chair*)   I have the powder here – take it!

Zheleznov   Get out!

Vassa   Just think, the whole town will come to court to see you. You'll be sentenced to hard labour and die a wretched, lingering death in jail. This way there's no pain, no shame, it's over in an instant. Your heart stops, and you fall asleep.

Zheleznov   Never! Let them arrest me! I don't care!

Vassa   And the children? And the disgrace?

Zheleznov   I'll join a monastery, I'll shave my head, I'll be a hermit, I'll live in a cave . . . But I won't die . . .

Vassa   Humbug! Take the powder.

Zheleznov (*gets up*)   I won't! I won't take anything from you!

Vassa   Take it yourself, then.

Zheleznov   Or you'll poison me?

Vassa   Please, Sergei, think of your daughters! They've their whole lives ahead of them. Children shouldn't pay for their fathers' sins.

Zheleznov   Or their mothers' either.

Vassa   Leave me out of it. Listen to me, Sergei, don't imagine I'll keep quiet in court. I'll tell them about the whores you brought to my house and what you got up to with them, and how you paraded them in front of your daughters, and taught your own daughters to drink –

Zheleznov   That's a lie – it was your brother! It was Prokhor who taught them to drink!

Vassa   You damaged Lyudmilla so badly she can't grow up or do anything or concentrate for a second . . .

Zheleznov   While Natalya's the image of you, of course!

Vassa   Just remember, I'll tell the court everything – the whole town will know!

Zheleznov (*stands up, muttering*)   Let me pass! You make me sick! Let me go! (*Pushes past her and makes for the door.*)

Vassa (*follows him*)   Take the powder, Sergei!

Zheleznov   No!

Both exit. **Liza** *appears at the door holding an assortment of locks on a tray. Behind her stands* **Prokhor** *holding a huge barn padlock.*

Prokhor (*morosely*)   What was all that about?

Liza   I don't know, she was trying to get him to take some powder.

Prokhor   What powder?

Liza   Medicine, I suppose.

Prokhor   What medicine?

Liza   How would I know?

Prokhor   There's nothing wrong with Sergei, you fool, he's in cracking form! He and I were up till four in the morning playing cards and drinking brandy!

Liza   She must have meant bicarbonate then.

Prokhor   Bicarbonate for brandy, you fool? Who asked you anyway? Just leave the locks on the table and go. You're useless, you never notice anything! I don't know why I keep giving you presents.

Liza   A fine one you've given me! Soon everyone will notice!

Prokhor   You're lucky it wasn't Pyatyorkin. Now move that chair from the sun or the leather will fade – sixty-five roubles it cost me.

Liza   What, the sun?

Prokhor   The chair, my girl, it was a present to my sister, the sun costs nothing . . . Wait, don't be funny with me – the sun indeed, remember your place! I can see my sister's been spoiling you.

Liza (*leaving the room*)   I'm not making your bed tonight.

Prokhor   Just go. (*Leafs through some papers on the desk, sneezes, then breaks into song.*)

'In autumn's windswept twilight
Wanders a lonely maid
Bearing the fruit of a love that won't fade . . .'

Natalya (*enters*)   What a lovely day . . .

Prokhor   I don't know about that, it's not started yet. Why are you running around like a jackal with your hair unbrushed?

Natalya   Have you heard the news?

Prokhor   What news?

Natalya   The Captain's had it.

Prokhor   What are you talking about?

Natalya   Sunk. Scuppered.

Prokhor   Well, well, whatever next!

Natalya   He's going to be tried.

Prokhor (*frightened*)   Who told you?

Natalya   Evgeny Melnikov.

Prokhor (*sits down heavily*)   Dammit, he didn't get off! So this is what the Zheleznovs have come to, and the ancient dynasty of the Khrapovs! Your father's done for us, we'll never live it down!

Natalya   I suppose he might get off.

Prokhor   That's not the point, it's the trial, the disgrace. They'll probably find him guilty anyway. The rich always are these days, it's the fashion now – it's a crime to be rich! But mark my words, it won't be him who's on trial, it'll be us Khrapovs!

Natalya   What can he do?

Prokhor   Nothing, apart from running off to America with all the other criminals.

Natalya   I mean, can't we bribe the court?

Prokhor   We've done that, my sister spent thousands trying to hush it up. She paid the police, the investigator, but it didn't work. Now I won't be mayor and you girls won't find anyone to marry you – even with your dowry. Your father's contaminated you, the swine! What an idiot she was . . . !

Natalya   Mother you mean?

Prokhor   Who else?

Natalya   She's not an idiot.

Prokhor   So what did she marry him for? He's almost twenty years older than she is.

Natalya   He's *your* friend – you talked her into it!

Prokhor   Good Lord, did I really? My head's like a sieve. I'm too easy-going, that's my problem – the artistic type. When I was young I dreamed of playing comic parts in operettas. While he . . . he was sailing the high seas! As if there's not enough shit in the ocean!

Natalya   Did she love him?

Prokhor   Bugger love! What kind of love makes a girl turn her back on her family? It's madness! It's fine for the gentry to marry gypsies and actresses, but it's not for us!

Vassa (*enters*)   What's not for us?

Prokhor   Natalya and I here . . .

Vassa   Yes, I can see Natalya's here.

Prokhor   How is Sergei?

Vassa   Not good, his heart's troubling him. Nata, get me some tea please.

Natalya   Why don't you say I'm in the way?

Vassa   All right, you're in the way. Now get me some tea.

Natalya *exits.*

Vassa (*to* **Prokhor**)   What are you sulking about?

Prokhor   I'll sulk if I want! You haven't stopped the trial!

Vassa   Don't tell the girls, I'll tell them myself.

Prokhor   Natalya already knows, she told me.

Vassa   And who told her?

Lyudmilla *slips into the room.*

Prokhor   Melnikov's son, Evgeny – I don't think they should spend so much time with him.

Lyudmilla   Why not? He's interesting and we're bored! All our girlfriends are sick and can't visit.

Vassa   Go and help Liza make the beds, will you?

Lyudmilla   But I want to stay here with you, Mother! Why are you always pushing me away?

Vassa   Work, Lyuda, I've a business to run.

Lyudmilla   Work, work! You never have time to talk to me!

Vassa   We'll talk while I drink my tea. Now run off, there's a good girl.

Lyudmilla   Honestly, I feel like crying. Now you'll shout at Uncle Prokhor for calling Papa a pervert!

Vassa (*strokes her daughter's hair and leads her to the door*)   It's not so bad to be a pervert, it just means being . . . different. Someone's got to be different. Like me – I've spent my life being different.

Lyudmilla   Don't laugh at me, I know what a pervert is! Uncle Prokhor's one!

Vassa *tries to push her out of the room and close the door, but* **Lyudmilla** *slips out from under her arm.*

Lyudmilla   Yes he is! He got Liza pregnant, and he says horrible things about Papa – he doesn't love him at all!

Prokhor   It's not true, we old men just don't have much love left in us!

Lyudmilla   And *you* don't love him either, do you, Mama?

Vassa   That's enough!

Lyudmilla   Why not? Uncle drinks too, and you love him! Drinking's a disease, Evgeny Melnikov says –

Prokhor   – the source of all bloody wisdom!

Lyudmilla   – he says it's like stomachache . . .

Liza *enters bearing a small samovar, followed by* **Natalya** *with a tray of tea things.* **Vassa** *embraces her older daughter then paces the room with barely concealed agitation, as if waiting for something to happen. She stops and stares at* **Prokhor**'s *locks.*

Vassa   Still playing with your toys, Prokhor? Aren't you bored of them?

Prokhor   It's not an expensive hobby – and it may be more than a hobby too!

Vassa   How's that?

Prokhor   Who knows? No one collects old locks – I'm the only one! The only brunette in a crowd of blondes. A lock and key mean something, like a bridle on a horse – things have to be locked up, if they weren't we'd have nothing left!

Vassa   Listen to you! It's not such a bad idea though. Pour me some tea, Natalya.

Prokhor *(watching her)*   You say I'm wasting my money, but d'you realise I paid seven roubles for this padlock here, and someone's already offered me twenty-five. If I collected thousands of them and sold them to a museum, I'd be a millionaire!

Vassa   All right, pigs might fly. (*To* **Lyudmilla**, *suddenly in a loud voice.*) Did you know I was fourteen when your father seduced me? We were married when I was sixteen. Yes, sixteen. When I was seventeen and pregnant with Fyodor, we were taking tea on Trinity Sunday – the virgins' feast – and I spilt some cream on my husband's boot. He ordered me to lick it off with my tongue, and I did, in front of all our guests. People didn't like our family much . . .

Lyudmilla   Oh, Vassa, do you have to tell us all this?

Natalya *observes her mother from behind the samovar.*

Vassa   Lord, he loved a joke! Lord, how he loved to enjoy himself.

Lyudmilla   Did he always enjoy himself, then?

Vassa   Remember how you drilled a hole in the wall, Natalya, so you could see your father enjoying himself?

Natalya   Yes I do.

Vassa   And you came running to me in tears, and said, 'Throw them out! Get rid of them!'

Natalya   Yes I do. What is this, a family tribunal?

Prokhor   You viper!

Vassa   That's good, Natalya, I'm glad you remember! If you don't remember, you die. I bore him nine children. Three survived. One was still-born. Two little girls died in their first year, two boys before they were five, another when he was seven. The reason I'm telling you this, girls, is so you don't rush into marriage.

Lyudmilla   You never told us before.

Vassa   I never had time.

Lyudmilla   Why did the others die and we didn't?

Vassa   You were lucky – I suppose. No, the others died because they were born weak, and they were born weak because their father was drunk and he beat me. Your Uncle Prokhor can tell you all about it.

Prokhor   Yes, he belted her all right. Many's the time I had to pull her away from the Captain with my bare hands. He learned how to flog his sailors, so he did it . . . properly!

Lyudmilla (*to* **Prokhor**)   So why did you never get married?

Prokhor   I did. But it's like the song: 'We find it easy to marry, but living together is hard . . .'

Lyudmilla   Why d'you sing everything in the same tune?

Prokhor   It helps me remembers the words. Four years I lived with my wife, that was enough for me. It's better to live alone and be your own master. Why keep horses when you can catch a cab?

Natalya   Will Fyodor live with us?

Vassa   I expect so – when he's better.

Natalya   And Rachel?

Vassa   What d'you mean? She's his wife!

Lyudmilla   Rachel's so lovely!

Natalya   But will they want to live here after Father's trial?

Vassa (*loses her temper*)   Stop asking questions, Natalya! You're too inquisitive!

Lyudmilla   Don't get angry, Mother, please!

Liza (*rushes in terrified*)   Vassa Borisovna . . . It's Sergei Petrovich . . . !

Vassa (*gives a slight start, then controls herself*)   Why, what's wrong? Does he want me?

Liza   I think he's – dead . . .

Vassa (*angrily*)   Don't be ridiculous!

She hurries out. **Lyudmilla** *and* **Liza** *follow.* **Natalya** *rises to her feet and looks at her uncle.* **Prokhor** *meets her gaze with a baffled stare.*

Prokhor   My legs are shaking – you go, Natalya, find out what's happening!

Natalya   If he's dead, I suppose there'll be no trial?

Prokhor   Off you go, I said! (*He remains alone on stage, drinking cold tea and mumbling to himself.*) Dear oh dear! Bloody hell, what a business!

Liza (*runs back in, speaking in a frightened whisper*)   I don't understand, Prokhor Borisovich! He was perfectly all right when I left him!

Prokhor   What's to understand? He was alive and now he's dead. Unless of course he's fainted.

Liza   Perfectly all right, he was – it must have been that powder, Prokhor Borisovich . . .

Prokhor (*stunned*)   Wha-at? You little . . . (*Seizes her by the throat in a frenzy and shakes her.*) Shut your mouth, slut! I'll teach you to make up stories! (*Pushes her away and wipes the sweat from his bald patch.*)

Liza   But you said I was to tell you everything . . .

Prokhor   Tell me what? You tell me what you see and what you hear. You've not seen anything now, understand? Nothing! Put it out of your head! You've made it up. The whole thing! Now get out of my sight, you little fool! Powder! I'll give you powder!

He pushes her out of the door, rushes about the room and goes back to the door, where he stops as if unable to take another step. **Vassa** *and* **Lyudmilla** *enter, followed by* **Pyatyorkin**.

Prokhor   Well, Vassa, is it true?

Vassa Yes. He's dead.

Lyudmilla Shall we take the plants to his room, Mother?

Vassa Yes, do that.

Pyatyorkin *rolls out the bay tree in the tub.* **Lyudmilla** *takes the geraniums off the window sills and goes out, returning a moment later.*

Prokhor Extraordinary thing to happen. There he was, right as rain -- he and I were up till four this morning . . .

Vassa Drinking brandy.

Prokhor That's right -- Liza was saying you'd given him some powder.

Vassa Yes, he had heartburn and asked for some bicarbonate.

Prokhor Bicarbonate! I see!

Lyudmilla You're terrible, Uncle Prokhor! Papa has just died and you're grinning all over! How can you?

Prokhor Don't upset yourself, Lyuda!

Vassa (*on the telephone*) Treble 0 8 451 Yes . . . Thank you . . . Who . . . ? Is that you, Yakov Lvovich? Be so good as to come at once . . . No, at once . . . Yes, Sergei Petrovich is dead . . . No, he was quite well . . . Yes, quite suddenly . . . No one saw what happened . . . Please do.

Prokhor (*with quiet admiration*) My God, Vassa, you're a genius!

Vassa (*astonished*) Stop blathering, you fool! Pull yourself together!

Act Two

A few months later. The same room. **Vassa** *is sitting in the leather armchair.* **Lyudmilla, Natalya, Anna** *and* **Evgeny Melnikov** *are on the couch. They have drunk tea, and the samovar and tea things are still on the table. It is evening and the lamp has been lit, but the rest of the room is in soft shadow. In the garden the moon is visible, and the dark outline of trees.*

Vassa Well, I've told you about the old marriage customs, and how husbands used to treat their wives . . .

Anna (*quietly*) What a terrible life.

Natalya And a stupid one.

Lyudmilla Why are people unhappy, Vassa?

Evgeny Because they're stupid.

Vassa I don't know why they're unhappy, Lyuda. Little Onegin and his Natalya know – because they're stupid. Some say clever people are unhappier than stupid ones, and I've seen that for myself, but –

Evgeny If you think the rich are cleverer than the poor –

Vassa Of course they are! But they lead mean, vile lives and they don't know how to forget everything and enjoy themselves like poor people do.

Anna That's true.

Natalya So we must live in poverty then?

Vassa That's right. You should try it, Nata. Marry Onegin here and see how you get on. He'll be a lieutenant in the infantry, and you'll be a regimental lady – you know the type. You won't get a penny from me, so you'll have to live on forty roubles a month. Out of that you'll buy clothes, shoes, food, drink, entertain guests. It'll cover the upkeep of your children too when you have them, and –

Natalya   I shan't have children. Why bring more misery into the world?

Vassa   Very wise, why indeed? So what are your prospects, young man? I'll tell you. Forty roubles a month and an orderly to make you stringy rissoles from cheap meat.

Evgeny (*sulkily*)   I might be transferred to the Navy . . .

Lyudmilla   I shan't marry at all, I'd be too scared. I'd rather travel the world looking at botanical gardens and hothouses and alpine meadows . . .

Natalya   It's all got to change – marriage, life, everything!

Vassa   Good idea, go ahead! Our Krotkikh will show you how.

Natalya   I don't need him to tell me we need a revolution!

Vassa   The revolution fizzled out, leaving a lot of spluttering logs and hot air.

Anna   Our new parliament you mean, the Duma?

Vassa   Right. Damp wood never burns. Krotkikh can teach us a thing or two though. For two hundred a month he helps me run my business, and for fifteen he'll help you make your revolution. That's one-fifty a lesson. When he came to work for me his trousers weren't even creased, but I saw him at the theatre the other night and his wife already had a bit of gold on her. That's the way to do it, girls! So you want to join the Navy, do you, Onegin?

Evgeny   I haven't decided yet. Why do you keep calling me Onegin?

Vassa   You'd better make your mind up – you're still a cadet! You should be an officer by now! I call you Onegin because –

Natalya   He's not a bit like him.

Vassa Isn't he, Nata? He's just as snooty . . . Well, all right, you know what he's like.

Natalya He's not like anyone.

Vassa What *is* he like then?

Evgeny (*offended*) I can't make you out — I never know when you're joking and when you're being serious.

Vassa Keep your hair on. Look, try and understand what I'm saying. We had a big strike down at the docks last month and the troops were sent in, and Vezlomtsev the locksmith said to the lieutenant, 'You earn forty roubles, Your Honour,' he says, 'and I get seventy-five – a hundred if I'm lucky. You serve the rich, and I'm richer than you are – so you've no right to give me orders!'

Evgeny I fail to see what's interesting about that.

Natalya Mother loves annoying people.

Vassa Yes, it's a fault of mine, I don't really like people much.

Lyudmilla Yes you do, Vassa!

Vassa I don't – I hate 'em! Never mind, we've had a nice chatter. Now run along, girls, I've work to do. Anna, you stay here. Clear off, the rest of you, I'll see you at supper! (*To* **Anna**.) Anna, is it true Melnikov's joined the League of the Russian People?

Anna Yes he has.

Vassa Silly fool, he only did it because of that idiot son of his! They want to kick the little pipsqueak out of the cadets. I'm afraid he'll be the ruin of my Natalya.

Anna I think she only took up with him because she's bored.

Vassa The wicked are never bored.

Anna   She's been very moody since Sergei Petrovich died, and all the rumours . . .

Vassa   They persist?

Anna   Yes.

Vassa   And you – believe them?

Anna   No I don't. But I was upset by Liza's suicide. I can't understand it. She was a lovely girl. She'd been with you since she was a child. We all liked her.

Vassa   It's my brother's doing. He must have scared her about something.

Anna   Had she – relations with him?

Vassa   He made her. So people don't believe she suffocated in the bathhouse?

Anna   Hardly anyone believes that, no.

Polya *enters.*

Vassa   What d'you want? Speak up, don't just stand there!

Polya (*mumbles*)   There's a woman come.

Vassa   At this time of night? Who is it?

Polya   She had a funny name – Moses or something.

Polya *follows* **Anne** *into her room, leaving the door open.*

Vassa   Wha-at? (*Hurries to the door, then turns back to* **Anna**.) Not a word about this to the girls, I want to surprise them. If anyone wants me I'm busy. (*To* **Polya**.) Take the samovar and heat it up. (*Exits.*)

Anna   Are you settling in all right?

Polya   It's hard work. I thought I'd just be attending to the young ladies, but the mistress needs a maid, and Prokhor Borisovich needs a servant. I can't wait on him, I can't!

Anna   Does he – bother you?

Polya *follows* **Anna** *into her room, leaving the door open.*

Polya   He's terrible – he has no shame! Tonight he's prowling round in his vest, singing the same thing over and over again. Last night when everyone was in bed, he was singing and clanking his locks. It's awful! What's the matter with him, Anna Vasilevna?

Anna   He's sick, an alcoholic – a drunk.

Polya   I'm grateful to you though, it's a very good house.

Anna   But not the people in it?

Polya   I don't judge people. I was judged in court and went to prison . . . Is it true what they say about the girl before me hanging herself in the bathhouse?

Anna   It's a lie, she suffocated. She went to take a bath and choked on charcoal fumes. She was pregnant.

Polya   So she *was* pregnant!

Lyudmilla *enters the office bearing a small circular bench. She is followed by* **Pyatyorkin**, *carrying a plant in a tub.*

Lyudmilla   Put it here, it needs sun – not there, here, in the middle.

Pyatyorkin   Yes, Miss, will this do? (*He is on his knee as he speaks to her.*)

Lyudmilla   Fine. My, what frightening hair you have. It must be very hard!

Pyatyorkin   It's not hard at all, Miss, would you like to stroke it? Go on, have a feel!

Lyudmilla (*passes her hand over his head*)   It's like a lion's mane!

Pyatyorkin   You're right there, Miss, everyone says that.

Lyudmilla   Who's everyone?

Pyatyorkin   You know, friends, people . . .

Lyudmilla   Why are you kneeling like that?

Pyatyorkin   I like kneeling before you!

Lyudmilla   How silly! I'd never get on my knees to a man!

Pyatyorkin   You don't have to, the man does it for you. You can do what you like with him, whatever your fancy desires . . .

Lyudmilla   Well, I don't desire anything with you. And I shan't.

Pyatyorkin   As you wish.

Lyudmilla   Wait here while I tell the gardener what to bring in. (*Exits.*)

Anna (*from her room*)   Don't shake the tree, Pyatyorkin, she's not for you!

Pyatyorkin   You're just jealous! You never know, it's worth a try, anything's possible!

Anna   If Vassa hears about your little tête-á-têtes . . .

Pyatyorkin   But she won't, will she?

Anna   . . . you'll be out on your ear before you know it.

Pyatyorkin   You won't squeal. Lyudmilla doesn't know the name of the game yet, and when she does it'll be too late. You keep your mouth shut, there's nothing in it for you. You get your cut, and if they sling me out it'll be worse for you.

Anna   Let them! I couldn't bear to have to serve *you* . . .

Lyudmilla (*returns*)   You can go now, Pyatyorkin. I don't need you any more.

Pyatyorkin (*exiting*)   I wish you joy on this day and for ever more!

Lyudmilla   Isn't he obliging!

Anna   Very.

Lyudmilla   He's a wonderful dancer too! You should see him!

Anna   All the same, Lyuda, I'd watch him if I were you.

Lyudmilla   Why, what can he do to me?

Anna   He can give you a baby.

Lyudmilla   Ugh, that's disgusting!

Anna   What is, a baby?

Lyudmilla   No, you are! (*Exits.*)

Anna (*calling after her*)   A baby, I said.

Vassa appears at the door with **Rachel** *and shoos away* **Anna** *and* **Polya** *with a sweep of her arm.* **Rachel** *is in her late twenties, strikingly handsome, elegantly but simply and austerely dressed.*

Vassa   Now, Rachel, sit down and tell me what brings you here and where you've come from.

Rachel   From abroad.

Vassa   So they let you in?

Rachel   I came with a woman musician – as her companion.

Vassa   On a false passport, I see. Well done! You're a clever girl. Brave too. And more beautiful than ever. Ah, with those looks . . . Never mind . . . So how's Fyodor? Tell me the truth.

Rachel   I always tell the truth, Vassa Borisovna. There's no hope. The doctors have given him two months, three at most.

Vassa   So the son of Captain Zheleznov is giving up the ghost!

Rachel   Yes. He's so thin, he knows there's no hope but he's funny and cheerful as ever. How's my Kolya?

Vassa   So this is the end of Fyodor Zheleznov. My son, the heir to my business . . .

Rachel   Is he asleep?

Vassa   Kolya? I don't know. I expect so.

Rachel   Can I take a peep at him?

Vassa   No, you can't.

Rachel   Why not?

Vassa   Because he's not here.

Rachel   Why? What's happened to him?

Vassa   Nothing's happened, he's in the country. He's living in a forest, surrounded by pine trees. It's better for him there. The town doesn't suit him, his glands are bad. He got his ill health from his parents.

Rachel   How far is it?

Vassa   Oh, about fifty miles.

Rachel   How do I get there?

Vassa   You don't, Rachel. Now listen, you and I have to talk.

Rachel   Is he dead?

Vassa   Of course not! There'd be nothing to talk about if he was! He's alive and well, a nice little boy, and clever too. So what do you want with him?

Rachel   I've decided to take him abroad with me. My sister's married to a chemistry professor in Lausanne and they've no children –

Vassa   I knew it! Rachel will dump that child on her relatives, I said. Well, I won't let you! You're not taking him!

Rachel   What do you mean! I'm his mother!

Vassa   And I'm his grandmother! Your mother-in-law.
The head of the family, understand?

Rachel   No, I'm sorry, I don't. You're not serious. It's . . .
barbaric! You're an intelligent woman. You can't mean
it . . .

Vassa   You're wasting your time. Just be quiet and I'll say
it again. You're not taking Kolya, got it?

Rachel   That's impossible!

Vassa   What can you do? Nothing! As far as the law is
concerned you're an outlaw and a revolutionary – you don't
even exist! If we turned you in they'd clap you in jail!

Rachel   You wouldn't, I don't believe it! You must give
me my son!

Vassa   Save your breath. I know what I'm doing.

Rachel   No . . .

Vassa   Don't shout, keep calm! You're not having Kolya
– I've other plans for him.

Rachel   What are you – an animal?

Vassa   Don't shout, I said! And don't insult me, I'm not
an animal. An animal feeds her babies, then sends them off
to forage for themselves . . . We're talking about beasts of
prey here, not rabbits. But you wouldn't make your little
one fend for himself and nor will I. No, my grandson will
inherit the Khrapov Zheleznov shipping line – the sole heir
to a multimillion rouble business! His aunts, Natalya and
Lyudmilla, will get a small share – fifty thousand should do.
The rest goes to him.

Rachel   You're wrong if you think you can buy me off like
this – quite, quite wrong!

Vassa   Why should I buy you off, Rachel? I've never
disliked you, even when you took my son from me. He was

no good to me anyway as an invalid. Besides, I never liked him much, and I could see you adored him. Go ahead, love him, I said, it doesn't bother me! A sick man needs his happiness too. I was even grateful to you for taking him off me.

Rachel (*losing her temper*)   That's horrible and untrue! I can't believe you could be so cruel!

Vassa   Shout all you like, you only shout because you know I'm right. But tell me one thing -- what can you give your son? I know you, you're stubborn. You've got a dream and won't give it up. You want to stir the revolution -- I have to look after my business. You'll go to prison and your little boy will be an orphan, living with strange people in a strange country. No, Rachel, you'd better get used to it -- I intend to keep him!

Rachel (*more calmly, with icy contempt*)   Yes, you have the power to do it, I realise that. Just as you can report me to the police.

Vassa   That too, I can do anything. I'll play dirty if I have to.

Rachel   You *are* an animal! How can I touch your savage heart?

Vassa   People are worse than animals. The way some of them live drives you mad – you want to kill them, destroy their homes, tear the clothes off their backs, freeze them to death and starve them like cockroaches. Don't talk to me about animals!

Rachel   Damn you, there's something good in that anger of yours!

Vassa   You're a clever girl, Rachel, sometimes I'm sorry you're not my daughter. There, now I've said it! I always speak my mind.

Rachel (*looks at her watch*)   May I sleep here tonight?

Vassa   Of course you can, we won't throw you out! The
girls will be delighted to see you – they love you. But
remember, you're not having Kolya!

Rachel   We'll see about that.

Vassa   You wouldn't kidnap him, would you? No, you
wouldn't!

Rachel   I've nothing more to say. I'm exhausted, my
nerves are shattered . . . You're a callous, ruthless person.
When I listen to you I think maybe there is such a thing as a
criminal type.

Vassa   Of course there is! There's everything! You could
never invent anything worse than there is already!

Rachel   But time's running out for you and your class.
The masters are being driven out by a new force, a new and
terrible force that'll crush the life out of you, wipe you out!

Vassa   Well now, isn't that dreadful! You know, Rachel, if
I believed any of it I'd say – go ahead, take my money, take
my worldly wisdom, take the lot!

Rachel   You're lying!

Vassa   Yes, because I don't believe a word of it! You're
not as clever as you think. It's not going to happen! It can't!

Rachel   Are you sorry?

Vassa   Well, maybe a bit . . . Listen, I'll tell you
something. When my wretched husband lost the whole
business one night at cards – all the ships, the wharves, the
houses, everything – you won't believe it, but I was glad!
Then he pulled the wedding ring off his finger, put it on a
card, and won the whole lot back, plus a bit more. That was
when the whoring and drinking really started. For the next
fifteen years I carried the whole business on my back. It took
a lot out of me, but I did it for the children. I pinned all my
hopes on my children – and now my grandson is the point
of it all.

Rachel   So my son's to be sacrificed to your vile business! Imagine how I feel, knowing Kolya's the reason for your dirty deals . . . !

Vassa   You don't like it? Never mind, I didn't like a few things you said either. Let's have some tea -- and mind our manners in front of the girls!

Rachel   Yes, there's no need for them to know I'm here illegally, or about our quarrel. It's nothing to do with them.

Vassa   No need to tell them anything!

Polya *appears at the door.*

Vassa   Call the girls, Polya. We don't want the cadet – tell them quietly so he won't hear. And bring the samovar! Off you go. So we meet at last, Rachel!

Rachel   Not a pleasant meeting.

Vassa   It can't be helped. Only children know what pleasure is, and that doesn't last long.

Rachel   I can't believe what's happening.

Vassa (*kicks the chair irritably*)   What can't you believe?

Lyudmilla (*runs in followed by* **Natalya**)   Who is it, who is it? Oh, look, it's Rachel!

Natalya   Why didn't you send us a telegram?

Vassa   Nata loves asking questions. Wish her good day and she'll ask you why!

Rachel   You haven't changed a bit, Lyuda, you're as sweet as ever -- why, you haven't grown up at all these last two years!

Lyudmilla   Is that a bad thing?

Rachel   No, of course not! While Nata here . . .

Natalya   Has aged.

Rachel   You look – older . . . Though I suppose you're not supposed to say that about a girl.

Natalya   I'm wiser now.

Rachel   That's different.

The girls are delighted to see **Rachel** *and sit her next to them on the ottoman. She talks wearily, never taking her eyes off* **Vassa***, who sits calmly at the table pouring tea.*

Lyudmilla   So tell us everything!

Natalya   How's Fyodor? Is he any better?

Rachel   No, he's very ill.

Natalya   So why did you leave him?

Rachel   I came to fetch my son.

Vassa   And I say he can't leave the country.

Lyudmilla   Your little Kolya's such a darling, Rachel! Brave, clever . . . He's staying at Khomutova. It's a lovely place, in a huge pine forest.

Natalya   He was moved from Bogodukhovo, was he?

Lyudmilla   Bogodukhovo's lovely too! There's a grove of lime trees, and beehives . . .

Rachel   You don't know where he is, then?

Vassa   Oh, come to the table!

Rachel   So tell me, Lyudmilla, how are you?

Lyudmilla   I'm very well! Now it's spring, Mama and I are working in the garden. She comes to my room first thing and says, 'Get up!' We drink tea and go straight out. You wouldn't believe what a lovely garden it is, Rachel . . . !

Anna *enters, nods to* **Rachel** *and says something to* **Vassa***. Both leave the room.*

Lyudmilla   It's so lovely it takes your breath away – all covered in dew and sparkling in the sun like a brocade vestment! Two years ago we ordered a hundred roubles' worth of seeds . . . No one in town has flowers like ours. I read gardening books and I'm learning German. We work in silence, like two nuns. We don't say a word, but we know what each other's thinking. Then I start singing, and when I stop Vassa shouts, 'Go on singing!' And I can see her face in the distance, and it's so kind and gentle . . .

Rachel   So you're happy?

Lyudmilla   Yes! I'm ashamed to be so happy! It's amazing!

Rachel   What about you, Nata?

Natalya   Me? I'm amazed too.

Prokhor (*comes in very drunk, with a guitar*)   Goddammit, if it isn't Rachel! (*Singing.*) 'Whence art thou from, oh lovely child?' My, my, prettier than ever . . . !

Rachel   *You* haven't changed . . .

Prokhor   No better no worse, still a few tricks up my sleeve.

Rachel   Having fun, eh?

Prokhor   Definitely. That's my trade. Simple fun is my strong suit, it's in my blood. Now Captain Zheleznov's gone, I must defend the family honour by drinking for two.

Rachel   Was he very ill?

Prokhor   Yes, very, he was dead!

Lyudmilla *guffaws.*

Rachel   I mean, had he been ill for a long time?

Prokhor   The Captain? He wasn't ill at all! Went out like a light! May his soul rest in pea-ce!

Natalya   Stop it, Uncle, it's disgusting!

Prokhor   Disgusting to rest in peace? Don't lecture me, my girl! (*To* **Rachel**.) So where did you spring from, firebrand? Switzerland? Is Fyodor still alive?

Rachel   Yes, he's still alive.

Prokhor   Pretty ill, is he?

Rachel   Yes, very.

Prokhor   Zheleznov's heirs are a feeble bunch, we Khrapovs are made of stronger stuff! Your Kolya's a splendid little devil though! The things he picks up! Once Zheleznov and I were having a bit of a row over dinner. Next day I see Kolya and he says, 'Be off, you drunken brute!' You could have knocked me for six! It was still morning too, and I was sober . . . What are you drinking – tea? Only cab drivers drink tea. Well-bred people quench their thirst with wine . . . I've some Spanish port coming. It's excellent stuff, too good for the Dagos. Natalya here knows. (*Goes to the door as* **Vassa** *enters.*)

Vassa   What happened at the club?

Prokhor   The club? How d'you know?

Vassa   Someone just rang me.

Prokhor   There was a scuffle about politics, that's all . . .

Vassa   I suppose you'll be all over the papers again.

Prokhor   Nonsense, I only swiped him once. He was bellyaching about the Duma, so I punched him in the mouth.

Vassa   Listen, Prokhor –

Prokhor   I'll be right back. Then I shall listen to you lecture me . . . 'Oh torment me not without cause . . . !' (*Exits singing.*)

Lyudmilla   He's ever so funny, isn't he? He's drinking even more these days. He's even taught Natalya . . .

Natalya He taught me a long time ago.

Rachel What are you saying, Natalya?

Natalya It's true. I love wine, and I love being drunk.

Vassa You might add: and there's no one to whip you for it.

Natalya And there's no one to whip me for it.

Vassa Watch out, Natalya!

Natalya You told me to say it, so I did.

Vassa You're lucky I'm too busy to thrash the devil out of you.

Lyudmilla See how cheeky she's become, I think she's awful!

Vassa She says we should improve our souls and be intellectuals, but she's no better than a pig!

Natalya A pedigree pig is worth a lot of money.

Vassa (*angrily*) This is what our life is like, Rachel.

Rachel Yes, it's a rotten, stinking life, but it's no worse than you deserve.

Vassa Me? How dare you!

Rachel Not just you - your whole class, your sort.

Vassa Here we go again!

Rachel People abroad live worthless lives too, maybe more so, but they don't torment each other so much.

Natalya Do you mean that or are you just saying it to make us feel better?

Rachel I mean it, Natalya, I don't try to make people feel better. The world of the rich is rotten to the core, though they're better organised abroad than you are. It's all falling apart, starting with the family. Over there the family's locked in an iron cage – in Russia it's a wooden one.

Vassa   Rachel!

Rachel   Yes?

Vassa   Why don't you come and live with us? Fyodor will die soon, you said so yourself. Why are you throwing your life away – always on the run, hiding from the police? You could move in here, bring up your son. Look at my girls – they love you! And you love your son, don't you . . . ?

Rachel   There's something else though, something higher than all . . . all these – personal attachments . . .

Vassa   I know, I know. There's work, there's business . . . But sometimes when something's there for the taking and you let it slip away . . .

Rachel   You couldn't be talking about yourself, could you?

Vassa   What do you mean?

Rachel   You might feel exhausted by the business, but the stupidity of it, the cruelty – that's something you'll never feel. I know you. In the end you're nothing but a slave. You're strong and you're clever, but you're a slave. Possessions are ruined by rot and rust, and possessions will be the ruin of you.

Vassa   Very clever I'm sure, but not true! Now I'll tell you what I'd like, and I don't mind my girls hearing it. I'd like the governor of the province to take out my chamber pots for me, and the priest to say prayers not for the holy saints, but for my evil soul, sinner that I am.

Rachel   That's Dostoevsky – not you.

Natalya   Mother hasn't read Dostoevsky – she hasn't read anything!

Vassa   What d'you mean, Dostoevsky? I'm talking about myself – about my public humiliation. The girls know all about it, I was just telling them . . .

Prokhor (*enters with two bottles of wine*)   Here we are! Now let's do this properly! Some for you, Vassa? You won't regret it. It's splendid stuff.

Vassa   Why not! Come to the table, girls, let's have a drink! My daughter-in-law is here! Pour it out, Prokhor . . . Now tell us who you thrashed at the club!

Prokhor   Your tenant, young Melnikov. I socked him in the jaw. And someone else too. To hell with them! They'll live!

Vassa   Did you know Melnikov senior has joined the League of the Russian People?

Prokhor   So what? My name's in the phone book, but I don't boast about it. Pass your glasses, please!

The telephone rings.

Vassa   That'll be for me. (*Picks up the receiver.*) Who? . . . Yes, speaking . . . Which boat? . . . Why? . . . The fools! . . . Who loaded it? . . . In Ufa? . . . Terentiev? . . . Sack him at once . . . ! My presence, why? . . . They've impounded the barge? . . . What else besides leather? . . . Everything? . . . The swine! . . . The hygiene officials? . . . The inspector too? . . . I'll come right away . . . (*Slams down the receiver.*) Now you all sit here quietly while I sort this out. One of our barges has been impounded – the confounded agent loaded the hides without getting them stamped by the hygiene inspectors. There are basts and fibres on board too, I must go. (*Exits, meeting* **Rachel**'s *eye as she leaves.*)

Prokhor   She'll have to pay them off. The river police are bandits and the others are no better. What the hell, let's have a drink. You'll like this one, Natalya, it's even better than your favourite. (*Sings in the 'sixth voice'.*)

'Fill the glasses to the top,
Pour the wine to the very last drop . . .'

Act Three

*A few minutes after **Vassa***'s departure. ***Prokhor*** is smoking a cigar. ***Lyudmilla*** happily munches sponge cakes, dipping them in a saucer of jam. ***Natalya*** sits next to ***Rachel***, a glass in her hand. ***Rachel*** is thoughtful.

Prokhor   This is how we live, Rachel, never a moment's peace. The police have it in for us! (*Chuckles.*)

Rachel   Are you mayor yet?

Prokhor   I did aspire to the post, then I asked myself what the devil I needed the responsibility for. I'm happier as I am, footloose and free.

Natalya   You're not free – you got cold feet and ducked the elections!

Prokhor   It's terrible how our Natalya loves to taunt me, and everyone else too. So young, and already a witch. Very like . . . Anyway, she's right – I'm a prudent man. And after the Captain's death . . .

Natalya   After Father died people said he'd poisoned himself, or that we'd poisoned him to avoid the trial.

Lyudmilla   It's not true!

Prokhor (*uneasily*)   Complete nonsense, of course! The whole business was thrown out by the court.

Natalya   For lack of evidence. But Uncle was petrified of the rumours and thought he wouldn't get elected –

Prokhor   That's enough, Nata!

Natalya   Whereas he should have said to hell with the rumours and what people said.

Prokhor   *She's* like that – *she's* against everyone!

Rachel (*strokes **Natalya**'s hand*)   Quite right too!

Natalya   Just because it isn't proved, Rachel, does it mean someone's not guilty?

Rachel   Of course it doesn't.

Lyudmilla   Do we have to be against everything, Rachel? Can't we live . . . ?

Natalya   In a fools' paradise, like Lyudmilla Zheleznova?

Lyudmilla   There's no point insulting me, I shan't lose my temper! Oh, Rachel, I hate all this . . . being mean and angry with each other all the time . . .

Natalya   She prefers sponge cakes and jam!

Lyudmilla   You're jealous because you've no appetite! You wouldn't be so cross if you ate more!

Prokhor (*sings*)

'I bear no grudge, though my heart is breaking,
O love for ever lost . . .'

As well as liking cakes and jam, our little Lyudmilla has a fondness for military uniforms, especially covered in feathers like a Red Indian.

Lyudmilla   No I don't!

Prokhor   Drink up, here's to the death of families, the past and everything else – we'll bury it! Now let's make mayhem while the boss is away. I'll show you a real dancer, Rachel – he'll take your breath away. Lyudmilla, fetch Pyatyorkin . . . !

Lyudmilla   Oh, Uncle, how lovely!

Prokhor   . . . with his guitar! (**Lyudmilla** *exits. He turns to* **Rachel**.) When will you see your son?

Rachel   Is he far away?

Prokhor   Ten, twelve miles or so. Nice little chap. Shocking health, but otherwise all right.

Rachel   His grandmother won't let me have him.

Prokhor   She's right – what d'you want with him? You're on the run!

Rachel   What do you think, Nata?

Natalya   Tell her she must give him to you – and if she doesn't, kidnap him!

Prokhor   Oho!

Natalya   You must get him away from here! You can see what we're like, you can see –

Rachel   Kidnap him . . . No, I couldn't do that.

Natalya   Why not?

Rachel   I have other things to do – a more important cause . . .

Natalya   More important than your own son? Why did you have him then? It's ridiculous!

Rachel   Yes, I suppose it was a mistake.

Natalya   What 'cause' anyway? You mean what you told me about two years ago? I remember that.

Rachel   But – you don't believe in it?

Natalya   No, I don't.

Rachel   It's only because you don't understand. For me, the cause is my life. And even if I lose – if I never see Kolya again –

Prokhor   Stop that! You must kidnap him, Rachel, it's a capital idea! It'll knock the stuffing out of my sister! Nata and I will help you, and I've my man Pyatyorkin – nothing will stop him!

Rachel   Don't . . . !

Prokhor   Alyosha Pyatyorkin? He could kidnap an archbishop – a child's nothing!

Rachel   Don't turn my son into a game!

Lyudmilla *reurns with* **Pyatyorkin**.

Prokhor   Here he is now – a brave soldier, served fearlessly in the rear. Alyosha, let's do 'Bird of God'! This is for Europe mind, so no mistakes!

Prokhor *takes the guitar from* **Pyatyorkin** *and tunes it.* **Lyudmilla** *brings in a balalaika and a tambourine, and hands the tambourine to her sister.*

Prokhor   Now then girls, soft and sad! Especially the tambourine – make it hum, don't bang it.

Lyudmilla   We know.

Prokhor   Here we go. (*Sings a crude a capella pastiche of Pushkin's poem 'Gypsies' in the sixth voice, with* **Lyudmilla** *and* **Pyatyorkin** *taking the second.*)

'Little bird of God so small,
Knowing neither grief nor care
Help us in our daily toil,
As we strive for love's sweet share.
You slumber through the night so dark,
But when the sun grows bright and strong
The voice of God you gladly hark,
And raise your voice in merry song.

Oh lady mine, oh lady fair,
Lady with the blushing air . . .'

Come on, Alyosha, let it rip! Go wild!

'All the way from Rostov town
Came a lady of renown.
Came another from Gomel,
No one knew her half so well.

Oh lady mine, oh lady fair . . .'

Pyatyorkin *dances a wild Russian dance to great comic effect.* **Lyudmilla** *strums and sings along enthusiastically.* **Prokhor** *is in his element.* **Natalya** *mechanically bangs the tambourine and looks at* **Rachel**, *sitting on the sofa looking dazed.*

'Now the lady's occupied.
Went abroad to have a spree
Ended up in gay Paree
Where a Frenchman she espied . . .'

Natalya   That's enough!

Prokhor   Why?

Natalya   I don't like it.

Lyudmilla   Pooh, you're so moody!

Rachel *stands up and moves away. After a moment* **Natalya** *joins her and they stand at the window together.*

Natalya   Well?

Rachel   Terrible.

Natalya   I'd sooner kill my son than leave him here.

Rachel (*puts an arm round* **Natalya***'s shoulders*)   I can't take him with me . . . abroad . . . without Vassa Borisovna's help.

Natalya   Uncle will see to it, he's longing for a chance to hurt her. He'll kidnap Kolya and we'll smuggle him out to you.

Rachel   But where? I don't know where I shall be! If I do get back to Switzerland I'll only be there a few weeks . . . I can't live in Russia, it's impossible for me to bring him up here. It's better for him in Lausanne with my sister.

Prokhor (*stops* **Pyatyorkin** *and shouts at* **Rachel**)   What's wrong? Don't you like it?

Rachel   No.

Prokhor   Where's your soul!

Rachel   Your singing's unbearable.

Prokhor   I apologise. I'm second to none when it comes to cards and wine, but nature didn't bless me with a good voice. I have a gentle soul, but my voice is hard and grating.

Get out, Pyatyorkin, you wretch, we're not appreciated!
Rachel, will you come upstairs and see my locks?

Rachel I've already seen them.

Prokhor Well, you must see them again! I've thirty-seven
padlocks, four fortress locks, and forty-two piano locks, a
unique collection! Come on anyway, we must have a chat.
(*Takes her by the arm, she follows reluctantly.*)

Natalya (*to* **Lyudmilla**) What's the matter with you?

Lyudmilla Nothing. Just tired.

Natalya Go to bed then.

Lyudmilla I'm so sad I could cry.

Natalya So cry yourself to sleep.

Lyudmilla It's always like this when Vassa's out. I'll wait
up till she gets back.

Natalya Why do you always call her Vassa now?

Lyudmilla Because I love her. And you don't.

Natalya No, I don't.

Lyudmilla And she knows it.

Natalya She'd be blind not to.

Lyudmilla But you're so alike – you're exactly like her!

Natalya Which is why we don't get on.

Lyudmilla She loves you.

Natalya She loves to bully me.

Lyudmilla You bully her too.

Natalya I get my own back.

Lyudmilla You are silly! So is Uncle Prokhor – telling
Rachel to kidnap Kolya!

Natalya Don't breathe a word to Mother, understand?

Lyudmilla I certainly will!

Natalya Why?

Lyudmilla Maybe I won't – I don't want to upset her.

Natalya (*sighs*) You're a saint – a freak, not like the rest of us!

Vassa (*enters*) What are you two doing up so late? Ugh, Prokhor's been smoking cigars again. How many times have I asked him not to smoke in my room. You seem the worse for drink, Natalya.

Natalya I can stand upright, can't I?

Vassa (*pours herself a glass of wine*) Is the tea cold? Pour me some, will you? (**Natalya** *pours*.) A hundred roubles down the drain! Thieves, pirates – they all had their hands out. So what have you been up to?

Natalya Drinking tea.

Lyudmilla And Pyatyorkin danced, and Uncle tried to get Rachel to kidnap Kolya!

Vassa Fancy that, how amusing! And what did she say?

Lyudmilla She didn't want to. She's so boring these days, not half as much fun as she used to be. She's horrid. Clever people always are.

Vassa I see. So you think I'm stupid?

Lyudmilla You're not clever or stupid, you're just a normal woman.

Vassa I don't know what you mean. Worse than a fool I suppose! All right, so I'm a normal woman. Take the samovar and tell them to heat it up. Natalya, do you want to go abroad?

Natalya You know I do.

Vassa You can then. And take Anna with you.

Natalya   I'm not going with Anna.

Vassa   Why not?

Natalya   Because I'm sick of her.

Vassa   Well, you're not going alone. Now listen here, my girl . . .

Natalya   Yes?

Vassa   Oh, I haven't time to talk to you now.

Natalya   Oh? So how will you find time for Kolya?

Vassa   He won't need much.

Natalya   He'll need more than I do.

Vassa   Go abroad with Anna, then you can see Fyodor.

Natalya   Sorry, it doesn't appeal to me.

Vassa (*shouts at the top of her voice*)   Be silent, devil!

Natalya   Very well, I'll be silent.

Rachel (*enters the room*)   Whatever's the matter?

Vassa   You're right, I shouldn't have shouted. What's the use? They torment me to death . . . I've this pain in my heart . . . So, Rachel, I hear Prokhor suggested kidnapping Kolya?

Rachel   He was drunk.

Vassa   Drunk or sober, it's the same with him. Why don't you go to bed, girls? It's late.

Lyudmilla   But what about supper?

Vassa   I don't want supper, I'm just thirsty – I'd love some hot tea. All right then, lay the table. (**Lyudmilla** *and* **Natalya** *exit.*) So did you think about what I said, Rachel?

Rachel   You must let me have my son, Vassa Borisovna! I have to take him abroad.

Vassa   Don't start, you're not having him and that's that!

Rachel   What do you want with him? How will you bring him up?

Vassa   We'll manage, we're well set-up – we'll get him professors, the best governesses. Don't worry, he'll get an education.

Rachel   But you won't teach him what a decent person should know. He'll live in this house, surrounded by balalaikas, guitars, rich food, an alcoholic uncle and two aunts, one of them warped and bitter, the other damaged and unable to grow up. I know a bit about your class, Vassa Borisovna, here in Russia and abroad – and it's sick! You live like machines, you're slaves to business and the things other people make for you. You hate and despise each other and never stop to ask what you're doing and what it's all for – even the best and cleverest of you only go on living because you're haunted by death . . .

Vassa   Have you finished? Now you listen to me. What I don't understand is why that clever little brain of yours is so stupid when it comes to life! Class, class – that's all you ever talk about! My manager Krotkikh knows a lot more about it than you do. He says revolutions are all very well if they serve that class you're forever on about. The revolution you want is moonshine – and it's illegal! Krotkikh has it all worked out. The socialists must tell the workers to throw their weight behind trade and industry. That's what he thinks, and he's no fool – as far as that's concerned. He's still a fool when it comes to business.

Rachel   Your little Krotkikhs are two a penny, lecturing the workers to be meek and mild and support the bosses. You let these loyal slaves of yours do quite well for themselves, don't you?

Vassa   Don't you understand – I'm just a businesswoman. I, Vassa Zheleznova, have nothing to do with that class! You say it's dying? It doesn't bother me. I'm all right, I run my own business, no one can stop me, no one can frighten me. I've put enough by to see me out, and there's a huge fortune waiting for my grandson when I die. That's it, the sum total of my wisdom on the subject. I shan't give Kolya to you, he's mine! Now let's have supper, I'm tired.

Rachel   I don't want to eat, I'd choke on your food . . . Where shall I sleep?

Vassa   Off you go. Natalya will show you. (**Rachel** *exits.* **Vassa** *gets up from her chair with difficulty, then sits down again and calls.*) Anna! (*No answer.*) Choke on my food! Poisonous creature! How dare she! (*Rings.*)

Polya (*enters*)   Your rang, madam?

Vassa   No, it was a devil under the piano. Where's Anna?

Polya   With the young ladies.

Vassa   Tell her I want her. (*Sits down again, listens, clutches her throat and coughs.* **Anna** *enters.*) What happened while I was away?

Anna   Prokhor Borisovich said he was going to kidnap Kolya.

Vassa   He suggested it himself?

Anna   Yes. First he said, 'She's right, what do you want with him?' Then the idea grew on him. He said, 'It'll knock the stuffing out of my sister!'

Vassa   What about Natalya?

Anna   She was the one who suggested it.

Vassa   It can't be true, you're wrong!

Anna   No I'm not. When Rachel Moiseevna said you were keeping Kolya, Prokhor Borisovich said, 'She's right,' and when Natalya suggested kidnapping him he was all for it.

Vassa   I see. He's determined to break me one way or another.

Anna   He said, 'My man Pyatyorkin could kidnap an archbishop.'

Vassa   He's a vicious dog, that Pyatyorkin.

Anna   He's a hard brute, without shame or honour . . .

Vassa   We'll have to soften him up then, won't we?

Anna   Are you ill?

Vassa   Why?

Anna   You don't look well.

Vassa   My daughters didn't notice anything. So Anna, would you like to go abroad?

Anna (*astonished*)   Me?

Vassa   Yes, you. With Natalya. Or on your own.

Anna   God, I'm so happy! I don't know how to thank you, madam!

Vassa   There's no need, you've earned it. You'd never lie to me, would you?

Anna   Never!

Vassa   That's good. You must take Fyodor a letter – don't show it to Natalya, mind. Write as soon as you get there and tell me how he is. Ask his doctors. You still remember your German, don't you?

Anna   Yes, I do.

Vassa   Good. If Fyodor's very ill, wait till he dies. But we'll discuss that later. Now you must go to the police and ask for Colonel Popov. No one else will do. Get them to send for him, say it's urgent . . .

Anna   But Vassa Borisovna –

Vassa   Let me finish. Tell him Rachel Moiseevna has returned from abroad – from exile. He'll know who you mean, he was the one who arrested her. Say if she's to be arrested again they must do it on the street, not in my house. Is that understood?

Anna Yes, but –

Vassa Just do as I say! If they come here she'll know it was you – or me. I don't want any more rumours, do you understand?

Anna I . . . can't . . .

Vassa (*astonished*) What do you mean, you can't? Why not?

Anna I just – can't.

Vassa Surely you're not sorry for her? Aren't you sorry for Kolya? They'll arrest her anyway – tomorrow or the day after. You wouldn't disobey me, would you?

Anna No, heavens above! You know I'd give my life for you! (*Mutters.*) Why should I care about that little Jew? She's always despised me!

Vassa (*suspiciously*) What's that? What are you mumbling about?

Anna I just don't want to go this late.

Vassa Rubbish, they won't eat you! (*Looks at her watch.*) Well, it is rather late, Popov will be out playing cards. All right, you can go first thing in the morning – mind you're there by seven. Make sure they wake him up for you.

Anna Thank you, thank you, Vassa Borisovna! (*Seizes her hand and kisses it.*)

Vassa (*wipes her hand on her skirt*) You're dripping with sweat, you imbecile – look, it's running off your nose . . .

Anna *mops her face and goes out.*

Vassa Rachel keeps ranting about class. Class, my foot! It's me she's getting at, it's me she hates! She stole my son like a gypsy stealing a horse. Now I'm stealing her son, and she's not getting him back! (*Falls silent, thinking.*) Lord, I feel ill. I must be tired . . . I'd better drink some raspberry juice . . .

Lyudmilla (*enters*)   Supper time, Vassa!

Vassa   You love your food, don't you!

Lyudmilla   Yes, I love eating!

Vassa   I've another treat for you too – not food this time, something better!

Lyudmilla   Mother, you're so . . .

Vassa   I decided to buy old Princess Kugusheva's house – that'll give us a bit more land, eh?

Lyudmilla   Oh, Vassa, how lovely . . . !

Vassa   The young Prince has been losing at cards again . . .

Lyudmilla   God, that's wonderful . . . !

Vassa   . . . and the Princess is in a hurry to sell. I'll give her the deposit tomorrow. So now you can celebrate.

Lyudmilla   How d'you find time for it all? Now let's eat!

Vassa   I don't want anything, I don't feel well. I'll have some raspberry juice and go to bed. Eat without me!

Lyudmilla   Don't you want some tea?

Vassa   Yes, bring in the samovar, I'm very thirsty . . . Where's Rachel?

Lyudmilla   She's locked herself in the yellow room. She doesn't want supper either. I think she's horrid, she's so stuck-up!

Vassa   Run along now Lyuda. (**Lyudmilla** *exits. Alone on stage,* **Vassa** *moves around the room cautiously, as though treading on ice, clutching the back of the chairs, coughing and groaning.*) What was I doing? So much to do . . . (*Makes as if to sit down, then* *changes her mind and stands with her back to the door.*) Should I call the doctor . . . ?

Pyatyorkin *enters drunk and dishevelled. He sticks out his tongue at his mistress and pulls a face, then picks up his guitar and plucks the bass string.*

Vassa (*starting*)   Who's that? What d'you want?

Pyatyorkin (*thickly*)   My -- my guitar.

Vassa   Get out of here!

Pyatyorkin   I'm going. No need to talk to me like that, I'm not a dog. I don't live in my master's kennel. (*Exits.*)

Vassa   Idiot . . . devil . . . !

Vassa *sits down heavily on the ottoman, tries to loosen her jacket and slumps sideways. For a few seconds there is no sound.*

Anna (*enters with a tray bearing cups and a teapot*)   Shall I take them to your room?

She stands waiting for an answer. The tray begins to shake in her hands, rattling the cups. She carefully puts the tray on the table and bends over **Vassa** *to look at her face, then straightens up and gasps.*

Oh my God, Vassa Borisovna – what is it?

Listens for a moment, then runs to the desk and opens a drawer. She rummages through it, finds some money and hides it in her blouse, then opens a safe on the table, and stuffs more money in her clothes. Grabbing some keys, she slips them in her pocket, slams the lid of the safe and runs out of the room. After a moment **Natalya** *runs in, followed by* **Prokhor**. **Anna** *and* **Pyatyorkin** *appear.*

Natalya (*feels her mother's face, speaking unnaturally loudly*) She's dead.

Prokhor   Well, bless my soul . . . First Zheleznov, now her! The rumours will start again . . . Hell, what a business . . .

Natalya   Will you be quiet!

Prokhor (*murmurs*) We must watch Anna. We need the keys, Nata. And the key to the safe. Anna knows where they are. See if they're in Vassa's pocket.

Natalya No, I won't! Go away!

Prokhor Why should I?

Anna (*in tears*) Maybe she's fainted, Natalya Sergeevna.

Natalya Ring for the doctor . . .

Anna I rang. Oh God, what shall I do?

Prokhor The key, bitch, where's the key to the safe?

Natalya Has Rachel been told?

Anna Must we tell her, Natalya Sergeevna?

Natalya You – worm! (*Runs out of the room.*)

Anna (*sobbing*) What did I say? What did I say?

Prokhor Don't whine! I need the key to the safe! Where is it?

Anna Prokhor Borisovich, I have served you loyally for thirteen years . . . (*Rummages in* **Vassa**'s *skirt.*)

Prokhor You'll get what you deserve . . .

Anna I gave my youth to you . . . Here's the key.

Prokhor (*goes to the safe, addressing* **Pyatyorkin**) Now don't let anyone in, boy . . . Wait a second . . . (*Suddenly beams with joy.*) Well, how d'you like that – I'm guardian to her heirs! Now we'll have some fun! (*Leers at* **Anna**.) We won't be needing you now! Your luck's run out! You can pack your bags and go! I'm sick of the sight of you, dirty spy!

Anna You'd better not, Prokhor Borisovich, you'll regret it . . .

Prokhor Enough! You've taken your cut – stolen it rather! Now hop it, be off!

Anna   I beg your pardon, I've something –

Prokhor   I know, that's what I said . . .

Rachel *and* **Natalya** *enter.*

Rachel (*to* **Prokhor**, *who is rummaging through the papers on the table*)   What are you stealing?

Prokhor   It's mine. I'm taking what's mine.

Polya *enters with* **Lyudmilla**.

Rachel   Yours? What's yours?

Lyudmilla (*breaks away from* **Polya** *and throws herself at* **Vassa**)   Mama! Ma-ma!

The Zykovs

Characters

Antipa Ivanovich Zykov, *a timber merchant*
Sofia Ivanovna Zykova (*Sonya*), *his sister*
Mikhail Zykov (*Misha*), *his son*
Anna Markovna Tselovaneva, *a widow*
Pavla Tselovaneva (*Pasha, Pashenka*), *her daughter*
Gustav Egorovich Hevern, *Antipa's business partner*
Shokhin, *mounted forest patrol*
Vasilii Pavlovich Muratov, *forest warden*
Tarakanov, *Antipa's bookkeeper*
Stepka, *the Zykovs' servant girl*
Palageya, *Tselovaneva's maid*

Act One

The small drab drawing room in **Tselovaneva**'*s house. In the middle of the room is a table laid for tea. Standing by the wall between the doors to the kitchen and* **Tselovaneva**'*s bedroom is another table set with wine, vodka and refreshments. To the right of this is a small harmonium, with framed photographs and vases of dried flowers. On the walls are postcards and a watercolour portrait of* **Pavla** *dressed as a convent choirgirl. Two windows look on to the street and the front garden.* **Tselovaneva**, *a neat, trim woman in her forties, sits at the tea table. She is visibly agitated and keeps peering out of the window.* **Sofia** *paces the room deep in thought, an unlit cigarette between her teeth.*

Tselovaneva (*fidgets with the cups*)   They're taking their time.

Sofia (*glances at her watch*)   Yes . . .

Tselovaneva   I wonder why you never married, Sofia Ivanovna?

Sofia   I haven't found one I like, if I find one I'll marry him.

Tselovaneva (*sighs*)   There are so few interesting men in this part of the world.

Sofia   Interesting ones aren't unusual, I want someone serious . . .

Tselovaneva   No offence, but you're pretty serious yourself, like a man. You should find yourself a nice quiet one.

Sofia (*grudgingly*)   What for? To catch mice?

Tselovaneva *smiles and looks embarrassed; she seems ill at ease with* **Sofia**, *clearly anxious to make a good impression but unsure how.*

Sofia (*frowning at her, hands behind her back*)   Tell me, who put it out that your Pavla's a – simpleton?

Tselovaneva (*hurriedly, glancing behind her in a low voice*)
That was my late husband – I went along with him so they
wouldn't bother her. She's outspoken – she says what she
thinks, men don't like that. And then he – my husband – he
suspected she wasn't his . . .

Sofia   Really?

Tselovaneva   It's common knowledge. He'd get blind
drunk and shout it to the world. He was jealous because I
formed an attachment to this man, a sectarian . . .

Sofia   You mean Shokhin's father?

Tselovaneva   So you did know!

Sofia   Not in connection with you, I just knew about him
– that he was persecuted.

Tselovaneva (*sighs*)   No connection? (*Quietly.*) I'll say he
was persecuted . . . (*Glances quickly at* **Sofia**.) My husband
used to stare at her and suddenly he'd yell, 'She's not mine!
I'm a vile person and you' – that's me – 'you're a witch!'

Sofia (*distractedly*)   Why did he say that?

Tselovaneva   God knows.

Sofia   Did he beat you?

Tselovaneva   Of course he did! It didn't matter about
me, it was Pavla I worried about. I managed to get round
him though and sent her to the convent. She's all I have
now . . .

Palageya (*appears at the kitchen door*)   They're coming!

Tselovaneva   You made me jump, devil! You'd think it
was the police coming!

Palageya   Shall I bring the samovar?

Tselovaneva   I'll tell you when we need it. Go away!

Mikhail (*flushed and tipsy, with a tired smile on his clean-shaven
face, to* **Palageya**)   Move, woman, don't block up the door!

He pinches her. She shrieks, he gives a whinnying laugh.
Tselovaneva *purses her lips.* **Sofia** *frowns at her nephew from the harmonium.*

Mikhail *(goes to the tea table)*   Mother, it's hot!

Tselovaneva *(mutters)*   What do you mean, 'Mother'?
(Loudly.) I'm afraid she's not very bright . . .

Mikhail   Who isn't?

Tselovaneva   Palageya, my servant.

Mikhail   Oh, just her? I'll make a note of that. *(Turns to the table with the wine.)*

Sofia *tries out some bass notes on the harmonium.*

Tselovaneva *(anxiously)*   Make a note of what?

Sofia   Nothing, Anna Markovna, it's a joke.

Tselovaneva   I never get jokes.

Palageya *(calls from the kitchen)*   A fellow on horseback's
arrived . . .

Sofia   That's Shokhin to see me, Anna Markovna.

Shokhin *(at the door)*   Shokhin here.

Sofia *(in a stern voice)*   I'd have come to the door, Yakov!

Shokhin *(bows)*   My pleasure. Everyone well, I hope?

Tselovaneva *(goes to the window)*   Don't mind me.

Sofia *(to* **Shokhin***)*   So?

Shokhin   He told me to say he'd write to you.

Sofia   That's all?

Shokhin   That's all.

Sofia   Thank you.

She jots something in a notebook at her waist. **Mikhail** *winks at* **Tselovaneva** *and pours* **Shokhin** *a glass of vodka.* **Shokhin** *drinks furtively and frowns.*

Mikhail   What are you so down in the mouth about, Yakov?

Shokhin   I don't get paid enough – I want a word with you, Sofia Ivanovna.

Sofia   Why?

Shokhin (*moves closer to her*)   Your warden told the engineer yesterday that we should all be arrested for letting the rivers run dry and ruining the land . . .

Sofia   I see. Run along . . .

Mikhail   Go, slave!

Shokhin *leaves.*

Tselovaneva   Was he talking about Muratov?

Sofia   Yes.

Tselovaneva   He's a hard-hearted gentleman. He quarrels with everyone, he's always drunk and his only pleasure is cards. Why doesn't he marry? He has a good job, he should marry! It seems no one likes family life these days.

Mikhail   What about me? I'm getting married!

Tselovaneva   You mean your father told you to . . . (*She blurts this out and goes off to the kitchen looking embarrassed, muttering to herself.*)

Sofia (*to* **Mikhail**)   You're behaving outrageously!

Mikhail   I'll stop then. You like my fiancée?

Sofia   She's a lovely girl – sweet and virtuous. What about you, do you like her?

Mikhail   Yes I do, I feel sorry for her really – what sort of husband am I for her?

Sofia Are you serious about her?

Mikhail I don't know, maybe.

Sofia Good. Maybe she'll make you think about yourself – it's time someone did!

Mikhail I think of nothing else . . .

Sofia It's all a game to you, isn't it?

Mikhail It's human nature. My fiancée plays at being sweet and virtuous . . .

Sofia (*stares at him*) What are you saying? She's trusting . . .

Mikhail A cat's trusting too, but play tricks with it, and . . . !

Sofia What d'you mean, tricks?

Mikhail You know what? Father should marry her and I'll step aside!

Sofia Nonsense!

Mikhail (*smirks*) It doesn't matter, if he can't marry her now, he'll have her later. Like you say, she's – trusting.

Sofia Stop! That's a disgusting thing to say! (*Walks away from him, upset.*)

Mikhail (*laughs quietly, drinks a glass of wine and declaims*)

'I tried to catch a flower
Reflected in the stream
But all my hand pulled out
Was something wet and green . . .'

Sofia What's that about?

Mikhail Nothing, it's a joke.

Sofia Look here, Misha, life's serious . . . !

Antipa *and* **Pavla** *enter from the hall.* **Antipa** *is in his late forties, with a greying beard, black eyebrows and curly hair receding at* *the temples.* **Pavla** *wears a loose blue dress with no waistline, like a cassock, and a blue gauze scarf over her head and shoulders.*

Pavla   I always tell the truth . . .

Antipa   Really? We'll see about that.

Pavla   But I do! Where's Mother?

Tselovaneva (*from the kitchen*)   Coming, coming . . . !

Antipa *goes to the table with the refreshments.* **Pavla** *smiles and goes to* **Sofia**.

Sofia   Tired?

Pavla   It's hot, I'm thirsty.

Sofia   You made the dress yourself?

Pavla   Yes, why?

Sofia   It suits you.

Pavla   I like feeling free.

Antipa (*to his son*)   You're drinking too much, it'll make you stupid.

Mikhail (*grins*)   The bridegroom should show every side of himself!

Antipa *grabs him by the shoulders and whispers roughly to him.* **Mikhail** *grins.*

Sofia (*to* **Pavla** *quietly*)   Which is the better-looking?

Pavla   The older one.

Antipa (*sharply*)   Shut up, you!

Sofia (*quietly*)   What's wrong, Antipa?

Pavla *clings to her.*

Antipa (*embarrassed*)   Forgive me, Pavla Nikolaevna, I said it for your own good . . .

Pavla   Why?

Antipa   Well, see, this gentleman here . . .

Tselovaneva (*carries in a pie on a plate*)   Sit down, everyone, tuck in!

Pavla (*to* **Antipa**)   You must be kind or I'll be afraid of you.

Antipa (*chuckles affectionately*)   You're always talking about kindness, little girl. My sweet child . . . (*Moves closer and says something to her that the others can't hear.*)

Mikhail (*although tipsy, realises he's in the way and struts around the room grinning. To his aunt*)   Phew, it's poky in here, like a chicken coop!

Tselovaneva (*watches her guests with a look of alarm. To* **Sofia**)   Please come to the table – you call them, they won't listen to me!

Sofia (*thoughtfully*)   I like your daughter . . .

Tselovaneva   God help her, you must look after her, teach her . . .

Sofia   Of course I will, we women must stick together.

Pavla (*shocked*, to **Antipa**)   But what about people?

Antipa   What do you mean?

Pavla   What would they think?

Antipa (*hotly*)   To hell with them, they can think what they like! What do I owe them? Grief and insults. See these hands? With these hands I've built my life! People can hang themselves! (*Downs a glass of vodka and wipes his mouth with a napkin.*) You're like a daughter to me, you're my future. 'Be kind,' you say. It's the fourth time I've met you and you always say that. You lived like a nun for five years – you'll change your tune when you've been with people a bit. Sometimes you look at this town and feel like burning it to the ground . . .

Pavla   Then I'd burn too.

Antipa   I'll – I wouldn't let you!

Tselovaneva   Come, Mikhail Antipovich, drink up, why don't you eat something?

Mikhail   Because my old man didn't tell me to.

Antipa   What?

Mikhail   And my fiancée's not looking after me.

Pavla (*blushes and bows*)   Let me fill your glass . . .

Mikhail   And yours.

Pavla   I don't like vodka.

Mikhail   Well, I do, very much!

Pavla   They say it's bad for you . . .

Mikhail   Don't you believe it. Your health!

Antipa   People don't know what good health is these days, do they, Anna Markovna? They're soft.

Tselovaneva   I don't know what you're talking about. My Pashenka . . .

Antipa   Not her, my son -- he's hardly drunk a drop but his eyes are dull and his face is stupid.

Sofia   Really, Antipa, listen to yourself.

Tselovaneva (*shocked*)   The boy's young . . .

Antipa (*to his sister*)   It's true. Anna Markovna remembers how we knocked it back in the old days. Her dear husband used to drink for weeks on end . . . (*To* **Tselovaneva**.) Youth, youth, what does it matter, youth passes . . .

A strained silence. Everyone looks at each other, waiting for someone to break it. **Sofia** *stares at her brother and* **Pavla**. **Mikhail** *lights a cigarette and stares drunkenly at his father.* **Pavla** *glances fearfully at everyone.* **Antipa** *goes to the table with the refreshments.* **Pavla** *takes the teapot off the samovar.*

Tselovaneva (*fusses round the table, whispers*)   Oh,
Pashenka, I don't like it . . .

Sofia (*quietly, to her brother*)   You shouldn't drink so much,
Antipa.

Antipa (*sullenly*)   Leave me alone.

Sofia   Just watch it.

Antipa   Mind your own business, I know what I'm doing.

Sofia   Do you? (*They eye each other.*) What are you doing?

Antipa   He's no match for her. We can't do anything
about him, but why destroy her?

Sofia (*steps back*)   Listen, if you intend . . .

Antipa   Stop making trouble and putting ideas in my
head.

Mikhail (*sniggers*)   It's all arranged but nobody's happy,
everyone's whispering . . . !

Antipa (*angrily*)   Your aunt's being solemn again. Pity
there aren't more people.

Pavla   See, you do need people.

Antipa   You caught me out! You're stubborn, Pavla
Nikolaevna. I like that – a woman should be stubborn.
Stand up for yourself against the world.

Pavla   And a man?

Antipa   A man's different, he's wild. Something grabs his
heart and he rushes at it like a bear – wherever it takes him.
Maybe life's cheaper for him . . .

Tselovaneva   Won't you drink some tea?

Antipa   Or something cold.

Mikhail   I recommend champagne.

Antipa   That's the first sensible thing you've said all day. Run along and fetch some.

Mikhail   With pleasure. (*Lurches off to the kitchen calling* **Palageya**.) Come here, beautiful!

Antipa (*winks at* **Pavla**)   See? I've drunk three times more than him – that's me, more of everything.

Pavla   So what are you frightened of?

Antipa (*surprised*)   Frightened? What are you talking about?

Sofia *talks quietly and animatedly with* **Tselovaneva** *while eavesdropping on their conversation.*

Pavla (*notices this, cheerfully*)   Why do you want to make my fiancé look stupid?

Antipa   Am I? But he's my son . . .

Pavla (*lowers her voice*)   What are you looking at me like that for?

Antipa   We'll be living under the same roof, I want to know what you're like. You said it was nice and quiet in your convent. This place is like a convent too when Sofia isn't shouting . . .

Pavla   But – you're kind . . . aren't you?

Antipa (*frowns*)   I don't know, maybe, it's probably more obvious to others. It fascinates me how you go on about kindness though. No, I don't pride myself on my kindness. (*Passionately.*) Perhaps there's something kind in me but what can I do with it? There's no place in this life for kindness. Give money to a beggar and he'll spend it on drink. No, Pavla, I don't like people. I've one good person working for me and that's my bookkeeper, he used to be in the police force . . .

Sofia   Tarakanov? Thanks a lot!

Antipa   Shut up, you're not like me, you're different. God knows what you are. We're talking about kindness but you're not good or bad, you're . . .

Sofia   A fine recommendation.

Antipa   She's almost twenty years younger than me, Anna Markovna, but I go to her in my hour of need like a mother.

Sofia   What's got into you, Antipa? You're so talkative.

Antipa   So what, I feel like it. Tarakanov was sacked from the police for being good – it's true. He's clever and knows a lot but he can't work, he's incapable of it. He's just an amusing spectacle, something nice to look at – in the old days he'd have been a court jester.

Sofia (*smiles*)   A court jester? Whatever next!

Antipa   It's how I see him. Sofia's not one of us – she was married for six years to a member of the gentry. she's got noble blood in her now!

Sofia   Stop it, Antipa.

Antipa   No, you're a clever woman, good at business, mistress of everything – but you're a woman, free as a bird. Fly off and leave me alone, there's nothing to stop you. A man never knows what tomorrow will bring, but take it from me, women of your sort know even less!

Tselovaneva   And what about Mikhail Antipovich?

Antipa (*sulkily*)   My son? I don't think there's much good there, to be honest – and we're planning an honourable deal, so we must be honest. What's he achieved? Nothing. He's a quitter. He scribbles his poems and plays his guitar, he dropped out of technical college because he didn't study. Studying means sticking at something – well, I'm not much good at that myself.

Pavla (*distressed*)   What must you think of me, talking about my fiancé like that?

Antipa (*quietly, as if to himself*)   Good question . . .

Tselovaneva (*anxiously*)   My dears, please listen to me, her mother . . .

Sofia (*sternly*)   Listen to reason, Antipa, think what you're doing.

Antipa (*rises to his feet, as though inspired*)   I'm not capable of reason, leave that to others – I just know what I want. Come, Pavla Nikolaevna, I want a word with you . . .

The three women stand up. **Pavla** *smiles and walks into the next room with* **Antipa** *as if in a dream. He walks heavily with a solemn, morose expression on his face. The door doesn't close and he is heard crying: 'Sit down, wait! Let me collect my thoughts!'*

Tselovaneva (*falls into a chair*)   Lord, what does he want, Sofia Ivanovna! What's happening?

Sofia (*paces the room*)   Your daughter's an intelligent girl, as I understand it . . . (*Lights her cigarette, looks for somewhere to put the match.*)

Tselovaneva   But he wants her for himself!

Sofia   Wait . . .

Antipa (*shouts from the other room*)   He's no husband for you. You're the same age as him but you're older in your soul. Marry me! I'll love you and fight for you like a young man. I'll dress you in vestments and brocades. I've had a hard life and it wasn't the right life for me. Help me live differently, Pavla, teach me to be kind, refresh my soul with something good. Say you will!

Sofia (*agitated*)   Hear that? He speaks well. Older men know how to make love properly!

Tselovaneva   Properly? I don't understand anything. Merciful Virgin, I put all my faith in you, have mercy on my child and spare her grief, all mine is spent on her.

Sofia   We must be calm. What can we do, it's in his blood. And your daughter's evidently not against it . . .

Tselovaneva   I don't understand any of you. You come here for her engagement party to your nephew – and now this. (*Bursts into the room where her daughter is with* **Antipa**.) I need to hear – I'm her mother, I can't allow –

Antipa   You appear on my path as if sent by God, Anna Markovna. Listen . . .

They close the door. **Sofia** *paces the room biting her lips.*
Muratov's *face appears at the window. He is middle-aged, with thinning hair, a pointed beard and mocking eyes with deep bags under them.*

Sofia (*to herself*)   Oh my God.

Muratov   Greetings, madam.

Sofia   You – how did you get here?

Muratov   Your faithful servant Shokhin told me you were in, and I deemed it my duty to present myself . . .

Sofia   Through the window?

Muratov   We have country ways here, you know . . .

Sofia   Still enjoying the country life then?

Muratov   Ah, irony! Yes I am. And you . . . still matchmaking?

Sofia   So people know?

Muratov   Of course. And they know the bride's not entirely, how shall we say . . .

Sofia   And you've heard the rumours of my alleged romance with you?

Muratov   Yes indeed – people anticipate events . . .

Sofia   You didn't deny it then?

Muratov   Why should I? I'm proud of them.

Sofia   Did you perhaps start them?

Muratov   Excellent, most astute. When people talk to me like that I become audacious!

Sofia   All the same, please leave the window.

Muratov   Fine, I'll go. May I see you on Sunday?

Sofia   Yes, but you might as well not.

Muratov   Then I'll certainly come. My respects. I wish you luck and success in everything you set out to achieve.

Sofia   Don't forget copies of the inventory I asked for.

Muratov   I never forget anything.

Mikhail (*returning*)   It's impossible to find champagne in this town. Who's this I see?

Muratov   Why are you running around on your own, bridegroom? Saving yourself for the big day?

Mikhail (*makes a farewell gesture*)   I'll see you tonight.

Muratov (*winks*)   Ready for your stag night? (*Disappears.*)

Mikhail   Where is everyone?

Sofia (*looks closely at him*)   There, next door . . .

Mikhail   I'm excluded, am I? I heard Father ranting in there.

Sofia (*with something like contempt*)   It seems you're excluded everywhere.

Mikhail   I said it would be better this way, but why make trouble for a good boy? There goes my stag night. You look upset, Aunt Sonya.

Sofia   By you? Oh yes. More than upset, I'm horrified.

Enter **Pavla** *and* **Antipa**, *followed by* **Tselovaneva** *in tears.*

Antipa (*triumphantly*)   There, sister, we've decided . . . (*Clutches his heart.*)

Pavla   Sofia Ivanovna, please try to understand and forgive me . . .

Sofia (*embraces her*)   I don't know what to say, I don't understand you . . .

Antipa   Mikhail, don't be hurt. You're young, there are plenty more women . . .

Mikhail   I'm very glad – word of honour! Don't be angry, Pavla Nikolaevna, I know I'm no match for you!

Antipa   See, Anna Markovna, what did I say?

Pavla (*to* **Mikhail**)   We're still friends then?

Mikhail (*bows*)   Of course we are. (*Laughs drunkenly.*)

Antipa   Anna Markovna, don't upset yourself, I swear to God your daughter won't shed a single tear because of my crime.

Tselovaneva (*goes down on her knees before him*)   You're a good man, sir, you had a mother you loved. For your mother's sake, spare my daughter.

Antipa and **Pavla** *try to pull her up.* **Sofia** *turns to the wall and wipes her eyes with a handkerchief.* **Mikhail** *nervously downs several glasses of vodka.*

Pavla   Stop it, Mama, everything will be all right.

Antipa   I give you my word of honour, anything you like – just get up. I'll put twenty-five thousand in her bank account – how's that?

Sofia   That's enough, friends. Misha, pour us some wine. You and I are mothers now, Anna Markovna, though I'm rather old for such a bearded son. You're shaking all over, Antipa, as if you're in court.

Tselovaneva   My darling. (*Clasps her daughter and weeps silently.*)

Antipa   Let's sit quietly for a while, like before a journey.

Sofia   Not in here, it's too stuffy. Take them out to the garden, Pavla.

Pavla (*takes* **Antipa** *and her mother by the hand*)   Come.

Mikhail (*to* **Sofia**)   You want a drink?

Sofia   Not now. (*Puts a hand on his shoulder and strokes his hair.*) You poor child, what now?

Mikhail   It's all right, Auntie Sofia, I don't mind.

Sofia   Let's go to the garden.

Mikhail   No, I can't go.

Sofia   Why not?

Mikhail   I don't want to . . .

Sofia (*stares into his eyes, quietly*)   So you *do* mind?

Mikhail (*grins*)   It's Father I feel embarrassed for. He's a fine strong man, solid as steel, what does he need to chase honey cakes for?

Sofia (*goes out smiling*)   What can you do? A man needs a little pleasure, just a little . . .

Mikhail (*goes to the table and pours wine, murmurs*)   Why just a little? A little's depressing . . .

Act Two

The **Zykovs**' *garden. On the left is the wide verandah of a large mansion. Opposite,* **Pavla** *sits at a table under a lime tree sewing, with* **Mikhail** *and his guitar, and* **Tarakanov**, *an eccentric-looking old man with a long beard, wearing a canvas suit. At the end of the verandah, and almost concealed by it,* **Tselovaneva** *stands by a brazier in the garden making jam with* **Stepka**.

Tarakanov   It's because everything's topsy-turvy, people are living in turmoil, no one knows their place . . .

Pavla (*thoughtfully*)   A turmoil of ideas . . .

Tarakanov   Exactly.

Mikhail (*strums his guitar*)   Cut the philosophy, Matvei Ilich, tell us about real life.

Tarakanov   Without philosophy there's nothing because everything has a hidden meaning and we have to understand it.

Mikhail   Why?

Tarakanov   What do you mean, why?

Mikhail   Suppose I don't want to understand anything?

Tarakanov   You have to.

Mikhail   Well, I don't.

Tarakanov   The whims of youth.

Pavla   Please don't argue, talk simply.

Tarakanov   If they tell you to move out of the way and you don't listen, you . . .

Mikhail   Yes?

Tarakanov   You get knocked over.

Mikhail   I always move out of the way, Matvei Ilich, I'm – susceptible!

Pavla (*looks at him*)   It's bad to lose your temper, it makes you fall.

Tarakanov   I don't understand, what do you mean susceptible . . . ?

Tselovaneva (*peers from the end of the verandah*)   Stop spreading gloom, Pavla. You want some skimmings?

Pavla   No thank you, I'd rather have some with pancakes for supper.

Mikhail   Why just you? What if I like pancakes too?

Pavla (*sighs*)   Drinkers don't like sweet things.

Mikhail   That's an aphorism.

Pavla   What is?

Mikhail   What you just said.

Pavla   What's an aphorism?

Mikhail   Damned if I know.

Tarakanov   You're a strange young man, Misha.

Mikhail   Everyone's strange, it's impossible to understand people. You're strange yourself – you should be doing a proper job and taking bribes, instead of sitting here with us philosophising.

Tarakanov   I don't need bribes, I'm a single man.

Pavla   I thought you had a son . . .

Tarakanov   I disowned him.

Pavla   Completely? What for?

Tarakanov   Utterly, he doesn't love Russia.

Pavla (*with a sigh*)   I don't understand.

Mikhail   Matvei Ilich doesn't either.

Tselovaneva (*from the verandah*)   Listen how people speak to the old nowadays.

Mikhail   The old say they're living in turmoil, so they should think before they speak.

Tselovaneva   I only speak as I find.

Stepka *looks round and furtively slips two sugar lumps in her pocket.*

Pavla   Please don't annoy each other -- why do you do it?

Tarakanov   Because it's fun.

Mikhail   That's right.

Pavla   Misha, sing us your song about the girl . . .

Mikhail   I don't feel like it.

Pavla   Please?

Mikhail (*looks at her*)   I suppose I have to obey my – parents. (*Tunes his guitar.*)

Tarakanov *fills his pipe and lights it.*

Mikhail (*speaks the words in a sing-song voice, accompanying himself on the guitar*)

'Over the field a maiden walks
Who she is I do not know
She it is my heart awaits,
Tell me, maiden, where to go . . .'

While **Mikhail** *is singing* **Muratov** *appears on the verandah in riding breeches, with a whip in his hand. He frowns ironically.*

Tarakanov   What sort of maiden?

Pavla (*annoyed*)   Don't interrupt, it's a dream.

Tarakanov (*sighs*)   So why doesn't he marry her?

Pavla (*snaps*)   Stop interrupting.

Muratov (*steps into the garden*)   What a pretty picture – making jam, singing sweet verses. Good day, Pavla

Nikolaevna, delightful as ever. Hail to you, retired teacher of truth and goodness. Greetings, Misha . . .

They greet him in silence. He sits down next to **Pavla**. *She edges away.* **Tarakanov** *nods and goes to the bottom of the garden, looking back angrily at him.*

Muratov   I came through the house and not a soul was in sight.

Pavla   Auntie Sonya's in.

Muratov   Then I heard the soft sounds of the guitar. Whose song is it, Misha, yours?

Mikhail   Yes, why?

Muratov   Dreadful stuff – all right for domestic consumption, I suppose . . .

Pavla   Shall I call Auntie?

Mikhail (*smirks*)   Sit there, I'll get her.

Pavla   I'd rather . . .

Muratov   Why?

Pavla   I just . . . Well, all right.

Mikhail *puts down the guitar and hurries off.* **Muratov** *picks it up and looks quizzically at* **Pavla**.

Muratov (*strums*)   It's a fine thing to be an army clerk, don't you think? They're brave and they play the guitar and court the ladies beautifully.

Pavla   I don't know, I haven't met any.

Muratov   Students and hairdressers also love playing the guitar.

Pavla   Do they?

Muratov   You're a terrible Eve, Pavla Nikolaevna, where's your curiosity? Aren't you curious to know why I keep coming here?

Pavla (*confused*)   No I'm not.

Muratov   I'm sorry to hear that, I wish you were.

Pavla   You're old friends with Auntie Sonya.

Muratov   Ah, but my heart is young – and it's drawn to the young, just as yours is drawn, for example, to Mikhail. A very stupid lad, in my view –

Pavla   No he isn't!

Muratov   I know him better than you do, he gets drunk with me regularly . . .

Pavla   And I'm not drawn to him at all.

Muratov (*strums the guitar*)   'Old husband, cold husband . . .'

Pavla (*stands up*)   It isn't true!

Muratov   What isn't true?

Pavla   Everything. What you just said. I don't want to listen to you, you're doing it on purpose . . . !

Muratov   What am I doing?

Pavla   I don't know, making fun of me . . . (*Runs away.*)

Muratov (*watches her and takes out his cigarette case; sighs and taps the strings of the guitar with the end of his whip*)   Little fool.

Tselovaneva *peeps out and darts back again.* **Sofia** *comes out of the house, stops on the top step and takes a deep breath.*

Sofia   What a lovely day.

Muratov (*stands up to greet her*)   Hot and dusty. Greetings!

Sofia   What was Pavla so upset about?

Muratov   I've no idea.

Sofia   Don't play games, Vasilii Pavlovich, I know you.

Muratov   I find her amusing.

They sit down.

Muratov   So the idyll's turning into a drama?

Sofia (*sternly*)   Don't talk rubbish. Have you brought the papers?

Muratov   Alas, my clerk never lifts a finger.

Sofia   You're not exactly renowned for hard work yourself.

Muratov   I'm lazy because I choose to be – what's the point of working for idiots who don't appreciate the value of my labour?

Sofia   As you keep saying.

Muratov   I mean it.

Sofia   To be original?

Muratov   I live among lazy, dishonest, uncivilised people, and I find it unrewarding and disagreeable to have to work for them – I hope that's clear?

Sofia   Quite clear, but it does you no credit.

Tselovaneva *grabs* **Stepka**'s *ear and marches her down the garden.*

Muratov   Well, there's nothing to be done about it. Incidentally, your friend Hevern . . .

Sofia   Let's not talk about him . . .

Muratov   Why not?

Sofia   I don't want to.

Muratov   You don't want me to?

Sofia   No.

Muratov   Mm, intriguing, that's partly why I came, to tell you something about the gentleman.

Sofia (*calmly*)   The gentleman's name is Gustav Egorovich, and I respect him very much . . .

Muratov   What if he turned out to be an embezzler?

Sofia (*stands up; firmly and angrily*)   What do you want?

Muratov (*flustered*)   I was just . . .

Sofia   I told you how I feel about the man!

Muratov   And – if you're mistaken?

Sofia   I'll pay for my own mistakes, I understand people as well as you do.

Muratov   You don't understand how I feel about you though.

Sofia (*smiles*)   I think I do. I understand that you don't trust or respect me . . .

Muratov (*sighs*)   Oh, how wrong you are.

Sofia   Don't sigh at me, I'm not wrong. To you I'm a merchant, a former landowner's wife, abused and corrupted by him, rich and devious, with sinful thoughts, but a coward. And uneducated. Is it because I'm uneducated that you play the cynic with me?

Muratov   I'm not a cynic, just sceptical, like anyone with any intelligence.

Sofia   I remember when you first tried to seduce me when my husband was alive. (*With a sigh.*) If only you knew how I needed sympathy then, someone to be honest with me . . .

Muratov   I was as honest with you as I knew how.

Sofia   That's it, you didn't. I liked you – I thought you were a good, intelligent man . . .

Muratov   I was just more stupid then.

Sofia   I didn't give in to you, and for a while it fired your obstinacy, your pride.

Muratov   Not obstinacy – passion!

Sofia   Stop that, you and your passion.

Muratov   Why are we quarrelling?

Sofia   I'm sorry, I get carried away sometimes.

Muratov (*bows*)   Never mind, I'm prepared for more. This conversation was inevitable, I think.

Sofia   I think so too.

Muratov (*looks around*)   Go on then.

Sofia (*stares at him*)   Once I almost trusted your feelings . . .

Muratov   When was that?

Sofia   What's it to you? (*Stands up and walks around.*)

Muratov (*pauses*)   I'd like to know what you think of me, Sofia Ivanovna.

Sofia   Nothing good.

Muratov   Well, that's honest. And if it cuts me to the quick . . .

Sofia   What then?

Muratov   Who's to say what will happen . . . ?

Sofia (*thoughtfully*)   I realised your so-called fatal attraction to me was just a way of covering up your laziness and lechery, and justifying your wretched life.

Muratov   Not bad for a start.

Sofia   You're a very dishonest man.

Muratov (*rises in his chair, grinning*)   I might say, however . . .

Sofia (*goes to him*)   Dishonest. An honest man doesn't use things without paying for them or taking responsibility for what he takes.

Muratov I don't recall taking anything from you.

Sofia They say you're very strict about arresting people and enforcing the law, but I think it's because you despise them and they bore you and you want to get your petty revenge on them. You use the power that's been given to you like a drunkard, or my late husband . . . I'm not good with words, it's like they're someone else's on my tongue, but I've feelings and I tell you honestly, I feel sorry for you.

Muratov I don't thank you.

Sofia You live a terrible life.

Muratov Really?

Sofia You don't like anyone or anything.

Muratov That's true, I don't like people.

Sofia And you don't like your work.

Muratov That too. Protecting forests? No, it doesn't amuse me. Go on!

Sofia But it's what you trained to do.

Muratov I know, it was a mistake, so what? It's a common Russian mistake. The Russian man strives above all to escape his native milieu, it doesn't matter where or how he gets there. Are you through?

Sofia Yes.

Muratov So what's your conclusion?

Sofia Draw it yourself.

Muratov Maybe you hope I'll blow my brains out? Well, you're wrong. There are thousands like me in this life, madam, we call the shots. There aren't more than a dozen like you, you're irrelevant, superfluous, there's nowhere for you to go. In the old days you'd have joined the revolution, but no one needs a revolution now – draw your own conclusions from that.

Sofia (*smiles*)   I seem to have got under your skin.

Muratov   My skin, oh no.

Sofia   Have we finished?

Muratov (*peers at her*)   You're cleverer than I thought, I'm amazed you put up with all this – mediocrity. (*Sighs.*) All the same, something in my heart . . .

Sofia   Well, it's no use to either of us now.

Muratov   You've a simple view of people, madam, very naive!

Sofia (*angrily*)   Enough of your complexity, look where it's got you.

Muratov   You're angry, I'm off. I like getting angry but I don't like it when someone else gives themselves the luxury, particularly a woman. (*Saunters back to the house; stops on the steps to the verandah.*) We didn't quarrel, all right?

Sofia (*quietly*)   If you say so.

Muratov   I do. Until we meet again, in more pleasant circumstances, I hope. (*Goes off.*)

Sofia *paces, shrugs and grins.*

Stepka (*peers from the corner of the verandah*)   Sofia Ivanovna, Granny boxed my ears.

Sofia (*not looking at her*)   Come here, what did you do?

Stepka   I took a bit of sugar.

Sofia   You should have asked.

Stepka   She wouldn't have given it to me.

Sofia   You should have asked me.

Stepka   You weren't there.

Sofia   You should have waited.

Stepka   I know, I'm a fool.

Sofia (*strokes her hair*)   Yes you are.

Stepka   When will I be clever?

Sofia   You will, be patient. Someone's come, go and see who it is.

Stepka (*runs off*)   Ooh, it's your German.

Sofia (*walks to the corner of the verandah*)   Anna Markovna, what are you doing here?

Tselovaneva (*comes up the steps*)   While you were chattering my jam boiled over. You spoil that child, she steals sugar . . .

Pavla (*from the door*)   Auntie Sonya – someone's come to see you.

Sofia   I know, I'm coming. Why do you look so sad?

Pavla   Misha was telling me about his college . . .

Tselovaneva   Oho.

Sofia   We must make some cold snacks, they'll probably want something . . . (*Hurries inside.*)

Tselovaneva   Oh, Pavlenka, I wish we hadn't sold our little house.

Pavla   It's not important, Mother.

Tselovaneva   A place of your own, not important? (*Drops her voice.*) Sofia Ivanovna just gave the warden the brush-off, seems she's decided to marry the German instead.

Pavla (*thoughtfully*)   She's kind . . .

Tselovaneva   Everyone's kind, but not to us.

Pavla   And clever.

Tselovaneva   I think it's stupid if a woman's clever. You shouldn't spend so much time with Mikhail, Pavla . . .

Pavla   Don't, Mama, how can you! You're no fun any more, you're always angry. Who are you angry with?

Tselovaneva   There there, look at yourself, you'd better go in and tidy up. (*Returns to her jam.*)

Pavla *irritably pushes the guitar away.* **Shokhin** *comes on to the verandah holding a parcel.*

Pavla   Who do you want?

Shokhin   No one, I brought some sugar.

Pavla   Are you Shokhin?

Shokhin   Yes indeed, mounted forest patrol.

Pavla (*quietly*)   Did you kill a man?

Shokhin (*after a moment*)   Yes I did.

Pavla   God, poor you.

Shokhin (*in a low voice*)   They acquitted me.

Pavla   But you can't forgive yourself, can you? How did it . . .

Shokhin (*angrily*)   With the handle of an axe . . .

Pavla   I didn't mean . . .

Shokhin   Where shall I put it? (*Puts the parcel on the table and speaks quickly and sharply.*) You know what they did in 1907? They came to the forests and cut down people's trees . . .

Pavla   So you got them?

Shokhin   It's my job.

Pavla   My God. You'd kill someone for that?

Shokhin   They kill them for less.

Pavla (*looks at him and calls out in a frightened childish voice*) Mama!

Shokhin (*hurt, quietly*)   Don't be afraid of me, I didn't mean to hurt him . . .

Commotion in the house. **Shokhin** *looks round and runs off to the garden.* **Antipa** *comes out looking tired and dusty.*

Antipa   Who's that running off?

Pavla   Shokhin.

Antipa   Why?

Pavla   I don't know.

Antipa   Where's Mikhail?

Pavla   In his room probably.

Antipa (*walks down the steps and wraps his arms round her*) Why so sad?

Pavla   That Shokhin . . .

Antipa   Yes?

Pavla   He killed a man.

Antipa (*gloomily*)   I know he did, the fool. I hired a lawyer to get him off, and now he's my faithful dog. You want me to sack him?

Pavla   No, don't, he might hurt me . . .

Antipa   Silly child!

Pavla   Or someone else. Don't sack him . . .

Antipa   Oh, Pavla, I see you and my heart's twisted up with words and I can't get them out, but you know without words how I . . .

Pavla (*shyly*)   I will, be patient with me.

Antipa   I can wait. (*Sighs.*) Only, you see, I've not much time. Life's short, I want everything to open up to me at once.

Pavla   People say you've changed.

Antipa (*startled*)   Changed? How?

Pavla   I don't know.

Antipa   Who says?

Pavla   People.

Antipa   People! (*Whistles.*)

Pavla   They say you're neglecting the business.

Antipa (*smiles*)   It's my business, I'll do what I like with it. (*Stares at her, grasps her by the shoulders.*) Fancy a child like you talking about business.

Pavla (*quietly, looking over her shoulder*)   They say Auntie Sonya's taken over.

Antipa (*furious*)   If I find out who said that I'll knock his teeth out. I order you not to repeat this filth, you hear? No one will make me quarrel with my sister, never. Lies and gossip! (*Pushes her off.*)

Pavla (*hurt, moves away slowly*)   You're losing your temper again. Just talk to me, ask me what I'm thinking . . .

Antipa (*graps her shoulders again*)   Wait, don't be cross, I'll tell you everything. I was upset, that's all. Just talk to me about yourself, not other people. Other people are angry and jealous, they're unhappy because they're weak . . .

Pavla   Misha's weak, but he's not angry or jealous.

Antipa (*recoils from her*)   Why do you bring him into it?

Pavla   Because you talk badly of him.

Antipa   Badly? Because he didn't – look what it's come to . . .

Pavla (*anxiously*)   Please don't think . . .

Antipa (*stares at her*)   Think what?

Pavla (*embarrassed*)   You know, what we talked about on Thursday -- I'm not interested in him, he means nothing to me . . .

Antipa (*embraces her again, stares into her eyes*)   Good God, it never crossed my mind . . . You told me and that's that – thank you. I love you, Pavla – I can hardly breathe sometimes from the power of it. Come to the pond, let me kiss you . . .

Pavla (*quietly*)   What, in broad daylight? It is not nice.

Antipa (*leads her off*)   Yes it is -- come, bright dawn of my evening . . .

They go off. **Hevern** *comes on to the verandah and squints after them.* **Stepka** *carries out a silver bucket with ice and bottles.*

Sofia (*follows* **Hevern** *out*)   Get on with it then.

Hevern   You're in such a cheerful mood, it agitates me.

Sofia   Really? You like women to be depressed?

Hevern   Oh, you know who I like.

Sofia (*smiles*)   No offence, but I'd take you more seriously if you had more money.

Hevern (*frowns slightly*)   That's a very valuable asset of yours, Sofia Ivanovna, you speak your mind. But I intend to be richer. I understand that nowhere is it so important to be rich as in Russia, where only money confers independence and respect. I'm thirty-four now, and plan to have a hundred thousand by the time I'm forty . . .

Sofia   You bring too much maths into it.

Hevern   It's essential – if only so you don't chase after twenty-year-old girls when you're fifty. It can't make a family, and it's bad for business.

Sofia (*coldly*)   You think so?

Hevern   I'm convinced of it. Late marriages in Russia are never successful. When a man rushes home to his wife he loses business, and third parties may suffer from his rushing.

Sofia   Me, for instance.

Hevern   You of course. And me.

Mikhail *comes out and greets* **Hevern** *silently. He pours himself a glass of wine and sits on the top step, holding it to the light.* **Hevern** *looks him up and down.* **Sofia** *smokes a cigarette and watches him.*

Hevern   Caught any perch this morning, Misha?

Mikhail   Yes I did.

Hevern   How many?

Mikhail   One.

Hevern   Big?

Mikhail   About a pound.

Hevern   Terrible. Nothing wastes a man's time so much as fishing. (*To* **Sofia**.) I was talking to your Marshall of the Nobility yesterday, a most unusual character.

Sofia   Is he? Why?

Hevern   It seems he's been all over Europe, seen the art galleries and visited the museums, but he didn't visit the Reichstag. He doesn't understand, socialism is a historic phenomenon. He laughs at it when he should study it. You need more than the landowner's instinct and naked self-interest to fight socialism – to defeat the enemy we must know it!

Sofia (*thoughtfully*)   I'm not interested in socialism either.

Hevern   It isn't necessary for a woman. Yes, he's an odd one, he talks passionately about the aristocracy's honourable duty to Russia and it's all very beautiful, but offer him two thousand roubles and he'll sing a different tune.

Sofia (*laughs*)   Why two thousand?

Hevern   As an example, I mean.

Sofia   Is that what you gave him?

Hevern (*sternly*)   Why would I do that? (*To* **Mikhail**.)
You're on friendly terms with Pavla Nikolaevna, I believe?

Mikhail   She's a good person, kind and honest . . .

Hevern   That's very nice, but it seems to me that with
many Russians kindness is a sort of weakness of
character . . .

Mikhail   I don't know, you'd see it more clearly as a
foreigner.

Antipa *and* **Pavla** *walk up from the garden separately; both are
quiet and subdued. The other three fall silent and watch them.*

Antipa (*in a hoarse voice*)   When the heart isn't on fire and
just smoulders it's not life, my dear, it's . . . (*Turns to* **Pavla**
irritably.) You should wait before you speak!

Pavla (*wearily*)   First I'm stupid, then you tell me not to
speak.

Antipa   I'm talking about something else, understand?
(*Sees his son and straightens up.*) Well, have you done the
payroll?

Mikhail   Not yet.

Antipa   Why not? I thought I said . . .

Mikhail   The accounts for the Chernoramen holiday
home aren't ready.

Antipa   What do you mean, boy? Don't lie to me.

Sofia   I took them, don't shout. I wanted to check them.

Antipa (*goes up the steps to the verandah*)   Covering up for him
as usual. Why can't he check them himself?

Sofia *whispers urgently to him, he mumbles back.*

Hevern (*to* **Pavla**)   How are you?

Pavla   Very well, thank you.

Hevern   I'm glad to hear it.

Pavla   You mean that?

Hevern   What?

Pavla   Are you really glad when people are well?

Hevern (*surprised*)   To be sure I am. Why shouldn't I be?
It's in my interest for everyone around me to be happy!

Pavla   How simple and true that is.

Hevern   If things are simple it's usually because they're
true.

Antipa (*to* **Hevern**)   Shall we look at the plans?

Hevern   By all means.

Antipa   You come too, Mikhail. Sofia, did you know we
bought that forest from the Marshall?

Sofia   No, I didn't.

Antipa (*to* **Hevern**)   What, you didn't tell your partner?

Hevern (*frowns*)   I assumed . . .

Sofia (*to her brother*)   How much?

Antipa   Twenty-three . . .

Sofia   You said you wouldn't go above eighteen.

Antipa   I know, but another bidder turned up – I'll tell
you about it later. Come, Mikhail!

Mikhail *and* **Antipa** *go off followed by* **Hevern**. **Sofia** *smokes
thoughtfully and watches them.* **Pavla** *stands against the railings with
bowed head.*

Sofia   Sad?

Pavla   Just tired.

Sofia   What were you two talking about?

Pavla   It's always the same, he keeps saying how much he loves me.

Sofia   My little bird, come here.

Pavla   'I love you, I love you' – I know he does. There's no need to keep saying it all the time.

Sofia (*sadly*)   My child, it's bad if you can't say it all the time.

Pavla   Men are strange – the way that one looks at me.

Sofia   Which one?

Pavla   Gustav Egorovich.

Sofia   He looks at everyone like that, as if he owned them!

Pavla   Do you like him?

Sofia   He's all right, he's competent – you'd never be late if you were catching a train with him.

Pavla   I don't understand, are you joking?

Sofia   There's a lot you don't understand, my dear.

Pavla (*sadly*)   I know there is, I didn't think it would be like this . . .

Sofia   Tell me, why did you marry my brother?

Pavla   I thought it would be different. I'm afraid of everything you see, I'm always convinced something bad will happen. Until I was twelve I was frightened of my father, then I lived in the convent for five years and everyone was afraid there too. At first we thought we'd be kidnapped. In 1905 there were Cossacks stationed outside and they used to whistle at us every night – they didn't respect the nuns, they were drunk, singing songs, it was horrible. Everybody sinned against the rules and they were angry and afraid of each other, and of God too, they didn't love Him. I thought I couldn't live alone the way I wanted to and needed someone strong to protect me . . .

Sofia (*thoughtfully*)   And you thought Antipa was strong?

Pavla   He said so himself. Misha doesn't care about people, he's in his own world. And before we were engaged, all these men were after my money . . .

Sofia (*embraces her*)   To begin with I thought badly of you, remember?

Pavla   Yes, and I hated it. I was afraid of you, you used to look at me so sternly and I'd go into the corner and cry – I wanted to say 'I'm not bad, I'm not greedy', but I hadn't the courage.

Sofia   God help you, little girl, it's going to be hard for you here.

Pavla   It is already. Shokhin killed a man and walks around as if nothing happened.

Sofia   Don't be afraid of him, he's not a criminal, just unlucky.

Pavla   I thought I'd live a quiet life and everyone would be good and smile and know I didn't wish them harm . . .

Sofia   But they don't.

Pavla   Why not?

Sofia (*stands up and paces*)   They just don't . . . You said it very well – everyone should smile . . .

Pavla   You know, when it's Christmas Eve and everything's ready and you've cleared up and you're tired and happy, waiting quietly for the big day?

Sofia   But Christmas is months away, my dear, and nothing's ready.

Pavla   Oh Lord, Aunt Sonya, teach me.

Sofia   What?

Pavla   How to live with people.

Sofia   I don't know myself, life passes in a fog . . .

Pavla   So what do you want out of it?

Sofia   Me? (*Stops, speaks quietly with great emphasis.*) I'll tell you what I want – I want to sin and riot and break the rules and turn everything upside down and rise high above people, then throw myself at their feet and say, 'Dear people, my beloved people, I'm not your owner, I'm a low sinner, the lowest of the low! No one owns you, there are no masters, no rulers . . . !'

Pavla (*alarmed, quietly*)   Why would you say that?

Sofia   To free people from fear. There's no one to be afraid of now – but everyone's still frightened and oppressed, you can see it for yourself! No one dares say what they want to . . .

Antipa *stands in the doorway listening.*

Pavla   But I don't understand. You mean you'd destroy yourself?

Sofia   God destroyed His son for people, that's what Shokhin's father said.

Antipa (*comes from the door*)   What are you talking about?

Pavla   A-ah!

Antipa (*goes to her, in a hurt voice*)   What are you scared of, you've done nothing wrong. What were you talking about?

Pavla   Oh, you know . . .

Antipa (*to his sister, rudely*)   You should talk less.

Sofia *ignores him and paces to hide her agitation.*

Pavla (*soothingly*)   And you should shout less, Antipa Ivanovich. You're always shouting, there's no need for it.

Antipa (*more gently*)   It's not because I'm angry, I just have a loud voice. Hey, lady of the house, how about some tea? Tell them to lay the table. And some snacks . . . Run along, little girl! (**Pavla** *goes into the house; he follows her with his eyes and speaks to his sister in a reproachful tone.*) You're spoiling her for me, Sonya.

Sofia *walks past him in silence.*

Antipa (*repeats insistently*)   Don't spoil my wife for me, I said.

Sofia (*suddenly, sharply*)   Be quiet!

Antipa (*backs off*)   Wait, I . . .

Sofia   You thought everything would be sweetness and light with your young wife, didn't you?

Antipa (*sinks into an armchair*)   Why? Is she complaining?

Sofia (*more calmly*)   No, believe me, no. I'm sorry, I'm in a foul mood, something's troubling me.

Antipa (*quietly*)   You had me worried. Merciful Lord, I love that child so much, I'd give everything I have to be close to her.

Sofia (*paces again*)   It doesn't make either of you happy though, does it?

Antipa   It will, just wait, it will! (*Silence.*) Sonya?

Sofia   Yes?

Antipa   How does she get on with Mikhail – all right?

Sofia (*stands in front of him*)   Stop that right now, you hear? Forget it, don't put ideas into people's heads. Where's Hevern?

Antipa (*waves an arm at the house*)   In there, buried in the plans. To hell with him, I'm sick of him.

Sofia   You're a most accommodating partner for him, I must say.

Antipa (*alert*)   How so?

Sofia   You just are. You should keep your eyes open.

Antipa   Oh, that. I thought you were going to say you and he . . .

Sofia   Don't even think about it.

Antipa (*smirks*)   I can't make you out sometimes, Sonya.

Sofia   Listen, you shouldn't shout at Misha in front of Pavla.

Antipa   He drives me mad. What's he doing with his life?

Sofia   You think only of yourself.

Antipa (*thoughtfully*)   I don't want to hurt Pavla though.

Sofia   Then stop making fun of her mother.

Antipa   I don't like the woman.

Sofia (*stumbles against the railings*)   I'm exhausted.

Antipa (*jumps to his feet and goes to her*)   What is it, Sonya? Can I get you some water?

Sofia (*leans against him*)   I don't feel well.

Antipa   What? Lord, Sonya, what's wrong?

Sofia   Wait, oh God . . .

Antipa (*puts his arms round her*)   Come, my dear, lie down, rest . . . (*Leads her out.*)

Tarakanov *comes up from the garden.* **Mikhail** *appears on the verandah, pours wine and drinks.*

Tarakanov   Has the German gone?

Mikhail   He's Swedish. Or Greek.

Tarakanov   Makes no difference, he's a foreigner. Has he gone?

Mikhail   He's staying for supper.

Tarakanov   Hm, surprising.

Mikhail   What is?

Tarakanov   Has no one here noticed that he smells like a crook?

Mikhail   But everyone here's a crook.

Tarakanov   Not everyone, nine out of ten – and the tenth is a fool. Where's Sofia Ivanovna? She sees everything.

Mikhail   How should I know. (*Sits on the step and lights a cigarette.*)

Tarakanov *gesticulates, mutters and leaves.* **Pavla** *comes out of the house smiling, stops behind* **Mikhail** *and tickles his neck with the tip of her scarf.*

Mikhail (*without turning round, roughly*)   Look out, if Father sees there'll be hell to pay.

Pavla (*grimaces*)   Don't laugh, I'm young, I'm bored . . .

Mikhail   Everyone's bored.

Pavla   There must be a happy life somewhere!

Mikhail   Look for it then.

Pavla   Let's go to the garden.

Mikhail   I must get back to the office, I'll finish my cigarette then earn my bread by the sweat of my brow.

Pavla (*goes down the steps*)   Well, I'll go on my own, I'll walk for a week, a month – goodbye. Will you be sorry for me?

Mikhail   I've been sorry for you for a long time.

Pavla   You don't mean it. (*Goes down the steps, turns back and wags a finger at him.*) It isn't true!

Mikhail *watches her glumly and puts out his cigarette; stands up and sees his father standing behind him.*

Antipa   Where are you going?

Mikhail   To the office.

Antipa   What isn't true?

Mikhail   I don't know, I didn't get it . . .

Antipa   Didn't you? (*Looks grimly at his son as if about to say something, then waves him away.*) Go! (*Drops his head and walks slowly after* **Pavla**.)

Tselovaneva *looks round the corner of the house and shakes her fist at him.*

Act Three

Sofia's *study. A large desk and on the right a fireplace. On the left are two doors, a small one leading to her bedroom, the other to the inner rooms. On the back wall are two windows and the door to the verandah.* **Sofia** *stands by the desk holding some papers.* **Muratov** *is about to leave and taps his leg with a battered hat. A grey autumn day is visible outside, and bare branches sway against the window.*

Sofia (*thoughtfully*)   One more question.

Muratov (*bows his head*)   Ten if you want!

Sofia   Tell me simply and honestly, what made you give me these papers?

Muratov   I had a feeling . . .

Sofia   Leave feeling out of it.

Muratov   What do you want me to say? (*Shrugs and grins.*) You're very hard on me, Sofia Ivanovna, you won't let me say which feeling!

Sofia   Jealousy?

Muratov   The idea.

Sofia   Wanting to make trouble for me?

Muratov   Also no – I fear I can't explain it any way you'll understand that won't make you angry. (*Pauses.*) You definitely won't understand, I don't understand it myself.

Sofia   Nevertheless.

Muratov (*sighs*)   We don't see eye to eye, do we?

She shakes her head in silence and stares at him.

But those papers will prove that I'm right and you're wrong.

Sofia (*sighs*)   Evasive as usual.

Muratov   Kindly let me take my leave.

Sofia (*peers out of the window*)   Goodbye. Why are you so lightly dressed? It looks like rain.

Muratov (*laughs quietly*)   Don't let it trouble you!

Sofia   Why are you laughing?

Muratov   I have my reasons, madam. I'm going.

Sofia   Forgive me for not seeing you out. Will you look in at the office and sent Tarakanov to me?

Muratov *goes out.* **Sofia** *throws the papers on the desk, wipes her fingers with a handkerchief and presses them to her eyes.* **Antipa** *enters through the door from the garden wearing felt slippers, looking unhealthy and dishevelled, with his shirt collar unbuttoned under a thick jacket and no waistcoat.*

Sofia (*annoyed*)   You should knock before you come in.

Antipa (*calmly*)   That's new, am I a stranger here?

Sofia   What do you want?

Antipa   Nothing. (*Looks round the room.*)

Sofia (*examines him more closely, in a gentler voice*)   Why are you loafing around like a tramp?

Antipa (*sits in the armchair by the fireplace*)   You can dress me up when I die.

Sofia   What's got into you, Antipa?

Antipa   I don't like this old house of yours – it's not a house, it's a morgue. Smells like one too. I should never have moved in with you, I'm a stranger, I don't belong here . . .

Sofia   Stop it please, I've no time to listen to you.

Tarakanov *enters.* **Sofia** *hands him a thick file from the desk.*

Sofia   Matvei Ilich, please take out all the accounts and documents for Useka and the Chernoramen dacha. Do it now . . .

She sits at the desk and writes. **Tarakanov** *settles himself at a little table by the fireplace, puts on his glasses and goes through the file, then opens the newspaper.*

Antipa (*smiles at him*)   Anything new?

Tarakanov (*gloomily*)   China's mobilising.

Antipa   Against whom?

Tarakanov   Us – egged on by the Germans.

Antipa   You don't like the Germans, do you?

Tarakanov   No, I don't.

Antipa   Why not?

Tarakanov   They're cleverer than us.

Antipa   You should respect them then.

Tarakanov   I do, I just don't like them.

Antipa   You're a strange fellow, my friend.

Tarakanov   Everyone who's clever in this country is strange.

Antipa   You're right there. (*Thinks.*) You're strange though, and you aren't clever.

Tarakanov   That's not true.

Antipa   So why did you take off your uniform and leave the police?

Tarakanov   I've already told you.

Antipa   You have and you haven't.

Tarakanov   Turn away from evil and create good, they say.

Antipa (*strikes the arm of his chair with his fist*)   You don't create anything without evil, you fool! You must go to the heart of it, beat it, kick it, trample it to the ground and show it who's boss! That's what you must do, am I right, Sonya?

Sofia   You're right, don't bother me.

Tarakanov   It's just hot air, words, drumbeats. When the evil falls on your head you'll run like the devil.

Antipa   Not me. Life's a battle, my friend, I don't run away.

Tarakanov   We'll see.

Stepka (*enters through the door on the left*)   Antipa Ivanovich, the peasants have arrived.

Antipa   Which peasants?

Sofia   The ones from Kamenskoe.

Antipa   Scoundrels, I'll skin them alive!

Sofia   Wait, Hevern put them up to it, I know he did.

Antipa   Really? Are you sure?

Sofia   Of course I am.

Antipa (*exits*)   Bloody German.

Tarakanov   He's got more sense than you have . . .

Stepka   Sofia Ivanovna, give me a book to read.

Sofia (*writing*)   Ask Misha for one.

Stepka   He sent me away, he's singing in the young mistress's ear . . .

Sofia (*looks up, quietly*)   What did you say?

Stepka   They're sitting side by side on the sofa and he's singing her a song!

Sofia   Run along now – don't gossip!

Stepka   But I only told you! (*Exits.*)

Tarakanov (*mutters*)   Young mistress. What kind of mistress is she?

Sofia   You've known Muratov long?

Tarakanov   About ten years.

Sofia   What do you think of him?

Tarakanov (*peers at her over his glasses*)   In the old days I used to think he was good. He did a lot of useful work in the forest – drained it, cleared trees, gave the peasants firewood, that sort of thing. Then suddenly it was as if something hit him and he became blind and angry. Now he's a most unpleasant man. People around here are made of straw, they flare up and make a lot of smoke but no light or warmth.

Sofia (*listens attentively with her elbows on the desk*)   What exactly do you find unpleasant about him?

Tarakanov   Me? The same things everyone does – he doesn't like anyone, he upsets them and quarrels with them, he's a gossip and he's lecherous with women. Clever though
. . .

Pavla (*enters*)   Can I come in?

Sofia   Of course you can!

Pavla   The house is so cold . . .

Sofia   Tell them to light the fire then.

Tarakanov (*hands* **Sofia** *the papers she asked for*)   Can I go?

Sofia   Thank you. Send Stepka in on your way out, and Misha.

Pavla   Why are you all dressed up?

Sofia   I'm expecting a guest.

Pavla   Misha's written another poem.

Sofia   Any good?

Pavla   Yes. About a pine tree.

Sofia   Is he drunk?

Pavla (*sighs*)   Since this morning.

Tselovaneva (*at the door*)   No wonder the boy drinks himself stupid.

Sofia   Why?

Tselovaneva   Because he's been wronged.

Sofia   Lots of people have been wronged!

Tselovaneva   And they all drink. What do you think makes them drink? Your father drank because he was clever and no one gave him credit for it, so he arrested people to get his own back, like Muratov. They took him to court of course, but it made him worse. A man doesn't need much. A man's soul is like a child's, Sofia Ivanovna – like a flower in spring. Why did I come? Oh yes, did you give Stepka a yellow ribbon?

Sofia   Yes, why?

Tselovaneva   Nothing, nothing. She just tied it in her hair and was staring at herself in the mirror for half an hour in the kitchen, that's all!

Pavla   Stop it, Mother!

Tselovaneva   Doesn't bother me, take care of your things and extra care of others', I say.

Stepka *enters.*

Tselovaneva   Here's our little darling.

Stepka   You called me?

Tselovaneva (*leaving the room*)   Of course we did. What would life be without you?

Sofia   Light the fire, Stepka.

Stepka   Oooh, Granny doesn't like me, she's got a horrible temper. (*Runs out.*)

Sofia   Stepka's a lovely girl.

Pavla   She's the only cheerful one in this house, but she's far too cheeky.

Sofia (*goes to her*)   Ask Antipa to take you to Moscow.

Pavla   Why?

Sofia   For a change, to see what life's like in the city.

Pavla (*listlessly*)   Fine, I'll ask him.

Sofia (*puts her hand on* **Pavla***'s head*)   Don't you want to go?

Mikhail *slips in from the inner rooms, looks at them and sinks into the armchair. He sits and dozes, almost screened by the door curtain.*

Pavla   To travel? No, I want to sleep for a year or two, and when I wake up everything will be different.

Sofia   That's childish, Pavla, you must learn to make your own life. You can't expect others to do everything for you.

Pavla   Please don't be angry with me.

Sofia   You're young, you've a good heart. You feel sorry for people, don't you?

Pavla   I know what you're going to say and I don't like him at all, I just like the way he speaks.

Sofia (*steps back disconcerted*)   I didn't mean that, but since we're on the subject I must say it's not right the way you behave with him, he's not a child, it may end badly for you.

Pavla   But I'm bored. I've nothing to do all day and he makes me laugh.

Sofia   Go away with Antipa, I'll sort Misha out.

Pavla   Perhaps I could take Mother instead?

Sofia   Is it so hard to be with your husband?

Pavla *clings silently to her.*

Sofia (*lifts her face and looks into her eyes*)   I understand, darling, I had a husband too.

Stepka (*runs in*)   Sofia Ivanovna, the German's here –
dressed to kill.

Sofia   I see. (*Strokes* **Pavla**'s *face*.) Well, Pavla, you'd better
leave me.

Pavla (*runs out*)   Lord, I wish you luck . . .

Sofia   Thank you, my dear! Tell him to come in, Stepka.
(*Covers the papers on the desk and tidies her hair in the mirror. Notices*
Mikhail *in the armchair*.) Misha, how long have you been
there?

Mikhail   Ages.

Sofia   Did you hear what we said?

Mikhail   A few things – the German's arrived, the nun's
making up stories . . .

Sofia   Stories?

Mikhail   Of course, she never stops. She's still playing
with dolls and I'm a doll for her – and you, and Father.
She'll always be like that, all her life.

Sofia   You know you may be right.

Mikhail   Why did you call me?

Sofia   I don't need you now. Please go – I'll call you later.

Mikhail (*stands up*)   I'm off. Marry the German and send
us packing – all of us, including my romantic papa and his
second youth!

Sofia   For heaven's sake, go.

Mikhail   Hush, you must be in command of your
emotions. (*Passes* **Hevern** *in the door*.) Greetings, bearer of
culture and civilisation.

Hevern (*dressed extremely smartly with a diamond tie pin and a ring
on his left hand. He greets* **Mikhail** *silently, kisses* **Sofia**'s *hand
and follows her to the desk*)   You probably know the reason I
wanted to see you today.

Sofia (*sits down*)   I think so . . .

Hevern   That's very pleasing for me.

Sofia   Why?

Hevern   It avoids unnecessary explanations. Do you mind if I smoke?

Sofia   Of course not. (*Pushes matches and an ashtray at him.*)

Hevern (*takes a cigar from his cigarette case*)   I feel somewhat excited today.

Sofia   A glass of water?

Hevern   No, no, it's natural in the circumstances.

Sofia   Your appearance is certainly most inspiring.

Hevern   If only my ideas inspired the same confidence.

Sofia   You'd better tell me what they are then.

Hevern   That was the purpose of my visit! (*Lights his cigar.*) You know I respect your ideas, and that they correspond closely to my own.

Sofia   I'm flattered to hear it.

Hevern (*bows*)   I speak from the heart. You can't deny that I know Russia and the Russian people – I observe much and judge well! For eighteen years I have lived among you and studied you, and my conclusions are these: that Russia suffers pre-eminently from a lack of sound, healthy people capable of setting themselves clearly defined targets. Do you agree?

Sofia   Go on.

Hevern   There are a few people who believe in themselves and their powers, but there's too much metaphysics and not enough mathematics.

Sofia   As you've said before . . .

Hevern   It's what I think. Take you – a woman of character and intelligence . . .

Sofia   Thank you.

Hevern   I even think of you in allegorical terms – Sofia Ivanovna, the new Russia, healthy in soul, who given the right circumstances could accomplish miracles and do much valuable cultural work in the town.

Sofia   You're too kind.

Hevern   I'm serious. So there is a very profound purpose to the union which I am about to propose to you. It will be more than mere marriage. My energy and yours – oh, together we will be colossal! When two strong people understand their objectives, it's very important to Russia these days, when after discarding her dreams she must finally set about the simple task of living and put herself on a sure footing . . . Your brother is distracted by family matters and the business suffers, as I've had the honour of pointing out to you several times before in my concern to protect your interests . . .

Sofia   Are you going to talk about love?

Hevern   (*slightly confused*)   Excuse me, that's not the issue! We have something deeper. I have already explained my feelings to you on four separate occasions.

Sofia   Four, that many?

Hevern   Yes indeed, I remember them clearly. The first was in the garden of the Marshall of the Nobility on his name-day, when it rained and you got your feet wet. The second was here by the pond, sitting on the bench, and you embarrassed me by joking that the frogs were croaking about love too . . .

Sofia   The third and fourth times I remember.

Hevern   It may be true about frogs, but I . . . forgive me, it was an inexcusable joke. When a man's heart ardently desires . . .

Sofia   Let's end this conversation, Gustav Egorovich . . .

Hevern (*surprised*)   Why?

Sofia   Need I spell it out?

Hevern (*stands up, in an injured tone*)   You certainly do, when the other party doesn't understand. I shall consider it an insult if you don't . . .

Sofia   Very well. (*Stands up and paces the room.*) You offer me the chance to save Russia with you . . .

Hevern   You twist my words!

Sofia   Well, something of the sort. I don't consider myself up to the role. That's the first thing. And as it happens I don't think you're up to it either.

Hevern   Pardon me, which role?

Sofia   I don't know, philanthropist, cultural worker.

Hevern (*with a smile*)   Why not?

Sofia   Because you're a little thief.

Hevern (*more surprised than offended*)   I beg your pardon! I didn't expect . . .

Sofia   I know you didn't – these papers on my desk implicate you in a series of thefts.

Hevern   There are no such papers. (*Sits down. Angrily:*) They set me up.

Sofia (*stands at the desk, speaking calmly and with emphasis*)   I have a copy here of your contract with the Buyanov peasants, and I know about your deal with the Marshall.

Hevern (*shrugs*)   Oh that – just business . . .

Sofia (*more quietly, with an effort*) You told Tarakanov to make a false inventory . . .

Hevern Tarakanov is mentally ill.

Sofia And Shokhin, whom you tried to bribe. Is he ill too?

Hevern It's been blown up out of all proportion . . .

Sofia You dig deeper and deeper into my brother's pocket — are all these activities necessary for the new Russia?

Hevern (*mops his face with a handkerchief*) Wait, let me explain . . .

Sofia (*moves around the room, laughs*) Well, sir, what's to explain? It seems very clear to me, it's all there in black and white!

Hevern (*carefully puts out his cigar*) So in your view, I'm a dishonest man, unworthy of your hand in marriage?

Sofia (*stops amazed, laughs*) You are an extraordinarily naive man.

Hevern (*smiles, spreads his hands*) If I did something — inappropriate, it was only because I was so sure that your feelings for me . . .

Sofia I don't know where you got that idea from.

Hevern It seemed to me you considered me as your friend, and that our business interests were the same.

Sofia Well, you were mistaken . . .

Hevern Mistakes should be forgiven. I thought that given the way your brother runs things you wouldn't blame me, and that my foresight would . . .

Sofia (*goes up to him; quietly but firmly*) Hop it!

Hevern *flushes and lunges at her; she grabs something off the desk; for a few seconds they stand opposite each other in a silent stand-off.*

Hevern (*backs away*)   You're a very rude woman, you're –
ridiculous! (*Puts on his hat while still in the room and goes quickly to
the door.*)

Sofia *sits at the edge of the desk and covers her eyes with one hand,
briskly rubbing her knee with the other.*

Stepka (*in the doorway, looks at her and sighs*)   Shall I light the
fire?

Sofia (*in a muffled voice*)   No need. Oh, go on then.

Stepka   Shokhin wants to see you.

Sofia   Let him wait.

Stepka   He has to go to the forest.

Sofia   Leave me alone. All right, call him. Quick!

Stepka *runs off and bumps into* **Antipa** *in the door.*

Antipa   Devil got your tail? What happened, Sonya? The
German ran into the hall all green and spluttering and
almost knocked me over, and he didn't say sorry.

Sofia (*brusquely*)   He's robbed you of ten thousand this
year.

Antipa   Really? All power to him, it's human nature – and
Pavla still says we must be good and virtuous and people
deserve her heartfelt sympathy. Where is she anyway? Have
you seen her?

Sofia   You should go away on your own for a while.

Antipa   So you say. Why?

Sofia (*covers the papers*)   I don't know what's got into you,
Antipa, moping at home all day. Go away and leave me in
peace.

Antipa (*leaves the room, brusquely*)   I'll find a place of my
own . . .

Sofia *walks around tidying her hair.* **Stepka** *brings in an armful of kindling and lights the fire.* **Shokhin** *appears at the door.* **Sofia** *looks at him in silence.*

Shokhin   Shokhin here!

Sofia   Yes, what is it, Yakov? Hurry up!

Shokhin   Sack me. Let me go . . .

Sofia   All right. Wait – why?

Shokhin   Just sack me, I know what I'm doing.

Sofia   But why? I'm so sorry . . .

Shokhin   I'm sorry too.

Sofia   Has someone offended you?

Shokhin   No.

Stepka   He's lying, the nun offends him, that Pavla, the little hypocrite . . . !

Shokhin   Tell her to go.

Stepka   I'm off. (*Runs out of the room.*)

Shokhin   The truth is I don't get on with the young mistress, I'm afraid of her . . .

Sofia   Whatever for?

Shokhin   She makes me feel bad. I don't want her pitying looks. Of course I'm a guilty man but I don't have to feel judged every day. It's not judgement, it's torture. When she arrived in this house it was as if she put sand in the works. People feel bad with her around, and you're worn out, Sofia Ivanovna . . .

Sofia (*looks at him, not listening; quietly*)   Such lovely gentle eyes . . .

Shokhin   It's not her eyes, it's what she does! Believe me, nothing good will come of it.

Sofia   I don't mean hers.

Shokhin   She's a snake, creeping up and stinging where it hurts.

Sofia   Stop, that's enough.

Shokhin   You shouldn't trust the German either. He's foreign and has no shame. And as for the . . . deceased, and his wife and children . . .

Sofia   I'll see they're taken care of. Where will you go?

Shokhin   To the town. And then, I don't know . . .

Sofia   I feel so sorry for you.

Shokhin   And I you. You're all alone here, the master's drunk without wine. Goodbye, Sofia Ivanovna, God give you success in everything.

Sofia   Goodbye . . . (*Gives him her hand; he holds it and looks warily at her.*) Maybe you'll change your mind?

Shokhin   No. I'll stay away until she dies.

Sofia   Who? Why should she die?

Shokhin   What has she to live for? What's the point of living? Goodbye . . . (*Backs out of the room.*)

Sofia (*watches him leave, rubs her eyes and mutters*)   What a nightmare! (*Looks in the mirror and sees* **Pavla** *pass the door snuggling playfully against* **Mikhail**'s *shoulder; she calls to her in a quiet, frightened voice.*) Pavla!

They come in together.

Mikhail (*with an embarrassed smile*)   Ah, a fire, excellent!

Pavla   Why are you so gloomy, Auntie? (*Embraces her.*) Listen to what Misha's just written!

Sofia (*stares into her face*)   My child, I was telling you just today . . .

Mikhail   Oh, one of her talks.

Sofia   Will you please leave the room.

Mikhail (*sits on the floor in front of the fire*)   No, I won't.

Sofia (*wearily*)   You want to drive me mad.

Tselovaneva (*enters*)   I've been looking for you everywhere, you shouldn't hide yourself away. The master's on the rampage, yelling at everyone . . .

Sofia   Anna Markovna, I need to talk to them alone.

Tselovaneva (*offended*)   Fine, dear, I'm off. I'm only the mother . . .

Mikhail   There's nothing to talk about, Auntie Sonya, don't you want to hear what I've written?

Pavla (*narrows her eyes at* **Sofia**, *rocking on her feet*)   I've nothing to talk about either.

Sofia (*stares at them and goes to the desk*)   Let's sit quietly and calm down.

Pavla   Go on, Misha, read it.

Mikhail   I'm ready, stepmother.

Pavla   Don't. I've asked you not to call me that.

Mikhail   It's your legal title.

Sofia (*impatiently*)   Get on with it, Mikhail.

Mikhail (*smiles*)   Just a minute, I can't remember . . .

Pavla   I remember.

Tselovaneva (*whispers loudly from the door*)   Stop, your father's coming!

Sofia   Anna Markovna, I thought I . . .

Tselovaneva   What have I done now?

Pavla *clings to* **Sofia**; **Mikhail** *frowns and moves across the floor into the shadows.*

Antipa (*enters, scowls at everyone, his hands hanging by his sides and trembling slightly*)   Stop what? You're all here together – poems, talk, what's wrong with that? (*Bursts out in an anguished voice.*) To hell with you, don't be frightened of me. I'm a man like anyone else!

Sofia   Keep your voice down, Antipa.

Antipa   Be quiet yourself. Why do you always want to silence me? Why do people run away from me? Am I an animal? When a man's alone he becomes an animal . . .

Mikhail   Really, Papa, you should . . .

Antipa   What?

Mikhail   Give Shokhin a raise.

Antipa (*slowly*)   What's this, are you mocking me?

Mikhail   God, no, it'll cheer him up that's all!

Antipa   What's he babbling about, Sonya?

Sofia   He's joking. Shokhin's leaving us.

Antipa   Leaving? Where will he go?

Sofia   I don't know . . .

Pavla   That's good, I'm scared of him.

Antipa   You're scared of everyone, and there's no need for it. (*Thoughtfully.*) So Yakov's going. The business . . . Why is he going?

Mikhail   Why didn't I know about this?

Antipa   You don't know anything. The father sells timber and the son scribbles poems. What a comedy . . .

Mikhail   He's off again.

All are silent. **Pavla** *whispers something to* **Sofia.**

Antipa   You shouldn't whisper, it's rude.

Sofia (*wearily*)   Let's do something, eat, drink – Anna Markovna, make us some tea.

Tselovaneva   It's too early for tea.

Sofia (*quietly, to* **Mikhail**)   Misha, you must go and check Hevern's accounts.

Mikhail   What, now?

Sofia   Yes, now.

Mikhail   You always want to get rid of people. You take the best room in the house and you don't want us to sit with you.

Sofia   What nonsense.

Mikhail   No, it's not.

Antipa (*to* **Pavla**)   Why don't you say something?

Tselovaneva   There you go – she can't speak and she can't stay quiet.

Antipa   Shut up, old woman!

Tselovaneva   Oh Lord, Pashenka . . . !

Antipa   Troublemaker, busybody!

Sofia   Pull yourself together, Antipa.

Antipa   Hold your tongue, sister. I can see what's happening! Are you blind?

Pavla (*quietly, very firmly*)   Antipa Ivanovich, I asked you not to shout at my mother!

Antipa   See? She doesn't fall to pieces at my voice.

Pavla (*advances on him*)   You're an evil, wicked man and I don't love you. I'm afraid of you!

Antipa   Pavla, Pavla, God help you.

Sofia   Wait! Listen, Pavla . . .

Pavla   No, you listen to me – I love Misha.

Mikhail   Gosh! (*Moves deeper in the shadows.*) Don't listen to her, Father, she's making it up because she's bored . . .

Antipa *slumps silently in the armchair and gives his wife a fearsome look.*

Pavla (*trembling*)   Yes I do. Lord kill me for it, I don't care! I know he doesn't love me but I love him, he's better than anyone else, you can kill me if you like . . . !

Tselovaneva   Pashenka, what are you saying!

Sofia   Anna Markovna, I beg you to go.

Antipa   You go, Pavla, leave. Now! Take her, sister.

Sofia *embraces* **Pavla** *in silence and leads her from the room.* **Tselovaneva** *follows them like a silent shadow.* **Mikhail** *moves closer to the fireplace.*

Antipa (*sits as if turned to stone looking belligerently at the floor, mumbling*)   You're an old man, my friend, an old man . . .

Fidgets in his chair and loosens the collar of his shirt, takes a ruler from the desk, snaps it in two and throws it in the fire. Picks up a book, looks at it and tosses it on the floor. Takes a small revolver from his pocket, smiles and squints down the barrel. His face becomes calm and serious. Putting it on his knee, he grabs his beard with the other hand and closes his eyes. **Mikhail** *quietly jumps up and tries to snatch it from him.*

Antipa (*starts up*)   You?

Mikhail   Listen, Father . . .

Antipa   Get out of my sight!

Mikhail (*moves to the door*)   I don't want anything from her, you heard what she said, don't believe her . . .

Antipa   Never mind, it doesn't matter . . .

Mikhail   I know those thoughts. (*Points to the gun.*)

Antipa (*hurls it at the door*)   Imbecile! You think because of you I'd . . . Get out, you drunkard.

Mikhail   I'm not to blame. I know I'm useless. I feel ashamed with you, with everyone, but you must believe me, I don't want anything from my stepmother . . .

Antipa (*howls*)   Go, before I kill you. I renounce you, you're not my son! (*Throws himself at* **Mikhail**, *grabs him by the neck and shakes him.*) Put those filthy thoughts out of your head . . .

Mikhail   They're not mine, they're yours.

Antipa   Wha-at?

Mikhail   I'm older than you, I've done nothing wrong . . .

Antipa   You've ripped my heart out.

Sofia (*hurries in*)   Let him go, Antipa! Run, Misha!

Mikhail *runs off, grabbing the revolver.*

Antipa (*rushes blindly at his sister and embraces her*)   Quick, Mother, send everyone away. Hide her somewhere . . . Misha must go. A great crime's been committed . . . Do something! I'm suffocating!

Sofia *seats him in the chair and closes the door.*

Antipa   It's killing me . . .

A gunshot rings out. **Antipa** *jumps up and looks at the floor, unable to speak.*

Sofia (*rushes to the door*)   He took the revolver!

Antipa (*staggers back*)   Mikhail! My son . . .

Act Four

The same room. **Antipa** *sits in the chair by the fireplace, apparently drunk.* **Muratov** *paces quietly behind him smoking, deep in thought.*

Antipa What does the doctor say?

Muratov I don't know, we only just got here.

Antipa Did you? Oh yes . . .

Muratov (*glances anxiously at him*) He probably hasn't had time to examine him yet.

Antipa Sofia threw me out of his room. (*Pause.*) So why did you come?

Muratov I told you, the doctor was visiting and Shokhin galloped over on horseback . . .

Antipa Shokhin? He killed a man too.

Muratov So I drove here with the doctor hoping to be of use.

Antipa You?

Muratov Well, yes.

Antipa Where's Shokhin?

Muratov They sent him to town for dressings.

Antipa You've an explanation for everything.

Muratov There's nothing to explain.

Antipa Nothing at all. (*Grins.*) Tell me, my lord, you've no love for me, have you?

Muratov (*stops pacing for a second*) This is hardly the moment to discuss love.

Antipa (*slowly*) No? Excellent. In that case I'm not afraid to say I love no one. Only Sonya. I respect her very deeply.

(*Another pause.*) Saying you love someone's dangerous. The doctor, is he plastered?

Muratov   No more than usual.

Antipa   He won't hurt Mikhail, will he?

Muratov   Come, you know he's a fine doctor . . .

Antipa   Yes. And a good man too. Until you started drinking with him. You've harmed everyone around here, including Mikhail – you've a harmful character. Wait. (*Rises from his chair as* **Sofia** *hurries in with her sleeves rolled up.*)

Sofia   The wound's not serious, d'you hear, Antipa?

Antipa   Is it true? It's not serious?

Sofia   That's what I said.

Antipa (*sinks back into his chair*)   Thank you, Sonya . . .

Sofia (*murmurs to* **Muratov**)   Don't let him go anywhere.

Muratov (*nods and looks at* **Antipa**)   He's not exactly . . .

Sofia *crosses to her room.*

Antipa   What was she whispering about?

Sofia (*comes out of her room holding some towels*)   I said, he's not to let you go anywhere.

Antipa   Tell me then, not him.

Sofia *goes out.*

Muratov   So Misha will recover.

Antipa   Whereas I am mortally ill.

Muratov   It'll pass.

Antipa   When I'm dead. Don't try to comfort me, it won't help. (*Silence.* **Muratov** *frowns at him.*) You've studied, Vasilii Pavlovich, you know the law. Tell me why I'm a healthy man, hungry for work, too healthy perhaps, yet my son's a weakling and won't settle to anything – what law is that then?

Muratov (*grudgingly*)   Well, you know, it's like a pendulum – one generation works and the next is depleted, it's born exhausted . . .

Antipa   I don't get it.

Muratov   Possibly the father's exhaustion is passed on to his children in his juices.

Antipa   Depleted, generation, I don't know, words are – slippery . . .

Muratov   What's slippery about them?

Antipa   Some people work, others rust from lack of it, it's all wrong.

Muratov   Did you drink much when you were young?

Antipa   Me? No. My father drank. My wife drank, she came from a family of alcoholics. She wasn't happy with me, I was almost never at home – she always smelt of mint or tea leaves, she chewed them to cover the smell but it didn't fool me. The trouble with Mikhail is he's spoilt. He lived here with Sofia and she taught him to read books and write poems . . . (*Closes his eyes.*) He compared a pendulum to a bronze axe once, cutting the heads off the minutes. Funny, heads off minutes, like ants. Maybe it isn't funny . . . (*Seems to doze off.*)

Sofia *returns and gestures to* **Muratov** *from the door; he glances at* **Antipa** *and goes to her.*

Sofia   Misha wants to see him. I sent Pavla away but she might come back. She mustn't see Antipa now. Make sure she keeps away, understand?

Muratov   Of course. But why are you wasting yourself on these pointless dramas? It's appalling.

Sofia   Just go.

Muratov Think - is it right you should . . .

Sofia (*drily*) Are you going or not?

Muratov *bows and leaves;* **Sofia** *watches him in the mirror.*

Antipa (*raises his head*) What do you want from him?

Sofia Nothing.

Antipa Good. It's better to live as beggars than with people like him.

Sofia (*goes to him*) Listen . . .

Antipa Sonya, what's happened? Our father worked, I worked, I've made enough money for a thousand men, but what have I to show for it? Mikhail's a dead soul, you've no children . . .

Sofia It's no time to be talking of children.

Antipa Like the warden said, no time to discuss love.

Sofia He's a strange one to discuss love with, silly man! (*Rests her hand on his shoulder; he takes it and looks at her fingers.*)

Antipa A small hand but firm - ah, you should have been my wife . . .

Sofia (*pulls her hand away*) Misha wants to see you . . .

Antipa (*shudders and half rises in his chair*) Did he say it or did you make him?

Sofia He did.

Antipa Do you swear?

Sofia All right, I swear.

Antipa (*stands up*) I won't be able to look at him.

Sofia Let's go.

Antipa It's always hard to look at him. I don't understand, where did I go wrong? He's tired of life and I'm not. Is she there?

Sofia   No. You mustn't blame her for anything.

Antipa   I know, those types never get the blame, it's always people like us. I don't know her, Sonya, who is she?

Sofia   It's a bit late to ask now, she's just a young girl living in the dream of youth . . .

Antipa   I thought I'd find peace and happiness . . .

Sofia   Happiness doesn't come cheap.

Antipa   I didn't ask for much.

Sofia   It never seems much when you have it – let it go and you discover how precious it is . . . (*Hurriedly.*) I wasn't talking about you . . .

Antipa   I though there'd be children . . .

Sofia   That's new, did you just think of it?

Antipa   No, I'm always thinking of it, waiting . . . A wife without children, what joy is that?

Sofia *seems about to say something, then throws up her hands and turns her back to him.*

Antipa   What is it?

Sofia   Coming?

Antipa   Coming. Sonya, why are women always sick and wretched when they're with me? It's as if she loves me but won't open her heart to me, why?

Sofia   Stop moping!

Antipa   Me, mope? I used to be a good-looking man . . .

Sofia   But a rotten one for women.

Antipa   That's a lie!

Sofia   Think about it, you know I'm right.

Antipa (*looks at the clock on the wall*)   So what shall I say to Mikhail?

Sofia   You'll think of something.

Antipa   A pendulum is like an axe . . . I don't feel sorry for him, just ashamed of what I've become – and sorry I've destroyed myself for no reason . . .

Sofia *stands deep in thought.*

Antipa   Dammit, let's go . . .

Sofia (*decisively*)   I've changed my mind, you mustn't go.

Antipa   Why not?

Sofia   I'll say you're not well or having a nap.

Antipa   I might as well go.

Sofia (*sternly*)   I said no!

Antipa   Well, I . . . I'll leave it an hour, until my head's cleared. My thoughts are all over the place, Sonya, playing this terrible game with me . . .

Sofia   You talk too much! (*Hurries out.*)

Antipa (*walks around the room, goes to the desk, looks through some bills and mutters, then goes to the door*)   You don't understand everything either, my dear! (*Returns to the desk and picks up a document, throws it down, frowns, picks it up again and reads in a low growl.*)   Well I never. (*Chortles.*) Hey, Sonya, so that's it.

Shokhin *enters gingerly, holding a parcel; he sees his master and takes a step back.*

Antipa   Who is it?

Shokhin   Shokhin here with the dressings.

They eye each other in silence for a few seconds.

Antipa   So, Yakov, I killed a man.

Shokhin   It's happening all over the place, sir.

Antipa   My son too, eh.

Shokhin (*gloomily*)   It's too crowded, can't see who's who . . .

Antipa   So you're leaving us?

Shokhin   Not in anger.

Antipa   Let's leave together.

Shokhin   Where?

Antipa   Let me go with you. Have you anywhere in mind?

Shokhin   I haven't decided yet.

Antipa   Well, I'll go with you.

Shokhin   If you mean it, I'll wait. I take it you'll hand over the business to Sofia Ivanovna?

Antipa   Her? She'll sort everything out.

Shokhin   Yes, of course.

Antipa   We'll be pilgrims.

Shokhin   I'd make a bad pilgrim.

Antipa   Your father did his best to teach you.

Shokhin   So it seems. Where shall I put these?

Antipa   The dressings? Put them there.

Shokhin   I'm afraid . . .

Antipa   You usedn't to be afraid of anything.

Shokhin   That was before.

Antipa   It's hard living with people, Yakov.

Shokhin   We're not people any more, we're just judges and condemned.

Antipa   So it's settled? We're going?

Shokhin   If you want to, I've nothing to keep me here.

Stepka (*runs in*)   What are you doing, Horse? Give me that! (*Grabs the parcel, sees her master, gasps and runs off.*)

Antipa   See? They're all scared of me.

Shokhin   She's stupid, nice though.

Antipa   No point scaring the nice ones.

Shokhin (*goes out*)   Depends what with.

Antipa *stands on his own for a moment looking at* **Sofia**'s *portrait over the desk, then turns down the wick of the lamp and turns it up again.*

Pavla (*runs in*)   Sofia Ivanovna . . . (*Sees* **Antipa**, *steps back and bows her head.*)

Antipa (*goes to her slowly, places his palms on her forehead and pushes her head back, looking into her eyes*)   Well?

Pavla (*quietly*)   Beat me.

Antipa   You, gentle snake . . .

Pavla   Don't torture me, beat me. Quick, sir.

Antipa   Why should I? (*Raises his fist.*)

Pavla   I don't know . . . For being young, for making a mistake and thinking you were different, for not loving you . . . (*Covers her face with her hands.*)

Antipa (*grabs them and pulls them slowly apart; hoarsely*)   Go away, leave me! What have you done to me?

Pavla (*sinking to the floor*)   I've done nothing wrong . . .

Antipa (*lets go of her hands; as she falls he slowly raises his foot as though about to kick her, then squats on the floor lifting her head on his knees and stroking her hair, whispering*)   My child – don't be afraid. I won't touch you, little girl, wake up!

Sofia *and* **Muratov** *are audible behind the door.*

Muratov   What will happen to us . . . ?

Sofia   Stop talking nonsense . . . (*Comes in and throws herself at her brother.*)   What have you done?

Muratov (*backs off*)   God help us . . .

Sofia   Be quiet.

Muratov (*feels* **Pavla**'*s pulse*)   Fainted?

Antipa   I don't know.

Muratov   I'll call the doctor.

Sofia   Quick, he's in Tarakanov's cottage . . .

Pavla (*comes to, looks around; to* **Antipa**)   Go away. Sonya, take me away . . .

Antipa   Fine. (*Walks away from* **Pavla**, *goes to the door leading to the verandah and stands with his back to everyone in the shadows.*)

Sofia   What happened?

Pavla   He was going to beat me. (*Stands up and clings to* **Sofia**.) Antipa Ivanovich, you know I tried to love you . . .

Antipa   Don't say it.

Pavla   I wanted you to be kinder.

Antipa   Yes . . .

Pavla   But you've no kindness for anyone, you've no compassion. Why don't you love your son? Why are you jealous of him, why do you try to drive him away? Is it his fault he's weak and unhappy?

Antipa   Is it my fault I'm healthy? Is it my fault I don't pity hopeless people? I love business, I love work. On whose bones is this life built, whose sweat and blood water the earth? People like you have nothing to do with it. Can he take everything I've laboured for on his shoulders?

Sofia   That's enough . . .

Antipa   From my work and my father's, hundreds of people have lived and made their way in the world, and what does he do? I committed a sin, but didn't I run the business? You good people say every business is a sin against someone – it's not true! My father used to say wipe out poverty and you'll get rid of sin, and he was right.

Pavla People everywhere say bad things about you.

Antipa So what, let them, they're jealous because I've got money. Everyone should have money, everyone should be strong, no one should have to bow and scrape and envy each other. If people work they live independently without envy, and they're happy – if they don't, they sink into their own iniquity. That's what Sonya says.

Sofia *looks intently at him.*

Pavla And Misha?

Antipa (*more quietly*) Maybe I've wronged you. I saw you, I liked you, I wanted to be happy with you – didn't I deserve that?

Pavla Lord, why can't people live in peace together and love each other? We must live differently.

Sofia *moves distractedly from her.*

Antipa (*sulkily*) Go on then, live differently . . .

Pavla We must, my dears, we can't go on living like this, without love or compassion. My dear people, are we really enemies to each other? (*Silence.*) My God, there's justice somewhere, something bigger than this.

Antipa It's not ready for you yet . . .

Pavla But we must think about it and search for it . . .

Sofia (*quietly*) You don't just think about it, you work at it. You must work, Pasha, not search. You only find what you've lost . . .

Antipa (*gloomily*) Except when it's peace of mind.

Sofia Peace of mind isn't justice.

Pavla (*wails*)   I don't understand, I don't understand . . .

Tselovaneva *leads in* **Mikhail**. *He walks quite steadily, holding her shoulder with one hand, extending the other to* **Antipa** *in a conciliatory gesture.*

Sofia (*anxiously clutches his arm*)   What are you thinking of? Who said you could get up?

Tselovaneva   He begged me . . .

Pavla   Mother, what are you doing!

Tselovaneva   Take me downstairs, he said, I want to see my father.

Mikhail (*smiles*)   It's all right, Auntie Sonya.

Tselovaneva   He won't come to me, he said, I'll have to go to him . . .

Pavla   I don't understand . . .

Tselovaneva   You understood a lot. That's right, shout at your mother.

Mikhail   Wait, don't, it's my fault . . .

Sofia *helps him to the armchair.*

Antipa (*peers at his son like a bull about to charge; in a muffled voice*)   You shouldn't have . . . I was going to come to you but we were talking . . .

Mikhail   Listen, Father . . .

Sofia   It's bad for you to talk.

Mikhail   It's worse to say nothing.

Antipa   Did you hurt yourself badly?

Mikhail   Forgive me, Father . . .

Antipa   Stop, my friend, that's enough. God knows who's to blame.

Mikhail   I know . . .

Pavla   Who then, who?

Tselovaneva   Who else but poor defenceless people like us who've no one to stand up for us?

Sofia   Really, Anna Markovna, if you don't mind . . .

Tselovaneva   No, my dear, you won't touch me.

Antipa   Troublemaker. Meddling, jumped-up interloper! In Christ's name be quiet, or I'll . . .

Sofia   Antipa, stop it!

Antipa (*gasping*)   Pest, mildew, rust!

Mikhail   Take it easy, Father, it's not a tragedy, it's a farce . . .

Antipa   A farce you say! It's bad, Mikhail, it's all wrong.

Mikhail   Careful, Father, you'll injure yourself!

Muratov *appears at the door and makes signs at* **Sofia**; *she goes to him and they confer urgently.*

Sofia   The doctor? Hevern? Really?

Muratov   Yes. Said it was complete nonsense and people were living off the fat of the land with nothing to do but gossip all day, then he went off.

Sofia   But we need him here. Please send Shokhin after him on horseback.

Muratov *wrinkles his nose and leaves.*

Antipa (*to his son*)   What are you laughing about?

Mikhail   I want to say something kind to you, Father, from my heart . . .

Antipa (*embarrassed*)   Now then, better not, you must rest . . .

Mikhail   There, I understand you. Sometimes I even admired you quietly from a distance, and if you admire someone it means you love them . . .

Antipa (*incredulous*)   Listen, Sonya, hear what he said?

Pavla (*to* **Sofia**)   He shouldn't speak!

Sofia *stops her with a gesture.*

Mikhail   You're like an axe in the hand of God, in some mighty creative hand. And Aunt Sonya too. She's sharper than you are. People like me are just rust and mildew . . . I've thought a lot about it, Father, and I know now that there are no useless people, only dangerous people. You mustn't punish yourself . . .

Antipa (*touched, stands up and kisses him on the forehead; straightens up*)   Thanks, my friend, I feel better now, God bless you. A father, my friend Mikhail, isn't just a lump of meat, he's a human being with a soul, and is capable of love. Love is a beautiful thing, you must love . . .

Pavla (*weeps quietly*)   Lord, I don't understand.

Antipa (*exultantly to her*)   You see? (*Turning to* **Mikhail**.) Ah, how I know you, son. Even before you could speak I was worrying about you and thinking of you – he'll be a man like me, I thought. He'll take all my sins and my labours, and when I die there'll be someone to carry them on . . .

Mikhail (*deeply moved*)   But how can I? I'm not . . . Aunt Sonya . . . (*Slumps unconscious.*)

Sofia *hurries to him.* **Pavla** *jumps back terrified.* **Antipa** *drops to his knees.* **Tselovaneva** *hovers around her daughter.* **Muratov** *stands in the door.*

Pavla (*in a loud whisper*)   He's dead!

Sofia   Stop it!

Tselovaneva   They've done for him!

Antipa   What's wrong with him, Sofia? Where's the doctor?

Sofia   He left, get him some water.

Pavla (*rushes around*)   We should have gone to him! Cruel people.

Muratov (*quietly*)   Stop making that racket!

Pavla (*angrily*)   What are you doing here? I don't like you.

Muratov (*bows*)   It's of very little importance to me.

Mikhail (*opens his eyes*)   Put me to bed.

Sofia (*to **Muratov** and her brother*)   Take him!

Mikhail   It's all right, I can . . .

*His father and **Muratov** help him up.*

Mikhail (*wryly*)   See how they honour me!

Pavla (*to **Sofia***)   What am I to do? Tell me.

Sofia   Wait, Misha needs me.

Pavla   I think I'll die here too. Tell me what to do, where must I go?

Sofia   Work it out yourself, you're no wife to Antipa and no mother to Mikhail.

Tselovaneva   I told you we shouldn't have sold our little house.

Pavla   Not that again, Mother!

Tselovaneva   But where will you hide?

Sofia   You talk a lot about love, Pavla, but it seems to me you don't know the first thing about it. When you're in love, everything's straightforward – where to go, what to do, you don't have to ask anyone.

Tselovaneva   That's right, go wild, break the rules – fine advice they give you here.

Sofia   On a sunny day you don't ask why it's bright. The sun hasn't risen in your soul yet . . .

Tselovaneva   Rubbish! Don't listen to her, Pavla.

Sofia   You've done your daughter a lot of harm, Anna Markovna.

Tselovaneva   No I haven't, I'm her mother! Pardon me, dear, I was only . . .

Sofia (*leaves the room*)   It's no use talking to you, forgive me, I shouldn't have said it . . .

Tselovaneva   Fine, go on, run off to your lover!

Pavla   It's not true. She hasn't got a lover.

Tselovaneva (*calmly*)   She will, she will . . .

Pavla (*walks round the room*)   The sun hasn't risen . . .

Tselovaneva   Don't listen to her! What's the sun got to do with it? You should think how you're going to live, quietly and with pleasure . . . Everyone wants some pleasure in their life. You must leave that robber, and the lady's no friend for you, she's of the same stock. We're quiet country folk, you've got your own money, twenty-five thousand and we can find more. You can live as you like on that – your own rouble is more precious than a brother. I'm a prisoner in this house too – I'm forty-three, it's no life for me. What am I doing here?

Pavla   What's that got to do with it? Why did I ever leave the convent?

Tselovaneva   With your capital you could live like a lady in the convent and I'll go too. You've no better friend than your mother, she understands everything, covers up for you . . .

Pavla (*looks out of the window*)   Someone's coming . . .

Tselovaneva   We'd better go, the police will be here soon.

Pavla   The police? Why?

Tselovaneva   Why do you think? I sent for them.

Enter **Muratov**.

Pavla   How is he?

Muratov   Very tired, he's asleep.

Pavla   He won't die?

Muratov   In time he'll die, naturally.

Pavla   But when? Soon?

Muratov   I don't know exactly when.

Tselovaneva   You shouldn't make fun of our simple ways, sir.

Pavla   That's enough, Mama. So he's not in danger?

Muratov   It was a small revolver and a small bullet – grazed his rib and out the other side, nothing to worry about.

Pavla   Thank God, thank God. Vasilii Pavlovich, I think I was rather rude to you just now.

Muratov   Don't distress yourself, I know your Christian feelings . . .

Pavla   I don't remember what I said.

Muratov   It was nothing, I assure you.

Tselovaneva   Look at you, Pasha, you're a mess.

Pavla *(glances in the mirror)*   Heavens. Why didn't you tell me?

Tselovaneva   There was no time.

Pavla   Excuse me, I must go.

Muratov   By all means.

Pavla   Will Misha be up soon?

Muratov   I don't know. The doctor says his organism has been weakened by drink and loose living.

Pavla   How can you . . .

Tselovaneva   Run along, it's no business of yours . . .

Muratov *sits in the armchair by the desk, clutching his head like a man in pain.* **Sofia** *returns and stands beside him, her face tired and severe. He raises his head and straightens up.*

Sofia   You're tired?

Muratov   And you?

Sofia   A little.

Muratov   You should rest. I'll go in a minute, but before that may I be allowed to ask you one question?

Sofia (*not immediately*)   Well, what is it?

Muratov   I am applying to be transferred to the Vladykin forestry area – you know, where the warden shot himself.

Sofia   Yes, I know.

Muratov   Should I stay here, on the other hand, might I count . . . ?

Sofia (*strikes the desk*)   Absolutely not!

Muratov   Allow me to finish my sentence, please! I wanted to ask if I could count on your attitude to me changing?

Sofia   I understood the question.

Muratov (*stands up, smiles*)   Shokhin killed a man, but you treat him more kindly than you treat me.

Sofia (*after a moment*)   You're probably right. What is Shokhin? He's an honest animal. He thought it was his duty to kill someone who stole his master's property, then he understood what he'd done and will never forgive himself as long as he lives, and it's changed the way he sees people.

Muratov You're wrong, as usual . . .

Sofia In your forestry area, people like Shokhin have killed and injured dozens of people in the last seven years.

Muratov Not that many . . .

Sofia How many men have been jailed and families destroyed for a bundle of firewood? Have you counted them?

Muratov No, of course not! What are these statistics to you, madam? This is pure romanticism! How would you wish us to deal with thieves?

Sofia I don't know, but not like that. They don't steal from us anyway.

Muratov I see. So it's not a fact, just an illusion, as our dear doctor would say – another romantic . . .

Sofia We must stop arguing like this, it happens every time we meet . . .

Muratov You're wasting your breath with me.

Sofia (*stands up*) Listen, Vasilii Pavlovich, it's not easy for me to say this, but yes, I do think you're worse than Shokhin, worse than the drunkest peasant – you can turn a peasant into a person, but there's no hope for you.

Muratov You're a businesswoman, Sofia, romanticism doesn't suit you.

Sofia It's hard for me to see you as you are now, an educated, intelligent man with no love for people and no desire to work – it repels me. I've seen how you've deteriorated, how you lost your way and corrupted people.

Muratov A few minutes ago, Anna Markovna very wisely said that everyone needed a little pleasure in their life. What do all these people you say I've corrupted matter? I'll crush them, along with your nephew, or they'll crush each other, what's the difference?

Sofia   It's easy to be Mephistopheles in a country town, you should try being an honest man for a change.

Muratov   That's not bad. What is an honourable man then?

Sofia   I've nothing more to say to you.

Muratov   You mean you don't know -- you're terribly alone, alone and powerless!

Sofia   It isn't true, I know there are people who see life as I do. You needn't invent it, you just take what's around you into your heart. There's something bright in my heart, so it must be bright outside too. I've faith in people, and in a better life. I don't have much education, there's a lot I don't understand, but I feel life's a blessing and people are good. And you just tell lies about them and yourself . . .

Muratov   I speak the truth.

Sofia   It's a wicked, rotten truth then, the truth of lazy, vain people who are on their last legs.

Muratov   Until now that truth was considered immortal.

Sofia   But a new one will live and grow! There's another Russia, not the one you speak for. You and I have nothing in common, I'm no partner for you – we've finished, don't you think?

Muratov (*takes his hat from the mantelpiece*)   Pardon, I fear you'll break your neck on the way to this new truth of yours. Put these fantasies behind you and accept my hand – the hand of an interesting man!

Sofia *stares at him in silence.*

Muratov (*goes to the door*)   We'll go to Europe – Paris is a lot more amusing than Myamlin, I assure you. You're young and beautiful, they appreciate beautiful women in Europe. Think about it, so many pleasures await you. I'm not jealous, your escapades will amuse me, we'll burn the candle at both ends. How about it?

Sofia (*shudders with distaste; quietly*)   Go . . .

Muratov   You insult me . . .

Antipa (*behind him in the door*)   Hey, you, get out of my way!

Muratov   I will, sir, farewell.

Antipa   And farewell to you too! (*To his sister.*) Mikhail woke up, we had a good chat . . . (*Stares at her with his back to the door.*) What's that devil up to now? Why are you so nice to him?

Sofia   A long time ago – about six years ago, I liked the man.

Antipa   You were young. Do you want me to go?

Sofia   Wait, do as you like.

Antipa (*pause*)   Perhaps Mikhail won't drink so much now, what do you think?

Sofia   Sorry?

Antipa   All right, think your thoughts, I'm going.

Sofia   What did you say?

Antipa   That Misha might stop drinking now . . .

Sofia   I doubt it, hardly. Don't bother him, leave him to me.

Antipa   I'm prepared to leave everything to you. How about . . . her?

Sofia   You must let her go.

Antipa (*quietly*)   Where can she go?

Sofia   Wherever she wants.

Antipa *sits down in silence.*

Sofia (*goes to him*)   What's on your mind?

Antipa (*gloomily*)   We Zykovs don't divorce our wives.

Sofia   What sort of wife was she to you? You'd only have tortured yourself with her.

Antipa   It's no good, it's better if I go myself. I'll leave everything to you and follow my nose, there's nothing for me here. Ah, you should have had children.

Sofia (*turns away; brusquely*)   Who married me off to a dying man?

Antipa   All right, so I did! But you're rich now, the most powerful woman in the district, more powerful than all those hot-shot landowners' wives. And children don't always come from husbands . . .

Sofia   Your kindness comes too late!

Antipa   Sonya, Sonya . . .

Sofia   Don't Sonya me. You're not going anywhere, it's ridiculous!

Antipa (*thoughtfully*)   I feel ashamed of myself, it's all wrong. I'm not afraid of sin, but I don't like sadness and it's overwhelming me – I can't live with her, I can't work . . .

Sofia   It's hard for me too and my sadness is more bitter, but I – don't hide it. If you knew how it breaks your heart to lose respect for a person, if you knew how I searched for good people and believed I'd find them. Well, I didn't, but I'll go on searching, yes . . .

Antipa   We're both unhappy, Sonya, we're surrounded by enemies.

Sofia   If only they were clever. At least a clever enemy is a good teacher.

Antipa   What do they teach you?

Sofia   Resistance. My husband was my enemy but I respected him, he taught me a lot. (*Goes to her brother and puts her hand on his head.*) Come, we're on our own now, we'll live alone together. Maybe good people will come along and teach us. What do you think, are there any good people?

Antipa (*thoughtfully*)   You won't find goodness if you're not good yourself, isn't that what you say?

Sofia   So show me you're good. Pull yourself together. When did you give in to grief? You mustn't give in, you mustn't.

Antipa (*stands up, throws back his shoulders, looks at her and smiles*)   Everything's simple for you, isn't it, sister? Where do you get it from? God bless you, my one and only Sonya. Thank you.

They embrace; **Antipa** *brushes away the tears.*

We'll live another day, we'll quarrel. Now I've work to do, I'll make the earth shake!

Sofia   That's more like it. Go now, I want to be alone. Go, dear, we're friends, I'm glad.

Antipa   Don't say anything or I'll sob.

Shokhin (*appears in the door*)   The police chief is here with the witnesses.

Antipa (*angrily*)   The police? Who called them?

Shokhin   Anna Markovna sent your Vasilii for them.

Antipa   That woman, I'll . . .

Sofia   No you won't, keep out of it, I'll sort her out. Stay where you are.

Antipa (*incandescent with rage*)   I'll – I'll throw her out of the window, along with her daughter!

Shokhin *smiles broadly.*

Sofia   Don't let him go, Shokhin, you hear? Just sit here quietly together. (*Leaves the room.*)

Antipa (*rushes around*)   She called the police. What did she do that for? Why are you pulling faces?

Shokhin   Nothing.

Antipa   Nothing? You think I'm going with you now? No, others can run off, I'm staying where I belong. Setting the police on us . . . (*Stops before* **Shokhin**.) There's nowhere for you to go, forget it. You committed a crime against people and now you must pay for it!

Shokhin   I'll stay then, it probably wasn't the right time . . .

Antipa   It's criminal to waver. Look at our mistress, Sofia Ivanovna, and she's a woman.

Pavla (*runs in*)   Antipa Ivanovich, someone's come.

Antipa (*stops her with a gesture*)   I know, it's the police, your mother called them. Go, you've nothing to fear, God be with you . . .

Pavla (*fearfully*)   Where to?

Antipa (*turns his back on her*)   Wherever you like, I've work to do. Goodbye.

Pavla   Tell me where, though?

Antipa   Your mother will show you. Goodbye.

Pavla *slowly leaves the room.* **Shokhin** *moves out of her way.* **Antipa** *goes towards the door to the verandah with bowed head; he stops there and leans his forehead against the window.* **Shokhin** *breathes heavily.*

Egor Bulychev

Characters

Egor Vasilevich Bulychev (*Egorii*), *a wealthy businessman*
Aksinia (*Ksenia*), *his wife*
Varvara (*Varya*), *twenty, his daughter with Ksenia*
Shura (*Alexandra, Shurka, Shuryonok*), *eighteen, his illegitimate daughter, also living in the house*
Andrei Zvontsov (*Andryusha*), *Varvara's husband*
Glafira (*Glasha, Glakha*), *chambermaid*
Stepan Tyatin (*Stepasha, Stepochka*), *Zvontsov's cousin*
Mokei Bashkin, *Bulychev's business manager*
Vasili Dostigaev, *a rich merchant*
Elizaveta (*Liza*), *early twenties, his second wife*
Antonina Dostigaev (*Tonya, Tonka*),   ⎫   *the children of*
  eighteen   ⎬   *Dostigaev's first*
Alexei Dostigaev (*Alyosha*), *sixteen*   ⎭   *marriage*
Father Pavlin, *a priest*
Mother Melania (*Malasha*), *Ksenia's sister, Mother Superior at the convent*
Taisya, *Melania's orderly*
Yakov Laptev (*Yasha*), *Bulychev's godson, a revolutionary*
Donat, *forest warden*
Mokrousov, *a policeman*
Zobunova, *village wisewoman and healer*
Propotei, *a holy fool*
Doctor Nifont Grigorevich
Trumpeter

Act One

The dining room in **Bulychev***'s house. Dark bulky furniture. A wide leather sofa. Beside it stairs lead to the upper floor. On the right is an alcove and glass doors to the garden. A bright winter's day.* **Ksenia** *sits at the table washing tea things in a bowl.* **Glafira** *stands in the alcove arranging flowers. Enter* **Shura** *in dressing gown and slippers; her hair is tousled and red, like her father's.*

Ksenia   Really, Shura, have you only just got up?

Shura   Don't shriek, it doesn't help. Glasha, give me coffee! Where's the newspaper?

Glafira   I took it upstairs to Varvara Egorovna.

Shura   Bring it down! It's for the whole house, the devils!

Ksenia   Who are?

Shura   Is Papa in?

Ksenia   He's visiting the wounded soldiers -- you mean the Zvontsovs?

Shura   That's right. (*Goes to the telephone.*) One seven six three . . .

Ksenia   I shall tell them what you think of them!

Shura   Do that. Antonina, please!

Ksenia   See how she talks to me!

Shura   That you, Tonia? Let's go skiing . . . Why not? The show? Forget it. You phony widow . . . (*Replaces the receiver.*)

Ksenia   Why do you call that girl a widow?

Shura   Her fiancé died, didn't he?

Ksenia   She's still a virgin though.

Shura (*guffaws*)   That's what you think!

Ksenia   Ugh, you're disgusting!

Glafira (*hands her coffee*)   Varvara Egorovna will be down in a minute with the paper.

Ksenia   You know too much, Shura, the less you know the better you sleep – I knew nothing at your age.

Shura   So what's changed?

Varvara *sails into the room.*

Shura   My big sister's looking very swanky today. *Bonjour, madame, comment ça va?*

Ksenia   Tell her off, Varya. She's being frightful.

Varvara   It's eleven o'clock in the morning and you still haven't dressed or done your hair.

Shura (*sits down*)   Will this take long?

Varvara   You're becoming more and more impertinent, you care nothing for Father and the fact that he's ill, you exploit the fact that you're his favourite . . .

Ksenia   What does she care about her father's health? Wait till I tell him about your behaviour.

Shura   Thanks for the warning. Are you through?

Varvara   Why, you –

Shura   Not me, I'm not the fool! You're wasting your breath, Varvara Egorovna.

Varvara   Red-haired fool!

Ksenia   You show her, Varya!

Shura   And your character's going from bad to worse.

Varvara   We'll see about that, my dear. We must go to the kitchen, Mummy, cook's throwing a fit.

Ksenia   He's in a bad mood, someone murdered his son the other day.

Varvara   Well, it's no excuse, lots of people are murdered these days . . .

They exit.

Shura (*mutters*)   She'd throw a fit if they bumped off her precious Andryusha.

Glafira   You shouldn't tease them. Drink your coffee, I have to clear up. (*Goes out with the samovar.*)

Shura *leans back in her chair, closes her eyes and puts her hands behind her head.*

Zvontsov (*creeps down the stairs in bedroom slippers and grabs her from behind*)   What are you dreaming of, carrot-head?

Shura (*without moving or opening her eyes*)   Don't touch me.

Zvontsov (*murmurs*)   Why not? Don't you like it? You do, don't you? Tell me you like it.

Shura   No.

Zvontsov   Why?

Shura (*pushes him away*)   Get off me. You don't like me at all, you're just pretending.

Zvontsov   You want me to like you?

Varvara *appears at the top of the stairs.*

Shura   What if Varvara finds out?

Zvontsov   Sh . . . sh! (*Moves away. In a lecturing tone:*) Really, Alexandra Egorovna, you must take yourself in hand, get on with your studies . . .

Varvara   She prefers running around with Antonina blowing bubbles and making mischief, don't you, Shura?

Shura   I like blowing bubbles. What's wrong? Do you mind the soap?

Varvara   I mind you. How will you live? Now they're throwing you out of the Gymnasium . . .

Shura   Fat chance.

Varvara   And your friend's none too bright either.

Zvontsov   She wants to study music.

Varvara   Who, Shura?

Shura   No I don't.

Varvara   Where did you get that from, Andrei?

Zvontsov   I could have sworn she –

Shura (*leaving the room*)   I said nothing of the sort!

Zvontsov   Hm, strange. You're much too hard on her, Varya.

Varvara   And you're much too nice.

Zvontsov   What do you mean? You know my plan –

Varvara   The plan's one thing, but I'd say you're suspiciously nice to her.

Zvontsov   Your head's full of nonsense. Are jealous scenes necessary at such a time?

Varvara   Nonsense is it? So why did you come down?

Zvontsov   There's an advertisement in the paper and the forester's arrived. The peasants have trapped a bear . . .

Varvara   Donat's in the kitchen. What advertisement?

Zvontsov   This is intolerable, questioning me like a ten-year-old!

Varvara   Keep your temper. Father's back and you're still in your slippers.

Zvontsov hurries upstairs. **Bulychev** *walks in followed by* **Father Pavlin** *in a mauve cassock.* **Varvara** *greets them on her way out.* **Shura** *runs in wearing a padded green jacket and matching cap and heads for the telephone.* **Bulychev** *puts out an arm and pulls her to him.*

Bulychev (*sits at the table with his arm round her waist. She strokes his greying auburn hair*)   They came straight from the front. Some were so bad I couldn't look at them . . . Stop fidgeting, Shurochka!

Pavlin   Are you prospering, Shura?

Shura   I'd have shaken you hand but Papa grabbed me like a bear.

Bulychev   What use are they now? We had our share of useless men before this war.

Pavlin (*sighs*)   It's not for us to reason why . . .

Bulychev   We messed it up with the Japanese too – we're the laughing stock of the world!

Pavlin   Notwithstanding the carnage of war, it may enrich us with a wealth of experience . . .

Bulychev   Yes, yes, people die, others make a fortune.

Pavlin   And since nothing in this world is accomplished without the higher powers and God's will, what does our grumbling signify?

Bulychev   Stop preaching, Pavlin. Off skiing, Shura?

Shura   I'm waiting for Antonina.

Bulychev   Very well, if you're not gone in five minutes I'll call you.

Shura *runs out.*

Pavlin   The maiden has developed.

Bulychev   Her body's all right, very supple; pity about her face – her mother wasn't pretty. Clever, but ugly as sin.

Pavlin   Alexandra Egorovna's face is most unusual and not without its attractions. Would I be right in thinking her mother is not from these parts?

Bulychev   She's Siberian. You talk about God's will and the higher powers -- what about our new government, the Duma? Who made that?

Pavlin   Many believe that the Duma is a fatal error, and that it has taken those powers on itself to its own detriment, as it were. But it ill befits a servant of the Church to go into such matters, especially at a time when the priesthood is charged with the duty of inspiring a spirit of cheerfulness and love of throne and country . . .

Bulychev   Inspiring us into the shit, you mean . . .

Pavlin   As you know, I have persuaded our churchwarden to enlarge the choir. I met the other day with General Bettling, and requested a donation for the belfry in the new church that is being built in the name of your heavenly namesake and protector, Saint Egor . . .

Bulychev   Did he give it to you?

Pavlin   He refused, and even made an unpleasant joke about it. 'I don't like brass, even in military bands!' he said. Might your indisposition perhaps persuade you to give money for the belfry?

Bulychev (*stands up*)   You don't cure people by ringing church bells!

Pavlin   Who's to say? The causes of illness are a mystery to science. I've heard that in some foreign sanatoria they treat people with music. We have a retired fireman living in the town who plays some sort of horn . . .

Bulychev   What's it like?

Pavlin   A brass one, they say it's very big.

Bulychev (*smirks*)   Big is it? Does it make people better?

Pavlin   Quite a few, apparently. All things are possible, dear Egor Vasilevich. We live in a world of mysteries, in the darkness of innumerable indecipherable secrets. It seems to us there is light, and that it comes from our reason, but it is only for the physical eye and the spirit is shadowed by reason and is extinguished by it.

Bulychev (*sighs*)   What a lot of words you have!

Pavlin (*grows more inspired*)   Take the blessed healer Propotei – in what a state of joy that man lives, whom the ignorant call a fool!

Bulychev   There, you're preaching again! Goodbye, Pavlin, I'm tired.

Pavlin   I sincerely wish you good health. I shall mention you in my prayers . . . (*Goes out.*)

Bulychev (*clutches his right side, goes to the sofa, groans*)   Fat pig, stuffing his face with the blood of Christ. Hey, Glafira!

Varvara (*enters in evening gown and lorgnette*)   Yes, what is it?

Bulychev   Nothing, I wanted Glafira. What are you dolled up like that for?

Varvara   I'm going to a benefit concert for the invalids.

Bulychev   With those bits of glass on your nose? Your eyes don't need them, is that the fashion now?

Varvara   Papa, you must talk to Alexandra, she's being insufferable!

Bulychev   You're good, all of you, now go! (*Mutters.*) They're all insufferable, I'll survive the lot of them and throw them out on the street.

Glafira   You called?

Bulychev   Yes I did. Eh, Glasha, you're pretty, plump and pink, not like my Varvara, the trout.

Glafira (*peers at the staircase*)   Just as well, if she was pretty you'd be dragging her into your bed too.

Bulychev   My own daughter? What are you saying, little fool.

Glafira   You know what I'm talking about. You paw Shura like she's your girlfriend – like a soldier!

Bulychev (*startled*)   A soldier indeed! Are you mad? How dare you accuse her of that, are you jealous? So tell me, have you been in a soldier's arms? Well, have you?

Glafira   Don't change the subject. You called me?

Bulychev   Tell Donat I want to see him. Wait, give me your hand. Do you still love me even though I'm sick?

Glafira (*throws herself in his arms*)   My darling, you give me such grief. You mustn't be sick, you mustn't! (*Tears herself from him and runs off.*)

Bulychev *smiles gloomily and licks his lips; shakes his head and lies down on the sofa.*

Donat *enters.*

Donat   I wish you good health, Egor Vasilevich!

Bulychev   Thank you. What's the news?

Donat   Good news, we've surrounded the bear.

Bulychev (*sighs*)   Well, it gives me no joy, my hunting days are over now. Are they cutting wood?

Donat   A little, there aren't enough men.

Ksenia *enters, dressed very smartly with her fingers covered in rings.*

Bulychev   What do you want?

Ksenia   Dear God, you mustn't think about bears now, Egor, you're far too ill!

Bulychev   Be quiet. Not enough men you say?

Donat   There are only old men and boys. They gave the Prince fifty prisoners of war, but they can't work in the forest.

Bulychev   So they're working on the women instead?

Donat   That's right, the women are hungry.

Ksenia   I hear our villages are becoming hotbeds of debauchery.

Donat   What do you mean debauchery, Aksinia Yakovlevna? They've slaughtered all the men — someone must give them children, and it turns out the ones who did the slaughtering are doing it!

Bulychev   I suppose so.

Ksenia   But what sort of children will prisoners produce? Though if the man's healthy, of course —

Bulychev   — And the woman's a fool. You wouldn't want them with one like that.

Ksenia   Our women aren't fools, but the only healthy men now are lawyers like your son-in-law . . .

Bulychev   Men are wounded, dying . . .

Ksenia   All the more for those that are left then!

Bulychev   She's got it all worked out, hasn't she?

Donat   The Tsar can't get enough people to eat.

Bulychev   What do you mean?

Donat   I mean we can't feed our people but we still want to fight foreigners. What are we fighting for? We'll be destroyed for our greed.

Bulychev   You speak the truth, Donat. My godson Laptev says that, he says greed is the root of our problems.

Donat   He's right, that godson of yours, he's clever.

Ksenia   Clever? He's insolent, not clever.

Donat   He's insolent because he's clever, Aksinia Yakovlevna. He rounded up half a dozen deserters and found them all jobs – they're good workers and it keeps them out of trouble.

Bulychev   There'll be trouble if the police find out.

Donat   Mokrousov knows already, and he doesn't mind because it means less work for him.

Zvontsov *comes down the stairs.*

Donat   So about the bear . . .

Bulychev   The bear is yours to enjoy.

Zvontsov   Allow me to present the bear to General Bettling, Egor Vasilevich. You know what he can do for us.

Bulychev   I do, I do. Give it to Bettling, or the Bishop.

Ksenia (*giggles*)   Imagine the Bishop shooting a bear!

Bulychev   I'm tired, Donat, goodbye. Everything's gone wrong, hasn't it, my friend? Ever since I fell ill.

Donat *bows silently and leaves the room, followed by* **Ksenia**.

Bulychev   Send Shura in, Aksinia. What's on your mind, Andrei? Spit it out.

Zvontsov   It's about Laptev . . .

Bulychev   Well?

Zvontsov   It has come to my attention that he's been associating with undesirable people and making anti-government speeches to the peasants at the Koposov fair.

Bulychev   What peasants? We don't have any fairs these days. Why are you always complaining about Yakov?

Zvontsov   He's virtually a member of our family . . .

Shura *runs in with her skis and sits down.*

Bulychev   Virtually? You've never considered him one of us, have you? He's even stopped coming to dinner on Sundays. Leave me, Andrei, we'll talk later . . .

Zvontsov *exits.*

Shura   Was he squealing on Yakov?

Bulychev Mind your own business. Now sit down and listen to me, everyone's squealing about you too.

Shura Who's everyone?

Bulychev Aksinia, Varvara.

Shura That's not everyone.

Bulychev I'm serious, my darling.

Shura You don't talk to me like that when you're being serious.

Bulychev You're far too free and easy with people, you lounge around the house all day, you run around –

Shura How can I if I'm lounging around all day?

Bulychev You don't listen to anyone.

Shura I listen to everyone – I'm sick of them, redhead.

Bulychev Oy, redhead yourself. You shouldn't talk to me like that. I should punish you but I don't feel like it.

Shura Don't then.

Bulychev Life's not a holiday, Shura, you can't live like this.

Shura Why not? What's stopping me?

Bulychev Everything, everyone – you wouldn't understand.

Shura Explain it to me, then I'll understand and they won't be able to stop me . . .

Ksenia *enters.*

Bulychev What's the matter, Ksenia? Lost something?

Ksenia The doctor's come, he's in the hall with Bashkin. Pull your skirt down, Alexandra, what way is that to sit?

Bulychev (*heaves himself off the sofa*)   Call the doctor then, lying down hurts, it's like this weight on me . . . Off you go, young lady, don't break a leg.

Shura *exits with her skis.*

Doctor (*entering*)   Good morning to you! How are we feeling today?

Bulychev   Not so well. I don't think much of your treatment, Nifont Grigorevich.

Doctor   Shall we go to your room?

Bulychev (*walks beside him*)   Give me the foulest-tasting, most expensive medicine you can find, my friend, it's bound to make me better. If you cure me I'll build you a hospital and put you in charge and you can do whatever you like there . . .

They exit. **Bashkin** *enters.*

Ksenia   What does the doctor say?

Bashkin   He says the cancer's spread to the liver.

Ksenia   No, what next?

Bashkin   He says it's serious.

Ksenia   He would, that's what he's paid for. Everyone thinks their job is the most important in the world.

Bashkin   It's a fine time to be ill. Money's falling around as if out of an old pocket, beggars become millionaires, and your husband –

Ksenia   Yes, yes, people are getting rich.

Bashkin   Dostigaev's so fat he can hardly button his clothes and talks only of his millions, but your Egor Vasilevich walks around in a fog. The other day he said, 'My business has bypassed the real business.' What did he mean?

Ksenia   I know, he's been saying the oddest things.

Bashkin   And to think it was your and your sister's capital that got him started – he should be increasing it.

Ksenia   I made a mistake, Mokei, I've known for a long time that I made a mistake. I married Daddy's assistant but it was the wrong one – I'd have been happy if I'd married you. Lord, the trouble he's given me! He had his daughter by that woman and inflicted her on me, and he found the worst possible son-in-law for our Varvara. I'm afraid those two are planning to swindle me and turn me out without a penny . . .

Bashkin   Everything's possible, it's the war – there's no shame or pity in war.

Ksenia   You've been with our family the longest, Mokei Petrovich, Daddy set you up in business and put you on your feet – you must tell me what to do . . .

Zvontsov *enters.*

Zvontsov   Is the doctor still here?

Ksenia   He's next door with Egor Vasilevich.

Zvontsov   Any news about the cloth, Mokei Petrovich?

Bashkin   Bettling won't take it.

Zvontsov   How much more must we give him?

Bashkin   Five thousand, minimum.

Ksenia   Outrageous. He's an old man.

Zvontsov   Through Jeanne?

Bashkin   As arranged.

Ksenia   Five thousand more, just for that?

Zvontsov   Money's cheap these days.

Ksenia   In another man's pocket.

Zvontsov   Is my father-in-law agreeable?

Bashkin   That's what I came to find out.

Doctor (*comes out of* **Bulychev**'s *room, takes* **Zvontsov** *aside*) One moment please . . .

Ksenia   Oh, happy news, I hope?

Doctor (*frowns*)   The patient must lie down as much as possible – business, any kind of excitement or irritation are exceedingly dangerous for him. Rest, rest and more rest . . . (*Whispers something to* **Zvontsov**.)

Ksenia   Why don't you tell me? I'm his wife.

Doctor   Some things can't be discussed in the presence of ladies. (*Whispers again to* **Zvontsov**.) So I'll set it up for this evening.

Ksenia   Set what up?

Doctor   A consultation. A conference of doctors.

Ksenia   Oh Lord!

Doctor   Don't distress yourself, madam. Until this evening then, goodbye! (*Exits.*)

Ksenia   He's so severe. And what a cheek – five roubles for five minutes, that's sixty an hour.

Zvontsov   He says an operation will be necessary.

Ksenia   An operation? No, it's out of the question, I won't let them cut him.

Zvontsov   That's ignorance, Mother, surgery is science –

Ksenia   I spit on your science. There, you ill-mannered man.

Zvontsov   We're not talking of manners, Mother, but of your blind ignorance –

Ksenia   You're ignorant yourself!

Zvontsov *throws up his hands and moves away.* **Glafira** *rushes in.*

Ksenia   Where are you going?

Glafira   He rang from the bedroom.

Ksenia *goes out with her to her husband.*

Zvontsov   My father-in-law has certainly chosen his moment.

Bashkin   Yes, it cramps our style. These days clever people are pulling money from the air like conjurors.

Zvontsov   Mm – yes, and a revolution too.

Bashkin   I don't approve of that. We had one twelve years ago. Complete shambles.

Zvontsov   1905 was more a riot than a revolution, the peasants and workers were at home – this time they're all at the front. No, this one will be against the state – the governors and ministers and officials . . .

Bashkin   I hope to God it is. They're like leeches, getting their hooks into you and you can't pull them out.

Zvontsov   The Tsar's obviously incapable of running the country, even the business world says so.

Bashkin   And what about this peasant Grigorii who's put a spell on our Tsarina?

Zvontsov   You mean Rasputin?

Bashkin   Magic, witchcraft. I don't believe in it.

Varvara *listens on the staircase.*

Zvontsov   You believe in sweethearts and favourites though?

Bashkin   It's like a fairty tale, they say she has hundreds of generals . . .

Varvara (*comes down the stairs*)   What nonsense!

Bashkin   That's what they say, Varvara Egorovna – as for me, I say that without the Tsar we're nothing!

Zvontsov   He shouldn't be in Petrograd, he should be in our hearts. Is the show over?

Varvara   They cancelled it. An inspector came and said there'd be a trainload of invalids from the front this evening, about five hundred in all, and there's nowhere to put them.

Glafira (*runs in*)   Mokei Petrovich, he's calling for you!

Bashkin *goes out leaving his old winter cap on the table.*

Varvara   Why are you so open with him? You know he's spying on us for Mother! He's worn that old cap for ten years – it's disgusting, it's all greasy. I can't understand why you let that swindler into your confidence.

Zvontsov   I've got my work cut out with him, I need him to lend me the money for Bettling—

Varvara   But I told you, Liza Dostigaeva's arranging it through Jeanne – at half the price.

Zvontsov   Liza will cheat you.

Ksenia (*from her husband's room*)   Tell him to stay in bed. He's with Mokei, walking around swearing. Lord, Lord!

Zvontsov   Go on, Varya.

Bulychev (*bursts in wearing a dressing gown and felt slippers, with* **Bashkin** *in tow*)   What then? The war's no good?

Bashkin   Can't argue with that.

Bulychev   No good for who?

Bashkin   For us of course, the people.

Bulychev   But why's that? You say people are making millions out of it.

Bashkin   For the ordinary people I mean.

Bulychev   Oh, the peasants. They don't care whether they live or die, and that's the truth.

Ksenia   Stop shouting, it's bad for you.

Bashkin   How can you – what kind of truth is that?

Bulychev   I'm telling you the facts, and the facts are that my business is to make money, and the peasant's is to produce bread and buy goods. What other truth is there?

Bashkin   You're right of course, but –

Bulychev   But what? What goes through your mind when you steal from me?

Bashkin   You insult me.

Ksenia   Varya, for heaven's sake stop staring at him and make him lie down like the doctor said.

Bulychev   Perhaps you're thinking about the people when you do it?

Bashkin   You insult me in front of people too. I steal from you, do I? Prove it.

Bulychev   No need to, it's common knowledge, stealing's practically legal now. I've no reason to insult you, insulting you won't make you honest, it'll make you worse. Anyway, it's not you who does the stealing, it's the rouble – the rouble alone takes more than all of you put together . . .

Bashkin   Only your Laptev gets away with talk like that.

Bulychev   So he does. You can go now. Don't give Bettling any more, you've given him thousands already – enough for his coffin anyway. (**Bashkin** *exits. To* **Varvara** *and* **Ksenia**.) What are you two waiting for?

Varvara   We're not waiting for anything.

Bulychev   I see, in that case you can go about your business. If you have business, that is. My room's stuffy, Aksinia, tell them to air it, it smells of sour medicines. And get Glafira to bring me some cranberry kvass.

Ksenia   You know you're not allowed kvass.

Bulychev   Go, go, I know what I'm allowed.

Ksenia (*leaving*)   If only you did . . .

Varvara *and* **Ksenia** *go out.*

Bulychev (*walks round the table holding on to it. Looks in the mirror, speaking to himself*)   You look bad, Egor, and your face – it's not yours any more.

Glafira (*with a glass of milk on a tray*)   Here's some milk for you.

Bulychev   Give it to the cat, I want kvass.

Glafira   They told me not to give you any.

Bulychev   Never mind what they say, bring it. Wait. What do you think – will I die?

Glafira   You can't.

Bulychev   Why not?

Glafira   I don't believe it.

Bulychev   You don't believe it? No, friend, I'm in a bad way, very bad. I know it.

Glafira   I don't believe it.

Bulychev   You're stubborn. Well, give me kvass!

Glafira *goes out.*

Bulychev   And perhaps some orange brandy too, that's good for you. (*Goes to the sideboard.*) The swine, they've locked it! I feel like a prisoner, a criminal . . . !

Act Two

*The **Bulychevs**' drawing room. Two doors lead off it. **Zvontsov** and **Tyatin** are seated in the corner at a small round table with a bottle of wine.*

Zvontsov *(lights a cigarette)*   Got it?

Tyatin   To be honest, I don't like it, Andrei.

Zvontsov   You like money though, don't you?

Tyatin   Unfortunately, yes.

Zvontsov   Who are you worried about?

Tyatin   Myself, obviously.

Zvontsov   What's there to worry about!

Tyatin   Well, you know, I'm the best friend I have –

Zvontsov   Stop philosophising and think.

Tyatin   I do – I think she's a spoilt child and it won't be easy living with her.

Zvontsov   So divorce her.

Tyatin   Then she'll keep the cash.

Zvontsov   We'll make sure you get it – don't worry, I'll break her in for you.

Tyatin   To be honest –

Zvontsov   Then they'll have to marry her off in a hurry and increase her dowry.

Tyatin   Smart man. So what's the dowry?

Zvontsov   Fifty.

Tyatin   Thousand?

Zvontsov   No, buttons.

Tyatin   Really?

Zvontsov   And you'll sign a thousand of it to me.

Tyatin   A thousand?

Zvontsov   Roubles, idiot!

Tyatin   That's a lot!

Zvontsov   Take it or leave it.

Tyatin   Are you serious?

Zvontsov   Only idiots don't take money seriously.

Tyatin (*grins*)   Dammit, I've got to hand it to you!

Dostigaev *enters.*

Zvontsov   I'm glad we understand each other. It's important in these cruel times that a proletarian intellectual of your calibre –

Tyatin   Yes, yes! I'll be late for court . . .

Dostigaev   What's up, Stepasha?

Zvontsov   We were discussing Rasputin.

Dostigaev   Fate, eh? An illiterate Siberian plays draughts with our bishops and ministers and rakes in the loot – I have it on good authority that he never accepts less than ten thousand. What are you drinking? Burgundy? That's a heavy wine, you peasants, you should drink it at dinner.

Zvontsov   How did you find my father-in-law?

Dostigaev   No need to look for him, he wasn't hiding. Bring us a glass, dear boy.

Tyatin *goes out unhurriedly.*

Dostigaev   I must say he didn't look well. Can't be long now . . .

Zvontsov   That's what I think . . .

Dostigaev   Exactly. And he's afraid of dying, which means he must die soon. You should get ready, you can't sit around with your hands in your pockets these days. Everywhere you look the pigs are digging up the fence protecting the state -- even the governor smells revolution.

Tyatin (*returning with a glass*)   Egor Vasilevich is in the dining room.

Dostigaev (*taking the glass*)   Thanks, dear boy. He's come out, you say?

Zvontsov   The industrialists seem to understand their role anyway.

Varvara *enters with* **Elizaveta**, *expensively dressed and coiffed.*

Dostigaev   Absolutely. The Moscow ones anyway.

Elizaveta   You're drinking like fish in here and Bulychev's yelling like a madman!

Dostigaev   Why does America flourish? Because the country's being run by the industrialists.

Varvara   Jeanne Bettling told me quite seriously that cooks over there drive to market in motor cars.

Dostigaev   It's possible, though it's probably a fantasy. Still with your soldiers, Varyusha? You want to live under a colonel?

Varvara   That old joke. What are you dreaming of, Tyatin?

Tyatin   Oh, you know . . .

Elizaveta (*in front of the mirror*)   Yesterday Jeanne told me an amazing joke, a real beauty.

Dostigaev   Go on, what was it?

Elizaveta   I can't, not with men present.

Dostigaev   Must be a cracker then.

Elizaveta *whispers to* **Varvara** *and they giggle.*

Elizaveta   Husband! Are you going to sit here with that bottle until it's finished?

Dostigaev   So what? I'm not disturbing anyone.

Elizaveta (*to* **Tyatin**)   Remember the psalm, Stepochka – 'Blessed is the man that walks not in the counsel of the ungodly nor stands in the way of sinners . . .'

Tyatin   I vaguely recall it . . .

Elizaveta (*takes his arm*)   All these people are ungodly sinners and you're just a quiet boy dreaming of love and the moon, am I right? (*Leads him out.*)

Dostigaev   Little chatterbox!

Varvara (*to* **Dostigaev**)   Did you know that Mother and Bashkin have sent for Aunt Melania?

Dostigaev   Our Reverend Mother? The old battleaxe! She'll be dead against the Dostigaev–Zvontsov partnership and will want Dostigaev and Ksenia Bulycheva on the board . . .

Zvontsov   Chances are she'll want to pull out her capital.

Dostigaev   How much? Seventy thousand?

Zvontsov   Ninety.

Dostigaev (*whistles*)   Hers or the convent's?

Zvontsov   Damned if I know.

Varvara   How can we find out?

Dostigaev   Easy, you can find out anything these days – the Germans know the exact number of our soldiers at the front and how many fleas each one has.

Varvara   Please be serious!

Dostigaev   My dear Varya, I know as well as you do that you can't make war or business without counting the cash in your pocket. This is how we do it – there's a lady called

Sekleteya Poluboyarinova, a pillar of the Church, who prays with Bishop Nikander at his all-night vigils, and Nikander loves to talk about his money. Then there's a man on the Diocesan council who we can keep in reserve. Varya, you talk to Poluboyarinova, and if it turns out the cash belongs to the convent – well, I needn't tell you what that means . . . (*Looks at his watch.*) Where has my lovely wife disappeared to?

Glafira (*comes in*)   They want you in the dining room.

Dostigaev   Right you are, let's go. (*Exits.*)

Varvara (*stops as if pulling her skirt from the chair*)   Help me, Andryusha! (*Murmurs.*) D'you trust him?

Zvontsov   What do you take me for?

Varvara   The scoundrel! He fell into my trap about Auntie though, didn't he? How's Tyatin?

Zvontsov   I'm working on him, don't worry.

Varvara   He'd better get a move on then.

Zvontsov   Why?

Varvara   Well, we can't have the wedding too soon after the funeral, and there's Father's weak heart, and . . . I've my reasons . . .

As they exit, they pass **Glafira**, *who watches them with a look of hatred, then clears the glasses off the table.* **Laptev** *enters.*

Glafira   I heard rumours yesterday you'd been arrested.

Laptev   Really? They must have been wrong.

Glafira   Very funny.

Laptev   A hungry life but a funny one.

Glafira   Crack your jokes, they'll crack your head one of these days.

Laptev   They don't get you for a good one, but they'll break you for a bad one.

Glafira   Listen, Shura's in there with Tonka Dostigaeva.

Laptev   Brrr, not her.

Glafira   Shall I call Shura then?

Laptev   Why not. How's Bulychev?

Glafira (*angrily*)   Why Bulychev? He's your godfather.

Laptev   Don't be cross with me, Auntie Glasha.

Glafira   He's very ill.

Laptev   Is he? Listen, Glasha, my friends are hungry, could you give us a pound or two of flour, or maybe a sack?

Glafira   You want me to rob my master for you?

Laptev   It's not the first time. You sinned before and the sin was mine. The boys have nothing to eat. You work twice as hard as your master, you've earned it for God's sake.

Glafira   You and your speeches. They'll send Donat the flour tomorrow morning, get a sack off him. (*Goes out.*)

Laptev   Thank you! (*Sits on the sofa and yawns till the tears come to his eyes; wipes them away and looks round.*)

Ksenia (*comes in grumbling*)   They've run off like the devil from a church . . . (*Sees* **Laptev**.) Goodness, what are you sitting here for?

Laptev   Shall I walk?

Ksenia   Merciful God, you play hide-and-seek with us for a week and no one knows where you are, then you turn up unannounced – your godfather's ill, does he mean nothing to you?

Laptev   You want me to be ill too?

Ksensia   You've all gone mad and want to drive me mad too. How am I to understand anything! I hear they want to put the Tsar in a cage like Pugachev. Is it true, scholar?

Laptev   Anything's possible, absolutely anything.

Glafira (*appears at the door*)   Aksinia Yakovlevna, just a minute . . .

Ksenia   What now? I never have any peace . . . (*Goes out.*)

Shura (*runs in*)   Yakov!

Laptev   Dear Shura, I must go to Moscow tonight but I've no money, can you lend me some?

Shura   I've thirty roubles.

Laptev   Make it fifty?

Shura   I'll get it.

Laptev   Tonight before the train goes, please.

Shura   Listen, is there going to be a revolution?

Laptev   It's here already, don't you read the papers?

Shura   I don't understand them.

Laptev   Ask Tyatin.

Shura   Tell me honestly, what sort of person is Tyatin?

Laptev   Don't ask me, you've seen him every day for the last six months.

Shura   But is he honest?

Laptev   I suppose so.

Shura   Why do you hesitate?

Laptev   He's a ditherer and he's dull, and he's full of grudges . . .

Shura   Against what?

Laptev   He was chucked out of university in his second year and now he works for his cousin as a legal clerk. And of course Zvontsov is –

Shura   A crook?

Laptev   He's a constitutional democrat and a businessman, and pretty much all of them are crooks. Give Glafira the money, she'll see I get it.

Shura   Glafira and Tyatin are helping you?

Laptev   To do what?

Shura   You know what I'm talking about Yashka, I want to help you too.

Laptev (*surprised, puts a hand on her shoulder*)   What's come over you, girl, have you just woken up?

Shura (*angrily*)   Don't patronise me! You're an idiot.

Laptev   Maybe, but I want to understand.

Shura   Varvara's coming.

Laptev   We don't need her.

Shura   Quick, let's go.

Laptev (*puts a hand on her shoulder*)   What's happened to you, Shura?

They leave, closing the door behind them. A few minutes later the front door slams and **Shura** *returns, pulling* **Donat** *by the hand.*

Donat   Where are you dragging me, Shurok?

Shura   Tell me, do people respect Papa in town?

Donat   The rich are respected wherever they are, you make mischief everywhere . . .

Shura   Respect him or scared of him?

Donat   If they weren't scared of him they wouldn't respect him.

Shura   But do they like him?

Donat   I wouldn't know about that.

Shura   Is there anything they like about him?

Donat   Hard to say. The cab drivers seem to like him. He doesn't haggle and gives them what they ask for - and of course one cabbie tells another . . .

Shura (*stamps her foot*)   Are you laughing at me?

Donat   Why would I do that? I'm telling you the truth.

Shura   You've changed, you've become horrible!

Donat   I haven't changed, I'm too old to change.

Shura   You used to say good things about my father.

Donat   I'm not criticising him, every fish has its scales.

Shura   You're all liars! Go away!

Donat (*bows his head and goes out*)   Anger won't prove anything.

Alexei Dostigaev *enters, a dandy in jodhpurs and a Swedish jacket covered in straps and pockets.*

Alexei   Lovely as every, Glasha!

Glafira (*gives him a surly look*)   Pleased to hear it.

Alexei   Well, I'm not. (*Stands in front of* **Glafira**.) Loveliness doesn't please me unless I possess it.

Glafira   Get out of my way – please.

Alexei   The pleasure's mine. (*Steps aside, yawns, looks at his watch.*)

Shura   So you're chasing servants now?

Antonina *enters, followed by* **Tyatin**.

Antonina   He doesn't care what kind of fish they are.

Alexei   Servants are just as good as ladies when you get their clothes off.

Antonina   See how he talks, as if he'd been brought up in a tavern!

Shura   He was always lazy, but he wasn't always so bold with his words.

Alexei   And deeds!

Antonina   Liar! He's a coward. And I'm terribly afraid our stepmother is going to seduce him.

Alexei   I've no idea what you're talking about, little fool.

Antonina   And disgustingly greedy too. I pay him one rouble twenty kopecks for each day he doesn't say something vile to me, and he takes it.

Alexei   Tyatin, how d'you like my sister?

Tyatin   Very much.

Shura   What about me?

Tyatin   To tell the truth . . .

Shura   The truth, of course.

Tyatin   Not a lot.

Shura   Really, is that the truth?

Tyatin   Yes it is.

Antonina   Don't believe him, he's talking like an echo!

Alexei (*puts an arm round* **Antonina**'*s waist*)   You can have her, Tyatin, I'm sick of her.

Antonina   Beast! Go away. You look like a pregnant laundress in that jacket.

Alexei (*dances with her*)   My, what a lady! We're just jumped-up merchants' children. Stop chewing sunflower seeds, it's *mauvais ton.*

Antonina   Push off!

Alexei   With pleasure!

Shura (*to* **Tyatin**)   You mean you don't like me at all?

Tyatin   Why do you ask?

Shura   I want to know, I'm interested.

Alexei   Go for it, Tyatin, she's throwing herself at you. They're all desperate to be heroes' widows now – it means rations, a halo and a pension.

Antonina   He thinks he's so clever.

Alexei   I'll be on my way – Tonka, see me out.

Antonina   See yourself out.

Alexei   It's important, come on.

Antonina   Probably something stupid . . .

They exit.

Shura   Tyatin, do you tell the truth?

Tyatin   No.

Shura   Why not?

Tyatin   It doesn't pay.

Shura   If you say that, it means you do. Answer me truthfully, did they tell you to marry me?

Tyatin (*pauses to light a cigarette*)   Yes, they did.

Shura   And you knew they were wrong.

Tyatin   Yes.

Shura   I didn't expect this. I thought . . .

Tyatin   You think badly of me, obviously.

Shura   No, you're – wonderful! Or perhaps cunning? You're playing with the truth so as to take advantage of me?

Tyatin   I'm not capable of that. You're clever, artful, malicious – to be honest I'm frightened of you. You're a firebrand, like your father . . .

Shura   Tyatin, you're extraordinary! Or extraordinarily devious . . .

Tyatin   And you've an extraordinary face.

Shura   You're saying that to soften the blow – ah, you're cunning.

Tyatin   Think what you like about me, I'm convinced you'll end up doing something criminal – while I lie on my back with my paws in the air like a guilty puppy . . .

Shura   Why guilty?

Tyatin   I don't know, because I haven't teeth to bite you with?

Antonina (*runs back*)   Stupid Alyoshka pulled my ear really hard and grabbed all my money, little thief! I bet he spends it on drink. What's so funny?

Shura   Tonya, forget everything I said about him.

Antonina   Tyatin? What did you say? I've forgotten.

Shura   That he wants to marry me.

Antonina   What's so bad about that?

Shura   For money.

Antonina   Oh yes – that's terrible, Tyatin!

Shura   I wish you'd heard him when I questioned him just now.

Antonina   Was he very frightening? I only like frightening things. When I'm frightened I'm not bored. I lie in the dark waiting for a big snake to slip into my room . . .

Tyatin (*sniggers*)   The one in paradise?

Antonina   No, much more frightening.

Shura   What are you babbling about? You're funny though, everyone here just talks about the same old thing – Rasputin, the Tsarina, war, revolution . . .

Antonina   You'll either be an actress or a nun, Shura.

Shura   It must be hard being a nun, playing the same part all the time. No, I want to be a loose woman like Zola's Nana - I want to get my own back on people and lead them astray.

Tyatin   Shame on you – what for?

Shura   For the fact that Father's ill and I've got red hair – everything. I'll spread my wings when the revolution comes, you'll see!

Antonina   You think there'll be a revolution?

Shura   Yes! Yes!

Glafira (*runs in*)   Shura, Mother Melania's arrived. Egor Vasilevich wants to see her in here.

Shura   Ooh, my auntie. Better run to my room, children! Tell me, Tyatin, do you respect Brother Zvontsov?

Tyatin   He's not my brother, he's my cousin.

Shura   Answer the question.

Tyatin   I don't think most families respect each other very much.

Shura   That's your answer?

Antonina   Don't be boring!

Shura   You're funny too, Tyatin.

Tyatin   What can I say?

Shura   And your clothes are odd.

They go off. **Bulychev** *appears in the door through which the young people have left, and* **Mother Melania** *walks slowly and solemnly through the other, holding a crozier.* **Glafira** *bows her head and holds back the curtain for her.*

Melania   Still here, you whore? Haven't they thrown you out yet? They soon will!

Bulychev   Take her into your convent then, she's got money.

Melania   Mercy, Egor, I didn't see you. Lord, how you've changed!

Bulychev   Glakha, shut the door and make sure no one comes in. Sit down, Mother, what business do you want to discuss with me?

Melania (*sits down*)   Are the doctors no help? Ah, our soul waits for the Lord a year, a lifetime . . .

Bulychev   We'll discuss the Lord later, first business. I suppose you've come about your money?

Melania (*agitated*)   It's not mine, it belongs to the cloister.

Bulychev   What's the difference? What are you bothered about – afraid I'll die and it'll disappear?

Melania   It can't disappear, I just don't want it falling into the wrong hands.

Bulychev   You want to pull out your capital? Go ahead, you'll lose by it though. Roubles are breeding like lice on soldiers and I'm not ready to die yet.

Melania   We know not the hour or day of our departure. Have you written your last will and testament?

Bulychev   No I haven't.

Melania   Then do it. The Lord may call you at any moment!

Bulychev   What does He care about me?

Melania   My position forbids me to listen to such talk . . .

Bulychev   That's enough of that, Malasha, we know each other inside and out! Take your money, Bulychev's got plenty more!

Melania   I'm not pulling out, I'm transferring it to Aksinia. I'm informing you in advance . . .

Bulychev   Fine. But when I croak Zvontsov will stitch her up and Varvara will help him!

Melania (*leans forward and peers into his face*)   Lord, how you speak now. I hear a change in your voice – all the anger is gone!

Bulychev   It's gone in another direction. Let's speak of God and the soul. 'We plunder the years of our youth, in old age we turn to the soul . . .' You serve God day and night, as, for example, Glafira serves me . . .

Melania   Blasphemy! Are you mad? How does Glafira serve you at night?

Bulychev   You want me to tell you?

Melania   Sacrilege. Profanity. Come to your senses!

Bulychev   Don't bellow! I speak in simple human words, not like a prayer book. You told Glafira she'd be thrown out so you must think I'll die soon. Why? Dostigaev's nine years older than me and nine times a bigger scoundrel, but he's strong as a horse and has a first-rate wife. Of course I've hurt people and I'm an all-round sinner, but everyone hurts people, it can't be helped, that's life . . .

Melania   Repent not before me, Egor, but before God. People won't forgive you but God is all-merciful. Remember when bandits robbed the rich in the old days and surrendered to God what was His, and were forgiven?

Bulychev   Yes, and if you rob the people and give it to the Church, you're not a sinner at all but a righteous man.

Melania   Is there no limit to your blasphemy, Egor? You're no fool, you know that if the Lord doesn't allow it, the devil won't tempt you.

Bulychev   Thank you.

Melania   What do you mean?

Bulychev   You've set my mind at rest. It seems the Lord lets the devil tempt me, which means He's mixed up with him in my sinful ways.

Melania (*springs to her feet*)   Hold your tongue, Egor, if I report you to the Bishop . . .

Bulychev   What did I say?

Melania (*brandishes her crozier at him*)   Heretic. What's crept into your sick mind? Don't you understand, if He allows the devil to tempt you it means He's renounced you!

Bulychev   What for? Loving women and money and marrying your sister for her money, the fool, and because I was your lover? He'd renounce me for that? Shut your mouth, you old crow!

Melania (*advances on him in a fury*)   Merciful God, what are you saying . . . ?

Bulychev   You pray day and night when the bells tell you to, but you've no idea who you're praying to.

Melania   You're falling into the abyss . . . into the jaws of hell. Everything is collapsing! The forces of evil are toppling the throne. Get hence, Antichrist! The hour of judgement is at hand . . . !

Bulychev   The second coming? Squawk your head off! Fly back to your nest and smooch with your choirgirls. This is what I think of your money! (*Puts two fingers up.*)

Melania (*falls back horrified in her chair*)   You . . . You heathen . . . !

Bulychev   Glafira's a whore, is she? So what are you?

Melania   You're lying! (*Jumps up and advances on him with her crozier.*) Die like a dog, you worm!

Bulychev   Be off! Away from my sin!

Melania (*rushes out*)   Snake! Devil!

Bulychev (*growls and rubs his right side*)   Hey, Glafira!

Ksenia *enters.*

Ksenia   What's the matter? Where's Melania?

Bulychev   Flown off.

Ksenia   You didn't quarrel again, did you?

Bulychev   Do you plan to stay long?

Ksenia   You never let me get a word in, Egor, you've stopped noticing me, as if I was a bit of furniture. Why are you staring at me like that?

Bulychev   Get on with it then, speak up.

Ksenia   What's happening in this house? It's like the end of the world. Our son-in-law's turned his room upstairs into a tavern and there are crowds of people day and night – consultations, conferences . . . Yesterday they drank seven bottles of red wine and heaven knows how much vodka, and they were talking about the Tsar and his ministers, and Izmail the janitor's complaining and the police are worrying him to death with questions . . . What are you hanging your head for?

Bulychev   Go ahead, don't stop. I used to like drinking in taverns too . . .

Ksenia   Why did Malasha come?

Bulychev   You're a bad liar, Aksinia, you're too stupid. You know perfectly well you two have been planning this talk about money.

Ksenia   I can't think what you mean. I planned no such thing.

Dostigaev, Zvontsov *and* **Father Pavlin** *enter, talking animatedly.*

Dostigaev   Egor, listen to what Father Pavlin heard in Moscow.

Ksenia You'd better go to bed, Egor . . .

Bulychev I'm listening, Father.

Pavlin I've little good news for you, and even that is bad in my view, since it's impossible now to live the way we used to before the war.

Dostigaev No, I protest!

Zvontsov *whispers something to his mother-in-law.*

Ksenia She's crying?

Dostigaev Who's crying?

Ksenia The Reverend Mother.

Dostigaev What's up with her? Wonder what's moved our Malasha to tears!

Bulychev Go, see what the matter is. Sit down, Father, tell us everything.

Ksenia, **Zvontsov** *and* **Dostigaev** *exit.*

Pavlin A mighty turmoil has befallen Moscow. Even men of maturity and wisdom are convinced that the Tsar must fall soon due to his incompetence.

Bulychev He's been competent enough for twenty years.

Pavlin A man's power is enfeebled in the course of time . . .

Bulychev Remember in 1913 when the Romanovs celebrated their tercentenary and Nikolai shook my hand? The whole nation rejoiced, the whole of Kostroma.

Pavlin They did indeed.

Bulychev What's happened? Look at the Duma . . . No, it's not the Tsar, the roots are rotten . . .

Pavlin But the roots are the autocracy.

Bulychev   Autocracy means each man for himself, holding on to power by his own strength. Where's our strength gone? There's no sign of it in this war.

Pavlin   I fear the Duma is hastening its own demise . . .

Elizaveta (*appears in the door*)   Are you taking his last confession, Father Pavlin?

Pavlin   Gracious, what a question!

Elizaveta   Where's my husband?

Pavlin   He was here a minute ago.

Elizaveta   How solemn you are today, Father! (*Exits.*)

Bulychev   Father . . .

Pavlin   Yes?

Bulychev   We're all fathers, Pavlin, you , me, God, the Tsar, but we've no strength, we're waiting to die – not just me, this war, like letting the tiger out of its cage at the circus –

Pavlin   Enough, Egor Vasilevich, pray calm yourself!

Bulychev   How? Who will calm me? Show me how, Father. Show me your strength!

Pavlin   If you read the Holy Scriptures you will recall Joshua and the war in Jericho. War is the Law . . .

Bulychev   Dammit, what law? Stop the sun shining? It's humbug, fairy tales!

Pavlin   Wherefore does a living man complain for the punishment of his sins? We must accept retribution in the spirit of forgiveness and humility . . .

Bulychev   Did you accept it when your warden Alexei Gubin made trouble for you at the church? Of course you didn't. You went to court and hired Zvontsov to defend you and got the Bishop to intercede for you. What court can I go to about my death? Are you telling me you'll die peacefully, with a calm soul? No, you'll groan and howl –

Pavlin   Stop, these are the words –

Bulychev   Cut it out, Pavlin, your cassock's very pretty but underneath you're a man, like me, and the doctor says you've a bad heart from too much rich food.

Pavlin   What is the purpose of such speeches? Consider and tremble! From time immemorial it has been established . . .

Bulychev   Not very firmly it seems.

Pavlin   Lev Tolstoy was a heretic and was anathematised by the Church for his lack of belief, but in the face of death he ran off to the woods and died like an animal . . .

Ksenia (*returns*)   Egor Vasilevich, Mokei has come, he says the police arrested Yakov last night.

Bulychev   Thanks for the sermon, Pavlin, I'll call you later. Call Bashkin, Aksinia. Tell Glafira to give me some porridge and some orange brandy.

Ksenia   You're not allowed brandy.

Bulychev   I'll have what I like! Go! (*Looks round, chuckles and mutters.*) Holy Father, what an owl . . . You should smoke, Egor, it's easier with smoke in your eyes . . .

Bashkin *enters.*

Bashkin   How is your health today, Egor Vasilevich?

Bulychev   Better. So they've arrested Yakov?

Bashkin   Last night. Terrible business.

Bulychev   On his own?

Bashkin   Apparently there were about a dozen in all – a clockmaker and Kalmykova the schoolteacher who used to give Alexandra Egorovna lessons, and Erikhonov the stoker, another well-known agitator . . .

Bulychev   Oh, that crowd – down with the Tsar, was it?

Bashkin   They all want different things – with some it's just the Tsar, others want to destroy the rich so the workers can run the state –

Bulychev   Rubbish. They'd run it on drink!

Bashkin   Yes, quite.

Bulychev   But then on the other hand they might not.

Bashkin   Impossible. What can they do without the masters?

Bulychev   True. Where would they be without you and Vaska Dostigaev.

Bashkin (*eyes him*)   And you too, you're a master.

Bulychev   Absolutely. Tell me, what were they singing?

Bashkin (*sighs*)   'Let us renounce the old world . . .'

Bulychev   Yes?

Bashkin   'Let's shake its dust from our feet . . .'

Bulychev   It sounds like a prayer.

Bashkin   Hardly. They say they hate the Tsar and his church . . .

Bulychev   Well I never, the devils! (*Pause.*) Well, what do you want?

Glafira *brings in porridge and brandy.*

Bashkin   Me? To ask who I should put in Yakov's place.

Bulychev   Get Sergei Potapov.

Bashkin   He's of the same persuasion – no God, no Tsar, that sort of thing.

Bulychev   Him too?

Bashkin   Allow me to recommend former assistant police chief Mokrousov. He's been asking for some time to work for you, he's competent, reliable . . .

Glafira   The porridge is getting cold.

Bulychev   That thief? What's he after?

Bashkin   It's dangerous to be in the police force at the moment, a lot of them are getting out.

Bulychev   So the rats are leaving. Send Potapov tomorrow. You can go now. Glakha, has the trumpeter come?

Glafira   He's sitting in the kitchen.

Bulychev   I'll eat the porridge, then send him in. What's happening, why is the house so quiet?

Glafira   Everyone's upstairs.

Bulychev   Good. (*Drinks some brandy.*) What's wrong? You look sad.

Glafira (*clings to him*)   Don't drink, darling, it's bad for you. You must get better – give up everything and leave them, they're devouring you like worms.

Bulychev   Let go, you're hurting . . .

Glafira   We'll go to Siberia. I'll work and you'll get better. Why do you stay here? No one loves you, they're all waiting for you to die.

Bulychev   Stop, Glakha, you're upsetting me. I know, I see everything. I know what you mean to me. You and Shurka are all I have, the rest just stick to me like ticks. Maybe I'll get better. Call the trumpeter . . .

Glafira   Eat your porridge.

Bulychev   To hell with porridge – call Shurka too!

Glafira *goes out.* **Bulychev** *thirstily downs glass after glass of brandy. The* **Trumpeter** *enters, a skinny, sad, funny-looking man with a large bass tuba on his shoulder in a bag.*

Trumpeter   Good health to you, Your Honour.

Bulychev (*surprised*)   Sit down. Shut the door, Glakha. You're not what I expected.

Trumpeter   No, sir.

Bulychev   Not very pretty, are you? So how do you cure people?

Trumpeter   My cure is simple, Your Honour, but people are accustomed to buying medicines from the chemist and don't trust me, so I ask for my money in advance.

Bulychev   Good man! So you make people better?

Trumpeter   I've made hundreds better, sir.

Bulychev   It hasn't made you rich though.

Trumpeter   Doing good doesn't make you rich.

Bulychev   You're right there. What illnesses do you cure?

Trumpeter   All illnesses without exception are caused by bad wind in the stomach, so I cure that.

Bulychev (*chuckles*)   Excellent! Show me your trumpet.

Trumpeter   Will you pay me a rouble?

Bulychev   A rouble, let's see – Glakha, have you a rouble? Here, you don't ask much.

Trumpeter   That's for a start. (*Unstraps the bag and takes out his tuba.*)

Shura *runs in.*

Bulychev   Like a samovar. You like our healer, Shurok? Blow it then!

The **Trumpeter** *clears his throat, blows softly and coughs.*

Bulychev   That's it?

Trumpeter   Four times a day for five minutes, no more!

Bulychev   And if someone blows their breath out and dies?

Trumpeter   Never! I've cured hundreds.

Bulychev   I see. Now tell me truthfully, how would you describe yourself, liar or fool?

Trumpeter (*sighs*)   You don't believe me, like everyone else.

Shura   Don't offend him, Papa.

Bulychev   I'm not, Shurok! (*Laughs.*) Don't put it away! Tell me straight – liar or fool? I'll give you money! What's your name, healer?

Trumpeter   Gavril Uvekov.

Bulychev   Gabriel? (*Laughs.*)

Trumpeter   It's a very ordinary name, no one has laughed at it before.

Bulychev   Go on – liar or fool?

Trumpeter   Will you give me sixteen roubles?

Bulychev   Fetch it, Glakha, it's in the bedroom. Why sixteen, Gavril?

Trumpeter   I made a mistake, I should have said twenty.

Bulychev   So you're a fool?

Trumpeter   No.

Bulychev   A liar then?

Trumpeter   No, but you know yourself that a man can't live without deception.

Bulychev   Very true, my friend – sad but true.

Shura   Aren't you ashamed of tricking people?

Trumpeter   Why, if they believe it?

Bulychev (*excited*)   Hear him, Shurka? Father Pavlin wouldn't say that, he wouldn't dare!

Trumpeter   The truth costs more. But I swear on the Bible – it helps some people.

Bulychev   I believe you, give him twenty-five, Glakha – give him everything.

Trumpeter   I thank you humbly. Maybe you'll try it? It works, devil knows how, but it works.

Bulychev (*laughs*)   Show me then. Go on, harder!

The **Trumpeter** *blows and produces a harsh, deafening sound.* **Glafira** *looks anxiously at* **Bulychev**. **Shura** *puts her hands over her ears and laughs.*

Bulychev   Blow! Give it all you've got!

The **Dostigaevs** *and* **Zvontsovs** *bursts in with* **Bashkin** *and* **Ksenia**.

Varvara   What on earth's going on, Papa?

Zvontsov (*to the* **Trumpeter**)   Are you drunk?

Bulychev   Don't touch him! Don't you dare! The Angel Gabriel's trumpeting the end of the world!

Ksenia   I don't believe this. He's gone mad!

Bashkin (*murmurs to* **Zvontsov**)   What did I tell you?

Shura   Listen to them, Papa, they're saying you've gone mad. Go away, trumpeter, go away!

Bulychev   Don't go. Deafen them, Gavril! Blow harder! It's the end of the world . . . !

Act Three

The dining room. Everything seems to have been moved from its place. On the table are unwashed dishes, a samovar, bottles, packets from the shop. Several suitcases stand in the corner. **Taisya,** *a lay sister from the convent in a pointed peasant headdress, is unpacking one of them.* **Glafira** *stands next to her holding a tray.*

Glafira   Is Melania staying long?

Taisya   I don't know.

Glafira   How old are you?

Taisya   Nineteen.

Zvontsov *appears on the staircase.*

Glafira   You don't know anything, are you a wild animal or what?

Taisya   We're not allowed to speak to outsiders at the convent.

Zvontsov (*enters*)   Has our Mother Superior had tea? Better heat the samovar just in case.

Glafira *goes off with the samovar.*

Zvontsov   So the soldiers frightened you, did they?

Taisya   Yes they did, sir.

Zvontsov   What did they do?

Taisya   They killed a cow and threatened to burn down the convent. Excuse me. (*Grabs an armful of underwear and goes out.*)

Varvara (*from the hall*)   Terrible weather, slushy and wet! What were you talking about with the nun?

Zvontsov   The Mother Superior's presence in our house is most inconvenient . . .

Varvara   It isn't ours yet . . . Has Tyatin agreed?

Zvontsov Tyatin's either a donkey or pretending to be honest.

Varvara Wait, is Father calling? (*Listens at the door to his room.*)

Zvontsov The doctors say there's nothing wrong with his mind, but after that ridiculous scene with the trumpeter I've my doubts . . .

Varvara He's capable of worse. Tyatin's on friendly terms with Alexandra at least?

Zvontsov Yes, but I see nothing good in it. God knows what your little sister's up to, something unpleasant I expect.

Varvara You should have thought of that when she flirted with you. I suppose you enjoyed it too much.

Zvontsov She flirted with me simply to annoy you.

Varvara How sad for you. Pavlin will be poking his nose in in a minute.

Zvontsov There's too much God in this house.

Elizaveta *and* **Pavlin** *come in quarrelling, followed by* **Bashkin**.

Pavlin The newspapers are lying.

Elizaveta I tell you it's true.

Pavlin It has been established beyond doubt that the Tsar abdicated not of his own free will but under pressure of violence, having been captured on his way to Petrograd by members of the Social Democrat Party, yes indeed!

Zvontsov What conclusions do you draw from that?

Elizaveta Father Pavlin's against the revolution and for the war, and I'm against the war. I want to go to Paris. No more fighting. You agree, Varya? Henri Quatre said, 'Paris is better than war' – something like that, and he was right.

Pavlin   I draw no conclusions at all because the situation is too unstable.

Varvara   We want peace, Father Pavlin, peace. The rabble's going berserk, can't you see?

Pavlin   I do, I do! And our invalid? How is he in this department? (*Taps his forehead.*)

Zvontsov   The doctors find no evidence of dementia.

Pavlin   That's good. Though the only thing doctors generally find with any certainty is their fees.

Elizaveta   Spiteful man. Varya, Jeanne's invited us to dinner.

Bashkin   They've released the political prisoners and the police are suffering as a consequence.

Pavlin   Yes, quite extraordinary. What possible good can come of it, Andrei Petrovich?

Zvontsov   The forces of law and order are pulling together and will soon have their say. By forces of law and order, I mean those with the necessary economic . . .

Varvara   Listen, Jeanne asked if we'd . . . (*Pulls him aside and whispers.*)

Zvontsov   But she must see that puts me in a most awkward position – the Mother Superior on the one hand, the flirt on the other . . .

Varvara   Keep your voice down.

Bashkin   Andrei Petrovich, Mokrousov's here, the assistant police chief I told you about.

Zvontsov   What does he want?

Bashkin   He resigned from his job because of the danger and is applying for a forestry post with you.

Zvontsov   I don't know if that would be in order.

Varvara   Wait, Andrei . . .

Bashkin   Very much so, I'd think. Laptev will get out of prison and run wild, and as you know Donat is an unsuitable man for us – he's a sectarian and keeps prattling about truth and justice. What use is truth now, when –

Zvontsov   Rubbish. We are witnessing the beginning of a new order and the victory of truth!

Varvara   Don't interrupt, Andrei.

Bashkin   Yes, exactly, and justice.

Varvara   What should we do, Mokei?

Bashkin   I propose we hire Mokrousov, I've suggested it to Egor Vasilevich already.

Varvara   And?

Zvontsov *frowns and moves away.*

Bashkin   He didn't say one way or the other.

Varvara   Let's have him then.

Bashkin   Perhaps you'd like to take a look at him? He's waiting outside.

Varvara   Very well.

Bashkin *goes to the hall.* **Varvara** *scribbles something in a notebook.* **Bashkin** *returns with* **Mokrousov**, *a round-faced man in policeman's uniform with a revolver at his belt. He has startled raised eyebrows and is smiling at everyone but looks as if he would rather curse them.*

Mokrousov (*clicks his heels, to* **Varvara**)   Allow me the honour of presenting myself. Mokrousov at your service, ma'am.

Varvara   Delighted to meet you. So you're still in uniform, I heard they were disarming the police.

Mokrousov   It's true, it's dangerous to walk on the streets in uniform now so I wear a civilian overcoat, but I'm still armed. The mob is a little quieter now so I'm without my sword.

Varvara   When do you intend to start working for us?

Mokrousov   In my heart I have been your humble servant for some time. I'm ready to go to the woods at once, I'm a single man . . .

Varvara   You think the riots will go on much longer?

Mokrousov   All summer, I imagine. When the rains and frosts come, people won't want to hang around the streets any more.

Varvara   Only the summer? The revolution doesn't depend on the weather, does it?

Mokrousov   I beg to differ, ma'am. Winter will cool them off, you'll see.

Varvara (*chuckles*)   You're an optimist.

Mokrousov   We police are always optimists, ma'am, we know our power!

Varvara   You served in the army?

Mokrousov   Yes indeed, in the Buzuluk reserve battalion in the rank of second lieutenant.

Varvara (*gives him her hand*)   Well, I wish you all the best.

Mokrousov (*kisses it*)   I am deeply touched. (*Backs out of the room clicking his heels.*)

Varvara (*to* **Bashkin**)   He seems to be a complete idiot.

Bashkin   That's no bad thing, the clever ones are all very well but give them half a chance and they'll turn the country inside out like an old pocket.

Pavlin   The priesthood must be allowed to preach freely at all times, or nothing will be accomplished . . .

Bulychev *enters, supported by* **Glafira** *and* **Shura**. *All look at him in silence.*

Bulychev *(frowns)*   Why has everyone stopped talking? I heard you mumbling away in here . . .

Pavlin   We were startled by the unexpected appearance . . .

Bulychev   Of what?

Pavlin   Of a man being led . . .

Bulychev   The man's legs are paralysed, that's why he's led. Mokei, have they let Yashutka out of prison yet?

Bashkin   Yes, all the prisoners have been released.

Zvontsov   The political ones.

Bulychev   So Yakov's free and the Tsar's under arrest, what do you make of that, Father Pavlin?

Pavlin   I have little understanding of such matters, but in my humble opinion one should enquire exactly what those persons intend . . .

Bulychev   They'll elect a new tsar, that's what. Without one you'll fight like dogs . . .

Pavlin   Your appearance is more robust today, Egor Vasilevich. Evidently you are overcoming your, ah, ailment?

Bulychev   Yes, yes, I'm overcoming it. You, Mokei, husbands and wives, leave me, I want to talk to Pavlin. Don't go, Shura.

Bashkin *goes to the hall. The others go upstairs.*

Shura   You should lie down.

Bulychev   I don't want to. What is it, Pavlin, have you come about the belfry?

Pavlin   No, I looked in hoping to see an improvement in your health and was not disappointed. But of course, bearing in mind your generous and magnificent donations in the past to the glory of our town and its church . . .

Bulychev   Your prayers for me are no good, I'm much worse and I've no wish to pay God. I've given Him thousands and it hasn't helped.

Pavlin   But your donations . . .

Bulychev   What about death then? Isn't He ashamed?

Shura   Don't talk about it, Papa, you mustn't!

Bulychev   Be quiet, you, I'm not just talking about myself.

Pavlin   Why distress yourself with such thoughts? What does death signify when the soul is immortal?

Bulychev   So why is it squeezed into this dirty cramped flesh?

Pavlin   The Church considers such questions not merely futile, but –

Bulychev   Stop hiccoughing, man, talk to me straight. Shura, remember the trumpeter?

Varvara *comes on to the stairs and stuffs a handkerchief in her mouth to smother her laughter.*

Pavlin   Perhaps in the presence of Alexandra Egorovna –

Bulychev   Stop that! She has to live, she has to know, I've lived long enough to ask – why do you live?

Pavlin   I serve the Church.

Bulychev   I know you do, but death will come to you. What does it mean, Pavlin? What does death mean to us?

Pavlin   Your questions are idle and illogical. Forgive me, but it's time now to cast off earthly matters –

Shura   How dare you!

Bulychev   But I'm earthly! Through and through!

Pavlin (*stands up*)   The earth is dust.

Bulychev   Dust? Is your cassock dust? Is that gold cross dust? You're greedy for everything, and everything's dust?

Pavlin   You say evil, destructive things in the presence of the virgin –

Varvara *slips upstairs.*

Bulychev   Virgin, bah! Fools, they train you like they train hounds to catch hares! You grow rich from a penniless Christ –

Pavlin   Your illness makes you bitter, and you sting like an angry wasp. Goodbye! (*Goes off.*)

Shura   You should save your strength, Papa. How obstinate you are . . .

Bulychev   Nothing's lost, I never liked that priest! Keep your eyes open, you hear? I know what I'm doing.

Shura   I see everything, I'm not a child!

Zvontsov *appears on the stairs.*

Bulychev   After the trumpeter they decided I was mad, but the doctors said they were lying. Do you believe the doctors, Shura?

Shura   I believe you.

Bulychev   That's good. My mind's in good shape, the doctors know that, I just bumped into something sharp. Everyone wants to know about death, don't they – or life . . .

Shura   I don't think you're really ill at all – Glafira's right, you must leave this house. You need proper medical treatment but you never listen.

Bulychev   I listen to everyone. Let's try that healer, maybe she'll help. Ah, the pain, it gnaws my heart!

Shura   Don't, Father, you must lie down now . . .

Bulychev   Lying down's worse. Lie down and you give in and the battle's lost. And I want to talk. It's funny, I feel as if I've lived on the wrong street. I fell in with the wrong crowd and lived with them for thirty years. My father did a bad job on me, I don't want that for you, understand? I . . .

Shura   Talk to me quietly, Father, remember when you used to tell me fairy stories?

Bulychev   I never told you stories, I told you the truth. Priests, tsars, governors – what do we need them for? And God? Where's He? And good people? Good people are rare as false money. You see what they're like, messing things up and getting us into this war. What's it to me? They're no use to Egor Bulychev now, or you either – how will you live with them?

Shura   Don't worry about me.

Ksenia (*enters*)   Tonya and her brother have come to see you, Shura, with that man . . .

Shura   They can wait.

Ksenia   You'd better go, I need a word with Father.

Bulychev   Do I need it though?

Shura   Please don't talk too much to him.

Ksenia   I'll do as I please! Egor Vasilevich, Zobunova the healer is here.

Bulychev   Very well I'll see her, bring the young people in later, Shura.

Shura *exits.*

Ksenia   Now I must tell you that your Alexandra has been canoodling with Alexei's good-for-nothing cousin. You know yourself he's no match for her. We've taken in one pauper, and Lord, how he throws his weight around.

Bulychev   Really, Ksenia, you're like a bad dream.

Ksenia   God forgive your insults. You must forbid her to make eyes at him.

Bulychev   Anything else?

Ksenia   And Melania's staying with us.

Bulychev   Why?

Ksenia   A misfortune has befallen the convent, that's why – some runaway soldiers broke in and killed a cow and stole two shovels, a pickaxe and a length of rope. What are things coming to! And now Donat's keeping company with the undesirable characters living in the workers' barracks at the timber mill!

Bulychev   I notice that anyone I like is generally disliked by someone else.

Ksenia   You must make peace with her.

Bulychev   Melania? Why?

Ksenia   Why? For the sake of your health.

Bulychev   All right, we'll bury the hatchet. Forgive us our debts as we forgive our debtors.

Ksenia   Be nice to her. (*Goes out.*)

Bulychev (*mumbles*)   'Lead us not into temptation but deliver us from evil . . .' Lies! Devils!

Varvara (*enters*)   Father, I heard Mother talking to you just now about Stepan Tyatin.

Bulychev   You hear everything, don't you.

Varvara   Tyatin's a modest man, he won't expect much for Alexandra – he's an excellent match for her.

Bulychev   You're too considerate.

Varvara   I've checked him thoroughly.

Bulychev   Considerate of who though? Family devils!

Melania *and* **Ksenia** *enter.*

Bulychev   How about it, Malasha? Shall we make up?

Melania   I see, soldier. You insult everyone and everything for no reason and think you can change your tune when it suits you.

Bulychev   Forgive us our debts, eh?

Melania   It's not a matter of debts, think what is happening to your country. The Tsar, anointed by God, is being driven from his throne and his people have been cast into outer darkness. Their foolish hearts have turned from the light, and with their own hands they are digging the ground from under their feet. The other day the peasant women in Koposovo shouted in my face, 'We're the people! Our menfolk the soldiers are the people!' Can you imagine it? Since when have soldiers been regarded as people?

Ksenia   That's Laptev putting ideas in their heads . . .

Melania   Now the Governor has been robbed of his power, and in his place they've put that accountant Osmolovsky . . .

Bulychev   Another fat pig.

Melania   Yesterday Bishop Nikander said, 'We are living on the eve of catastrophic events. Is civil authority possible at such a time?' People have been ruled since biblical days by a hand armed with a cross and a sword . . .

Bulychev   In biblical days they didn't worship the cross at all.

Melania   Know your place. The Bishop knows better than you what was worshipped and when. The cross is a sword, and the Gospels are to be found in the same binding as the Bible. Those who are full of pride rejoice at the fall of the throne, but beware that your rejoicing turns not to tears of bitterness . . . Egor dear, I need a word with you in private.

Bulychev   Won't we shout at each other again? Let's talk then, but later. The healer's coming, I want her to make me better, Malasha.

Melania   Zobunova is a noted healer, the doctors have much to learn from her. You should also try the blessed Propotei.

Bulychev   I heard he was a fraud.

Melania   Mercy, what are you saying? You must see him.

Bulychev   Send for him then. I feel a bit better today. Just my legs . . . More cheerful somehow, everything makes me laugh. Call Zobunova, Aksinia.

Ksenia *exits.*

Melania   Oh, Egor, there's life in you yet.

Bulychev   What's left of me.

Ksenia (*runs in again*)   She says we're all to leave.

Varvara, **Melania** *and* **Ksenia** *go out.* **Bulychev** *grins and rubs his chest.* **Zobunova** *comes in. Making sure he notices but as if completely alone in the room, she twists her mouth and blows out of the right side, then clutches her heart with her right hand and flaps the other like a fin; she stops, and passes it over her face.*

Bulychev   Are you praying to the devils?

Zobunova (*in a sing-song voice*)   Wicked ailments and bodily griefs, fly off, be gone from this servant of God. On this day and hour, I banish you henceforth with my strong word for ever. Amen! Greetings, charitable man called Egorii.

Bulychev   Greetings, Auntie! Are you driving the devil away?

Zobunova   Lord, no, dear, what would I want with devils!

Bulychev   You have to, that's what! The priests pray to God and you're not a priest, therefore you pray to the devils!

Zobunova   These are terrible things you say. Only the ignorant say I study the evil arts.

Bulychev   Then you're wasting your time, Auntie. The priests prayed for me and God won't help!

Zobunova   You laugh, dear man, because you don't believe me.

Bulychev   I'd believe you if you came from the devil. You've probably heard I'm a cruel man, greedy for money and women . . .

Zobunova   I heard but I didn't believe it – you'll not grudge me good money?

Bulychev   I'm a great sinner, Auntie, God's washed His hands of me. So if you're not known to the devils, go back to your village and give the girls abortions. That's your trade, isn't it?

Zobunova   So what they say is true, you're a sinful, wicked man!

Bulychev   Tell me lies then, fire away!

Zobunova   I'm not versed in lies. Tell me what's hurting, where's the pain?

Bulychev   My stomach. The pain's bad. Here . . .

Zobunova   You see – only don't tell anyone, not a soul?

Bulychev   Not a soul, don't worry.

Zobunova   Well, there are yellow ailments and black ailments – the yellow ones the doctor can cure, but neither the priest nor the nun can pray the black ones away. The black ones come from bad energy, and there is only one remedy for them . . .

Bulychev   What doesn't kill me makes me better, eh?

Zobunova   The remedy's expensive!

Bulychev   Of course it is.

Zobunova We must deal with the powers of evil . . .

Bulychev Satan himself?

Zobunova Well, not directly, but . . .

Bulychev Can you do it?

Zobunova Not a word to anyone?

Bulychev Go to the devil, Auntie.

Zobunova Wait . . .

Bulychev Be off before I throw you out!

Zobunova Listen . . .

Glafira *(from the hall)* Be off he said, go! *(Comes in.)*

Zobunova Listen to her! Who does she think she is!

Bulychev Throw her out! Send her away!

Glafira So you're pretending to be a witch now?

Zobunova What about you and that face of yours?
Wicked people . . . ! *(Goes out muttering spells.)* No rest for the
wicked, no sleep . . .

Bulychev *looks round and sighs.* **Melania** *and* **Ksenia** *enter
with* **Taisya. Taisya** *stands by the door.*

Melania Didn't Zobunova suit you then?

Bulychev *eyes her in silence.*

Ksenia She's got a short temper too, her reputation's
gone to her head.

Bulychev Malasha, do you think God gets stomachache?

Melania Stop, Egorii.

Bulychev I expect Christ did, he lived on fish.

Melania You are provoking me, Egor.

Glafira The woman wants money for her pains.

Bulychev   Give it to her, Aksinia. Forgive me, Malasha, I'm going to my room. Fools make me tired. Help me, Glakha.

Glafira *leads him out.* **Ksenia** *gives her sister a questioning look.*

Melania   He's faking it, he's not mad at all. He's made the will you say?

Ksenia   Yes, but he . . .

Melania   Let him, it'll backfire on him if it's contested in court. We've Taisya, Zobunova, Father Pavlin, the trumpeter – any number of witnesses. We can prove he wasn't in his right mind.

Ksenia   But how . . . ?

Melania   I'll tell you how! You had to run off and marry him, didn't you? I said you should have married Bashkin!

Ksenia   But that was then. And he was such a lion! You were envious of him yourself as I recall . . .

Melania   Me? Are you mad?

Ksenia   Well, what's the point of raking it up now.

Melania   Merciful God, me envious?

Ksenia   What about Propotei? Do we really need him?

Melania   What are you saying? After all the time I spent persuading him. Don't make trouble for me, Aksinia! Get him ready and bring him out. Taisya!

Ksenia *goes out.* **Taisya** *moves from the door.*

Melania   Well, tell me what you've heard?

Taisya   I heard nothing.

Melania   Why not?

Taisya   She didn't say anything.

Melania   Good heavens, girl, you should have questioned her!

Taisya   I did question her, but she snarled like a cat and called everyone names.

Melania   What names?

Taisya   Liars, cheats, swindlers.

Melania   Why did she call them that?

Taisya   She said you wanted to drive him mad.

Melania   She told you?

Taisya   No, she told Propotei the simpleton.

Melania   And what did he reply?

Taisya   He just spoke in funny rhymes . . .

Melania   Give me patience – he's a holy fool, you dunce. Sit in the hall and don't move. Did anyone else come to the kitchen?

Taisya   Mokei . . .

Melania   Off you go. (*Goes to the door of* **Bulychev**'s *room and knocks.*) Egorii, the holy man has come!

Propotei *walks in supported by* **Ksenia** *and* **Bashkin**, *carrying a staff and wearing bark shoes, a long linen shirt down to his ankles and a mass of icons and brass crosses on his chest. His appearance is alarming; he has thick, long unkempt hair and a narrow beard, and his movements are jerky and abrupt.*

Propotei (*sniffs the air*)   Smoke, I smell smoke. It stifles the spirit.

Ksenia   No one's been smoking in here, sir.

Propotei *stands in the middle of the room and drones like a winter wind.*

Melania   Stop, wait for him to come out of his room first . . .

Propotei *stops droning.* **Glafira** *leads* **Bulychev** *from his room.*

Bulychev   So that's what you look like.

Propotei   I am here, do not fear. Stench and sin are in the air. (*Drones again.*) All will pass, all is dust. Grisha grew higher, hit the spire . . .

Bulychev   That's Rasputin you're talking about?

Propotei   Threw out the Tsar, destroyed the power! Debauchery, calamity. Ruin, ruin! (*Moans and points his staff at* **Glafira**.) Satan in female form stands before me. Get rid of her!

Bulychev   I will not. Babble on but know the limits. Melania, did you teach him to say this?

Melania   The idea. How can one teach a madman?

Bulychev   Sounds like you did.

Shura *runs down the stairs followed by* **Antonina**, **Tyatin**, *the* **Zvontsovs** *and* **Dostigaevs**. **Propotei** *hangs his head and silently makes signs with his staff on the floor and in the air.*

Shura (*runs to her father*)   What's this? He's putting on a show?

Melania   Be silent.

Propotei (*speaking with exaggerated effort*)   Tick, tock, knock, knock! Midnight's struck, wake the cock! Dog, God, the heretic wakes! Got out of bed, bumped his head, if he wasn't bad he would be good. Satan's come, it's Satan's day. Let Satan play, there's debts to pay . . .

Bulychev   Excellent. Spoken very fluently.

Melania   Don't interrupt, Egor!

Antonina (*regretfully*)   He's not so frightening after all!

Propotei (*shrieks*)   Die, die, kill a fly! Dance, dance . . . ! (*Stamps his feet and hums, at first softly then louder and louder.*) Hey hey, what do you say! Astarot, Askafat, Idumnei,

Stupumnei! Smack! Bang! Into the smoke! Egor, Egor, run away! Satan's devils out to play! Witch, bitch, stand in a ditch! Ride him Katama, stench and sin! Witch, bitch, save your skin . . .

Shura (*shouts*)   Clear off. Get rid of him!

Bulychev   To hell with you, Propotei, you want to scare me?

Zvontsov   End this grotesque performance immediately!

Glafira *rushes at* **Propotei**. *He swings his staff at her while continuing to whirl around the room.*

Propotei   Bitch, bitch, stand in a ditch! Tick, tock, the kingdom will die . . . !

Tyatin *grabs the staff from his hands.*

Melania (*tries to grab it off him*)   How dare you. Who are you?

Shura   Father, send them away. Why don't you say something?

Bulychev (*waves an arm*)   Hang on . . .

Propotei *sits on the floor droning and shrieking.*

Melania   Nobody touch him. He's going into a trance of ecstasy!

Dostigaev   He'll get a kick up the backside for it, Mother Melania.

Zvontsov   Stand up this minute and be off!

Propotei (*looks up sharply at him*)   Where to? (*Drones again.*)

Ksenia *weeps.*

Elizaveta   See? That's clever, he does it in two voices!

Bulychev   Go . . . all of you. You've seen enough.

Shura (*stamps on* **Propotei***'s foot*)   Step on it, freak. The show's over. Tyatin, throw him out!

Tyatin (*grabs* **Propotei** *by the scruff of the neck and drags him from the room*)   Come on, holy man, out you go!

Taisya   He wasn't so frightening today, he's usually much more frightening.

Melania   What are you jabbering about? (*Slaps her face.*)

Zvontsov   Aren't you ashamed, Mother?

Melania   What of, you?

Varvara   No need to get excited, Auntie.

Ksenia (*weeps*)   Lord, it's beyond belief . . .

Shura and **Glafira** *help* **Bulychev** *to the sofa. He lies down.* **Dostigaev** *watches him intently. The* **Zvontsovs** *lead* **Ksenia** *and* **Melania** *out. Distant singing is heard through the window.*

Dostigaev (*to his wife*)   Better go home, Liza, Bulychev looks bad. There's a demonstration on, we'd better join it.

Elizaveta   My, how he droned. I never imagined it would be like that!

They leave.

Bulychev (*to* **Shura**)   It was the Mother Superior's idea, wasn't it. Like a requiem for the living.

Shura   Do you feel bad? Shall I send for the doctor?

Bulychev   No need. The kingdom that clown thought up wasn't bad – if I wasn't bad I would be good . . . did you hear?

Shura   Don't, forget it.

The singing on the street grows louder.

Bulychev   I will. Run in and make sure they're not hurting Glafira. What are they singing?

Shura   Lie down, don't get up. (*Goes out.*)

Bulychev   Sin and stench, the kingdom will die . . . I can't
see . . . (*Stands up and gropes his way to the table, rubs his eyes.*)
Thy kingdom . . . Animals! Our Father! . . . (*Staggers.*) It's no
good. What sort of father are you? All people must die?
Well, let them. (*Shouts hoarsely.*) Shura, Glakha, Doctor! Hey,
someone, dammit!

Shura, **Glafira**, **Tyatin** *and* **Taisya** *run in;* **Bulychev** *hurls
himself at them. Outside the voices grow louder.* **Glafira** *and*
Tyatin *hold* **Bulychev** *up.* **Shura** *runs to the window and
throws it up. Revolutionary songs burst through and fill the room.*

Bulychev   Another requiem? Who are they, Shura?

Shura   Look! Come here!

Bulychev   Eh, Shura, Glakha . . . !

Methuen Drama Student Editions

Jean Anouilh	*Antigone*
John Arden	*Serjeant Musgrave's Dance*
Alan Ayckbourn	*Confusions*
Aphra Behn	*The Rover*
Edward Bond	*Lear*
Bertolt Brecht	*The Caucasian Chalk Circle*
	Life of Galileo
	Mother Courage and her Children
Anton Chekhov	*The Cherry Orchard*
	The Seagull
Caryl Churchill	*Serious Money*
	Top Girls
Shelagh Delaney	*A Taste of Honey*
John Galsworthy	*Strife*
Robert Holman	*Across Oka*
Henrik Ibsen	*A Doll's House*
	Hedda Gabler
Charlotte Keatley	*My Mother Said I Never Should*
Bernard Kops	*Dreams of Anne Frank*
Federico García Lorca	*Blood Wedding*
	(bilingual edition)
John Marston	*The Malcontent*
Willy Russell	*Blood Brothers*
Wole Soyinka	*Death and the King's Horseman*
August Strindberg	*The Father*
J. M. Synge	*The Playboy of the Western World*
Oscar Wilde	*The Importance of Being Earnest*
Tennessee Williams	*A Streetcar Named Desire*
	The Glass Menagerie
Timberlake Wertenbaker	*Our Country's Good*

Methuen Drama Modern Plays

include work by

Jean Anouilh
John Arden
Margaretta D'Arcy
Peter Barnes
Sebastian Barry
Brendan Behan
Dermot Bolger
Edward Bond
Bertolt Brecht
Howard Brenton
Anthony Burgess
Simon Burke
Jim Cartwright
Caryl Churchill
Noël Coward
Lucinda Coxon
Sarah Daniels
Nick Darke
Nick Dear
Shelagh Delaney
David Edgar
David Eldridge
Dario Fo
Michael Frayn
John Godber
Paul Godfrey
David Greig
John Guare
Peter Handke
David Harrower
Jonathan Harvey
Iain Heggie
Declan Hughes
Terry Johnson
Sarah Kane
Charlotte Keatley
Barrie Keeffe
Howard Korder

Robert Lepage
Doug Lucie
Martin McDonagh
John McGrath
Terrence McNally
David Mamet
Patrick Marber
Arthur Miller
Mtwa, Ngema & Simon
Tom Murphy
Phyllis Nagy
Peter Nichols
Joseph O'Connor
Joe Orton
Louise Page
Joe Penhall
Luigi Pirandello
Stephen Poliakoff
Franca Rame
Mark Ravenhill
Philip Ridley
Reginald Rose
Willy Russell
Jean-Paul Sartre
Sam Shepard
Wole Soyinka
Shelagh Stephenson
Peter Straughan
C. P. Taylor
Theatre de Complicite
Theatre Workshop
Sue Townsend
Judy Upton
Timberlake Wertenbaker
Roy Williams
Snoo Wilson
Victoria Wood